Seduction and Theory

Seduction and Theory

Readings of Gender, Representation, and Rhetoric

Dianne Hunter,
Editor

UNIVERSITY OF ILLINOIS PRESS
Urbana and Chicago

© 1989 by the Board of Trustees of the University of Illinois
Manufactured in the United States of America
1   2   3   4   5   C   P   5   4   3   2   1

This book is printed on acid-free paper.

Library of Congress Cataloging-in-Publication Data

Seduction and theory: readings of gender, representation, and
    rhetoric / Dianne Hunter, editor.
        p.   cm.
    Bibliography: p.
    Includes index.
    ISBN 0-252-01626-2 (cloth : alk. paper). — ISBN 0-252-06063-6 (paper :
alk. paper)
    1. Seduction—Psychological aspects.   2. Femininity (Psychology).
3. Seduction in literature.   4. Femininity (Psychology) in
literature.   5. Seduction in art.   6. Femininity (Psychology) in
art.   7. Feminism.   I. Hunter, Dianne, 1943–   .
    BF637.S36S43   1989
    155.3—dc 19   88-37602
                                                                CIP

Contents

Acknowledgments

I thank Madelon Sprengnether for inviting me to participate in the Modern Language Association convention session on "Seduction and Theory" which she organized in 1984, for which some of the work in this collection was initiated; and I thank her for the suggestive reading she gave the first draft of the manuscript. Celeste Schenck and Peter Rudnytsky read an early version of the book and offered useful criticism, for which I am grateful. Tony Weisgram, Claire Kahane, and Sheila Fisher read drafts of the introduction and made excellent suggestions for improvements. I appreciate the editorial help of Ann Lowry Weir and the careful copyediting of Carol Saller.

DIANNE HUNTER

Seduction and Theory

Introduction

This anthology represents a field of conflict within which the term "seduction" focuses a current debate concerning the status of woman—as the fetishized object of the male gaze on one hand, and, on the other, as a source of metaphor for deconstructive theory and practice. Into this debate, the collected essays strive to introduce the voicing of female subjectivities, carrying forward a critique of male-centered thinking. From a core of feminist commitment, these essays radiate in the directions of the visual arts, psychoanalysis, literary criticism, and postmodernist theory.

In the early history of psychoanalysis, "seduction" was a euphemism for incest. The seduction theory was the hypothesis that whenever there is hysteria, it can be traced back to an incidence of sexual abuse of the hysteric in childhood. This was Freud's position in 1896, when he "put forward the thesis that at the bottom of every case of hysteria there are *one or more occurrences of premature sexual experience*."[1] Freud wrote, "In order to cause hysteria, it is not enough that there should occur at some period of the subject's life an event which touches his [*sic*] sexual existence and becomes pathogenic through the release and suppression of a distressing affect. On the contrary, *these sexual traumas must have occurred in early childhood (before puberty), and their content must consist of an actual irritation of the genitals (of a process resembling copulation.)* . . . I have found this specific determinant of hysteria— *sexual passivity during the pre-sexual period*—in every case of hysteria (including two male cases) which I have analyzed" (*S.E.*, 3:163, Freud's italics). Freud stated, "*A passive sexual experience before puberty* . . . is the specific aetiology of hysteria" (*S.E.*, 3:152, Freud's italics).

Thus, in seeking to explain hysteria, Freud had to confront the issue of power abuse in patriarchy. Although he would later go on to revise this implicit radical critique of the patterns of fear and dominance associated with the onset of childhood sexuality, the questions raised by the psychodynamics of the traumatic scene associated with hysteria recur as central themes in studies of modernism, the visual arts, and postmodernist theory. Freud explicitly did not specify gender roles in the incestuous scenes he brought forward in 1896, but sexual passivity turned out to be his model of the feminine; and activity, including active looking, was for him masculine.

Patriarchal masculinity in modernist theory is associated with the power of the dominant subject whose gaze can both objectify and fetishize, and femininity is associated with taking pleasure in being dominated. Part One of this book presents three critiques of the assumptions behind this gender division.

In "The Uncanny Lure of Manet's *Olympia*," Charles Bernheimer draws our attention to the provocative image of the female body openly advertising its availability as an erotic commodity. Bernheimer speculates that the figure represents an overt acknowledgment that art is a form of prostitution and that Olympia's direct gaze back at her viewer challenges the dominance of male voyeurism.

Working along similar lines, Judith Mayne goes further in deconstructing the logic of the phallocentric gaze. She shows how resistance to the idea of woman-as-spectacle is part of the seductive appeal of the star persona of Marlene Dietrich, whose cool detachment comments ironically on the sexual politics of the look and the mechanics of performance. In *The Blue Angel*, Dietrich operates resistantly in articulating a cabaret performance mode that seduces through transgression of patriarchal boundaries. Reciprocally, the scrutiny of the professor who marries the cabaret star inspires an appeal to bourgeois respectability, transforming the carnivalesque performer into a conventional vamp, thus effecting her representability within the confines of patriarchal discourse.

Like Mayne, Sharon Willis uses and extends feminist film theory on the cinematic construction of the female body as seductive enticement. But in Willis's essay enticement is obsession with the male body and postmodern luxury spaces in *American Gigolo* and *To Live and Die in L.A.* Showing how these two films participate in a postmodernist ideology of undecidability, she analyzes cinematic seduction as part of collective libidinal channeling and mapping.

Willis points out that psychoanalytic grounding is fundamental to the most powerful discussions of subject construction in ideology, but that many psychoanalytic approaches succumb to a theoretical influence which has tended to confine itself to individual subjects. Psychoanalytic thinking pervades modern discourses, though classical psychoanalysis has been insistently and cogently criticized by, among others, cultural semioticians and feminists who point out that in seeking the meanings of mental distress in repudiated childhood wishes rather than in intrusive patterns of invasion, domination, and submission, psychoanalysis may lead away from the kinds of insights and commitments we need in order to effectively realign power, to avert it from rigidly defined class and gender boundaries. Flawed psychoanalytic focus on the private fantasy life of individuals has roots in the suppression of Freud's radically antipatriarchal discourse on seduction, his original theory that neuroses are caused by childhood experiences of adult sexual invasion—the so-called seduction theory.

But Freud later concluded that not all adult hysteria derives from actual childhood sexual abuse. He therefore renounced the seduction theory of hysteria's origin, though he did not fail to acknowledge the reality of "seductions." Of his altered views Freud wrote retrospectively in 1914, "Influenced by Charcot's view of the traumatic origin of hysteria, one was inclined to accept as true and aetiologically significant the statements made by patients in which they ascribed their symptoms to passive sexual experiences in the first years of childhood—to put it bluntly, to seduction. *When this aetiology broke down under the weight of its own improbability and contradiction in definitely ascertainable circumstances, the result at first was helpless bewilderment.* Analysis had led to these infantile sexual traumas by the right path, and *yet they were not true*" (*S.E.*, 14:17, my italics). Though the "ascertainability" of Freud's "definite" reality is bound to be problematic today, here he specifically asserts that he had found in certain cases a verifiable absence of child abuse though the patient had symptoms of hysteria, and moreover, a memory or scene of sexual submission in childhood had come up in analysis. Contrary to his previous view, Freud now conceded that hysteria could exist without an originary cause in an actual childhood sexual trauma in the personal past of the patient, and decided that the stories he had heard required another interpretation. He therefore sought a new explanation of the aetiology of hysteria and a new way of accounting for the many reports he had heard of children's sexual encounters with adults. Since he previously believed childhood to be a "presexual" period of life, Freud had assumed that if patients reported childhood sexual scenes those scenes must have been instigated by perverse adults. But when the high incidence of hysteria indicated to Freud an incredibly high number of "perverse fathers," he concluded that not all of these reported sexual scenes

had historical basis; many had been childhood fantasies, fantasies
Freud found he shared with his patients.

This sharing spurred Freud's theorization of the oedipus complex, and it also opened the way for analysis of how the interlocu-
tions of the psychoanalytic encounter imply verbal seduction, seduction by interpretation. Freud reasoned, "If hysterical subjects trace
back their symptoms to traumas that are fictitious, then the new
factor which emerges is that they create such scenes in *phantasy,*
and this psychical reality requires to be taken into account alongside practical reality" (*S.E.,* 14:17–18, Freud's italics). Ten years later
(1924), again recounting his change of view, Freud dropped the "If"
at the beginning of his previous account and wrote, "I was at last
obliged to recognize that these scenes of seduction had never taken
place, and that they were only phantasies which my patients had
made up or which I myself had perhaps forced on them. . . . When I
had pulled myself together, I was able to draw the right conclusions
from my discovery: namely, that the neurotic symptoms were not
related to actual events but to wishful phantasies, and that as far
as the neurosis was concerned psychical reality was of more importance than material reality" (*S.E.,* 20:34). Freud's description of the
scenes of seduction as "only phantasies which my patients had made
up or which I myself had perhaps forced on them" suggests that the
patients were mistaken about what they remembered or perhaps did
not actually remember, but which they had instead constructed or reconstructed once Freud had served as interlocutor. Freud concluded
that the reports he had heard of sexual attacks were the result not
of historical realities but either of patients' private fantasies that
disguised the truth of their forbidden childhood desires, or of the patients' having been misled by the suggestiveness of Freud's presence
as a doctor with a theory about how infantile sexual traumas cause
neurotic symptoms. Yet we may see that the shared fantasies were
the result of both historical realities (the social structures of domination) *and* of patients' fantasies; and the fantasies may represent
both childhood desires *and* a response to Freud's role as interpreter.

Freud's conclusion that "these scenes of seduction had *never
taken place*" constitutes, according to psychoanalytic orthodoxy, the
founding moment of psychoanalysis; though ironically, from the
point of view of a major group of psychoanalytic commentators, it
is in fact an unpsychoanalytic claim, since one of the central tenets
of contemporary psychoanalysis is precisely the inextricability of
fantasy and reality, and of perception and desire.[2] Freud's distin-
guishing "only phantasies" from what really took place has contrib-

uted to popular confusion of the seduction theory with the issue of the reality or fictitiousness of reported and unreported instances of childhood incest as well as other forms of sexual exploitation and abuse.[3]

One can believe Freud's theory of the oedipus complex without concluding as Freud does that memories of being seduced in childhood by adults are *only* fantasies. Clinical evidence indicates that the oedipus complex is mutual: the desire of the parent is transitional to the desire of the child; these desires are reciprocal, and may spill over into acting out.[4] Thus, of the mothers of certain patients, the psychoanalyst Masud Khan wrote, "It is not far-fetched to infer that the behavior of these mothers is both traumatizing and seductive. The role of actual infantile sexual seduction in the aetiology of hysteria was at first emphasized by Freud and later discarded. From the material of these patients it seems that the theory of actual seduction, as creating acute dissociation of the ego, is not so false after all."[5] Both Heinz Kohut and Anna Ornstein have urged psychoanalysts to recognize the diagnostic importance of *actual historical* disturbances *in the parents* of patients. Neither Kohut nor Ornstein nor Khan argues for abandonment of the theory of the oedipus complex, yet each points to parental instigation of neuroses.

Remarkably enough, the very passage in which Freud publicly introduces his theory of the oedipus complex leaves the question of who initiates infantile desire open to an ambiguous and equivocal reply. Freud writes, "In my experience, which is already extensive, the chief part in the mental lives of all children who later become psychoneurotics *is played by their parents*" (*S.E.*, 4:260, my italics). His phrase "in the mental lives" and the passive verb "is played" are the vehicles by which the active agency of oedipal desire gets shifted from the parents' to the child's psyche. Since in this passage Freud is discussing typical dreams and arguing for the universality of the oedipus complex, it may seem strange that he begins by specifying that he means "children who later become psychoneurotics." He says however that neurotics are not in this respect differentiated from human beings who remain normal. Neurotics do not create something absolutely new; they simply magnify feelings that occur less intensely in the minds of most children. We might conclude from Freud's blending of the neurotic and the normal that patients who report sexual seduction in childhood express in extreme form how all children may feel about being subjected to and channeled by adult dominance.

Part Two of this collection examines the psychodynamics and

some of the consequences of Freud's self-seduction in his turning away from evidence of how patriarchal domination of the family and the social order affects pathologically the position of children as subjects. In "Hysteria and the Seduction of Theory," Martha Noel Evans asserts that Freud avoided his unconscious identification with violated daughters of incestuous fathers by substituting a male child as protagonist in the oedipal theory that replaced the idea that childhood sexual abuse is the key to neuroses. Evans argues that Freud's theory of the oedipus complex served to ward off his identification with the position of the victimized, hysterical daughter, and that psychoanalytic theorizing may serve as a medium of display between men demonstrating their mastery of the feminine.

From a similar perspective, Shirley Nelson Garner discusses how Freud's homophobic love for Wilhelm Fliess led to his own seduction by Fliess's ideas, and Lawrence Frank argues that consequences of Freud's friendship with Fliess are traceable in his failure to bring forward evidence of infantile sexual abuse in the Dora case. Professor Frank thinks that because Freud unconsciously associated the repudiated, controversial seduction theory with the wild speculations of Fliess, clues that Dora had been a victim of her father's sexual advances toward her were ignored. Yet Frank believes that the case as Freud presents it leaves open the possibility that Ida Bauer ("Dora") was forced to perform fellatio with her father even though the announced theoretical project in the case steers away from the historical actualities of seduction, focusing instead on what Freud takes to be Ida's repudiated love for Herr K. Ida Bauer herself was not taken in by the enticements of Freud's ingenious interpretations; and the drama of these two well-matched adversaries has provoked numerous reconstructions of the significance of their encounter.[6] Though Freud intended the case history to be an exemplification of his theory that hysterical symptoms, like dreams, are compromise formations between a desire and its rejection by the ego, what he wrote was an exercise in the politics of interpretation, a patriarchal representation of female sexuality. In this aspect, Freud's psychoanalysis shows itself as part of an establishment empowering men.

Though the psychoanalytic discourse on seduction was eclipsed once Freud began to focus on repudiated childhood wishes, a return of the repressed is marked by the many studies of psychoanalytic history that seek to return to the early Freud, literally a French Freud, and by the insistence with which the idea of seduction and its link with psychoanalytic discourse recur in literary criticism and in the sociology of communications in popular culture.[7] Thus, Part Three of this book is organized around the theme of seduction of the reader. In "Seduction and the Voice of the Text: *Heart of Darkness* and *The Good Soldier*," Claire Kahane analyzes the literary representation of the speaking voice as an uncanny force. Since a narrator depends on the listener as an interlocutor who makes speech possible, the meaning of a narrative is the product of the listener as well as the teller. Kahane shows how Conrad and Ford locate their readers within a circle of oral storytelling and evoke seductive scenes of acoustic power. Within narratives that fulfill the drive to be heard, Kahane finds the figuration of masculine fears associating subjugation with femininity as an open ear of masochistic vulnerability to deathly silencing.

In analyzing the erotic poetics of Anne Sexton's "To John, Who Begs Me Not to Enquire Further," Alicia Ostriker develops the theme of undermined sexual difference in the mutuality of cooperating psyches required by seduction. She notes that the surmounting of the resistance that we associate with seduction and the ambivalence with which the seduced accedes to it seem to enact a regression from oedipal differences and distinct ego differences to a more fluid realm where the boundaries of self and other, speaker and reader, dissolve.

In contrast, Gabriele Schwab's cultural critique of *The Scarlet Letter* analyzes the way in which a seduction of the reader is effected by a polarization between the narrator of the novel and its protagonist. As part of this polarization, Hester Prynne achieves her persuasiveness as a saintly heroine from precisely the tendencies which the narrator condemns; and just as Hester's seduction of the parishioners leads to a reevaluation of her social role, so her seduction of the reader leads to a reading against the grain of the narrator's Puritan norms. In the same way that Hester manages to invert the cultural meaning of the letter which is supposed to codify her body for the communal gaze, she seduces us into resisting the values of the narrator. In binding together the theme of the reversibility of signs with the politics of the visible and the invisible, Schwab's essay points toward the preoccupations of Part Four of *Seduction and Theory* while at the same time reviewing the issues of Part One. And she contextualizes her analysis of *The Scarlet Letter* by tracing the psychohistorical and semiotic process by which the witchcraft patterning of male fantasies of seduction, particularly fantasies of women seduced by the devil, have persisted in unconscious politics.

The question of the relationship between gender and rhetoric organizes Part Four. The final three essays focus on rhetorical seduction as a thematic and performative issue within the discourse of what is regarded in America as French theory. In "Confessing Lacan,"

Susan David Bernstein analyzes the performative rhetoric of two American Lacanians who use the confessional mode as a strategy to appropriate the power of Lacan's textual and interpretive authority. Bernstein restages comically the seductive theatrics of her objects of analysis—Stuart Schneiderman's melodramatic representation of his privileged access to Lacan's Parisian consulting room and Jane Gallop's fits of paralysis before the baffling complexities of Lacan's obscurantist prose. Bernstein shows how seduction, motivated by the desire for knowledge difficult to obtain, pervades Gallop's and Schneiderman's transmissions of Lacanian theory; and she examines the gender politics of the difference between Gallop's enticing vexation as a reluctantly seduced and seducing reader-writer, and Schneiderman's straightforward exploitation of the power he finds inherent in his ability to write with authority in Lacan's name.

Andrew Ross critiques the neoconservative fear of democracy that fuels Jean Baudrillard's rejection of feminism and his characterization of America as an obscene desert. Ross deconstructs the cozenage of Baudrillard's delight in the dissolution of boundaries between the real and its simulation. Via the same operation that Sharon Willis condemns for the misleading effects of *American Gigolo* and *To Live and Die in L.A.*, mass seduction by appearances in the Baudrillardian world takes on hyperreal dimensions, and visibility is linked to power and domination. A champion of the manipulative power of representations and the reversibility of signs, Baudrillard subverts the materialism of Marxist discourses on production by idealizing seduction, for he sees himself as a skillful rhetorician exploiting inversions of codified cultural meanings to captivate the reader in a play of indeterminacy. For Baudrillard, says Ross, power lies in the symbolic world of appearances; and the feminine, like seduction, is the constituting form of this symbolic order.

Since to be conventionally feminine is to pose on display as the object of another's gaze, Baudrillard links himself rhetorically to contemporary discourses on woman by finding an equivalence between the reversibility of the meanings of signs and Joan Riviere's idea of womanliness as a masquerade.[8] Luce Irigaray, on the other hand, wants to uncover the mechanism by which feminine posturing represses women. In "Romancing the Philosophers: Luce Irigaray," Carolyn Burke demonstrates how Irigaray's amorous discourses with past masters of philosophy seek recognition of the speaking female subject. Irigaray moves beyond the seductive conventions of female masquerade and mimicry, and tries to insert the voice of a real woman into the closed system of the Western philosophy centered on male subjects. By deliberately blurring the distinctions between theory and poetry, masculine and feminine, writes Burke, Irigaray creates a fecund, caressive language that respects the bodily contours and inwardness of the other, seeking to know the other as a corporeal being within elemental forms of nature. Thus Irigaray's philosophy performs rhetorically its own thematics of female desire.

NOTES

1. Sigmund Freud, *The Standard Edition of the Complete Psychological Works of Sigmund Freud*, ed. and trans. James Strachey et al., 24 vols. (London: Hogarth Press, 1953–74) (hereafter cited as *S.E.*), vol. 3, p. 203 (Freud's italics). Subsequent references to Freud will be to this edition and will be documented parenthetically by volume and page numbers in the body of the text.

2. Freud, *S.E.*, 3:308–22; Jean Laplanche and J.-B. Pontalis, "Fantasy and the Origins of Sexuality," *International Journal of Psychoanalysis* 49 (1968), 1–18; idem, *Fantasme originaire: Fantasme des origines, Origines du fantasme* (Paris: Hachette, 1985); William Beatty Warner, *Chance and the Text of Experience: Freud, Nietzsche, and Shakespeare's Hamlet* (Ithaca: Cornell University Press, 1986), p. 70; idem, "Spectacular Seduction: The Case of Freud, Masson, and Malcolm," *Raritan: A Quarterly Review* 6, no. 3 (Winter 1987), 124–25.

3. As, for example, in Jeffrey Moussaieff Masson's *The Assault on Truth: Freud's Suppression of the Seduction Theory* (New York: Farrar, Straus, Giroux, 1984) and the media coverage by Ralph Blumenthal (*New York Times*, August 18 and 25, 1981) and David Gelman (*Newsweek*, November 30, 1981), who are far from isolated in their confusion of Freud's abandonment of the seduction theory with suppression of the recognition of the reality of child abuse.

4. Cf. Laplanche and Pontalis, "Fantasy and the Origins of Sexuality"; and see Neil Friedman and Richard M. Jones, "On the Mutuality of the Oedipus Complex: Notes on the Hamlet Case," in *The Design Within: Psychoanalytic Approaches to Shakespeare*, ed. M. D. Faber (New York: Science House, 1970), pp. 121–46; Milton I. Klein, "Freud's Seduction Theory: Its Implications for Fantasy and Memory in Psychoanalytic Theory," *Bulletin of the Menninger Clinic* 45, no. 3 (May 1981), 185–208; and Anna Ornstein, "Fantasy or Reality? The Unsettled Question in Pathogenesis and Reconstruction in Psychoanalysis," in *The Future of Psychoanalysis*, ed. Arnold Goldberg (New York: International Universities Press, 1983), pp. 381–96.

5. Masud Khan, *Alienation in the Perversions* (New York: International Universities Press, 1979), pp. 44–45. Cf. Heinz Kohut, *The Restoration of the Self* (New York: International Universities Press, 1977), p. 256.

6. These include Catherine Clément and Hélène Cixous, *The Newly Born*

Woman, trans. Betsy Wing (Minneapolis: University of Minnesota Press, 1986); the issue of *Diacritics* edited by Neil Hertz and titled *A Fine Romance: Freud and Dora* (Spring 1983); and the anthology *In Dora's Case: Freud—Hysteria—Feminism*, ed. Charles Bernheimer and Claire Kahane (New York: Columbia University Press, 1985).

7. Examples include Jean Baudrillard, *De la Séduction* (Paris: Galilée, 1979); Shoshana Felman, *The Literary Speech Act: Don Juan with J. L. Austin, or Seduction in Two Languages*, trans. Catherine Porter (Ithaca: Cornell University Press, 1983); Jane Gallop, *The Daughter's Seduction: Feminism and Psychoanalysis* (Ithaca: Cornell University Press, 1982); Ross Chambers, *Story and Situation: Narrative Seduction and the Power of Fiction* (Minneapolis: University of Minnesota Press, 1984); and Peter Brooks, *Reading for the Plot: Design and Intention in Narrative* (New York: Random House, 1985).

8. See Joan Riviere, "Womanliness as a Masquerade," *International Journal of Psychoanalysis* 10 (1929), 303–13; and Baudrillard, *De la Séduction*, p. 21.

PART ONE

The Politics of the Gaze:
The Visible and the Invisible

The Uncanny Lure
of Manet's *Olympia*

"What is art? Prostitution," declares Baudelaire in *Fusées*.[1] To no other art form does this remark apply more pertinently than to the representation of the female nude. In the nude, woman is put on display for the pleasure of a spectator presumed to be male. Her naked body becomes nude insofar as it is seen as an erotic object offered to the man's gaze, to his imaginary knowledge. The terms of that offering in the European artistic tradition are subject to conventions calculated to flatter the male viewer and to stimulate his fantasy of sexual domination. Thus, as John Berger has observed, "almost all post-Renaissance European sexual imagery is frontal—either literally or metaphorically—because the sexual protagonist is the spectator-owner looking at it."[2] The convention of not painting female body hair, Berger further notes, contributes to the representation of female submission by eliminating the hint of animal passion and physical desire suggested by hairy growth. The nude, like the prostitute, is an erotic commodity; her nakedness is valuable not for its marked individuality and subjective expression, but for its ability to feed male fantasies that erase woman's desiring subjectivity.

This ability is dependent on an ideological cover-up: the nude body is never overtly styled as a body for sale and imaginary possession. In the nineteenth century, the nude is typically a mythological figure or an odalisque, removed from the viewer's present and disguised through classical idealization or romantic exoticism. In contrast, Manet's *Olympia* (figure 1) represents the unmistakable image of a female body laid out for purchase, offered here and now, openly advertising its seductive availability. It is as if art had suddenly become self-conscious about its function as prostitution, as if the figure of Olympia were addressing a challenge to her male viewer: can you still fantasize me as an erotic commodity if I offer myself as such?

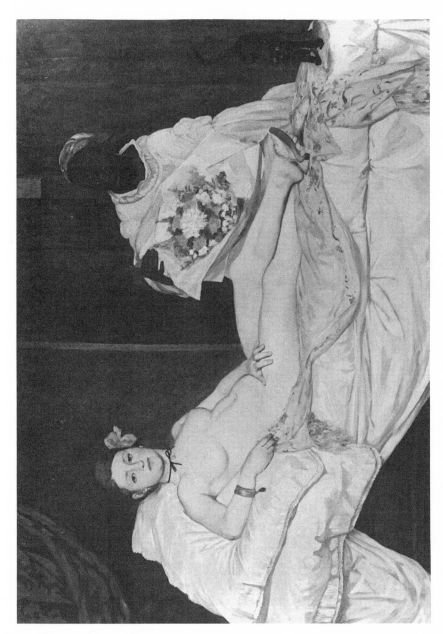

FIG. 1. Eduard Manet, *Olympia*, 1863. Musée d'Orsay, Paris.

Is your dominance as bearer of the look still assured if I return your gaze in full awareness of what it conveys, willing to accommodate your desire if the price is right? Can you contemplate my nudity as art when my naked body belongs to the degraded context of your urban experience, you "hypocrite voyeur"? Indeed, can you read me at all, given that I cannot comfortably be decoded through any signifying system of the mid-nineteenth-century discourse on woman?

The critical reception of *Olympia* when the painting was first exhibited at the *Salon* of 1865 suggests that the image was indeed nearly unreadable for contemporary viewers. After examining sixty different critical appraisals of *Olympia* published in the contemporary press, art historian T. J. Clark concludes that "if we apply the test . . . of some sustained description of the object in hand —some effort at controlled attention to particulars, some ordinary mobilization of the resources of criticism in 1865—then a response to *Olympia* simply does not exist."[3] What then was the content of the numerous journalistic reviews? In a word, scandal, a word that originates suggestively in the Greek *skandalon*, which means "trap, snare, stumbling block." The viewers of Olympia in 1865 reacted as if they were trapped by this provocative image, able to respond only with derisive hostility and contemptuous ridicule. The public, indeed, took such offense at this apparent affront to bourgeois morality that the painting had to be rehung high up out of retaliatory reach. Yet most of the painting's critics did not even identify Olympia as a courtesan, and none bothered to investigate the possible meanings of the image, be they generated in relation to contemporary social mores or to the great tradition of European painting. Even Théophile Gautier could do no better than stress the picture's essential meaninglessness: "Olympia can be understood from no point of view," he wrote in the *Moniteur*, going on to complain about the dirty color of the flesh, the absence of modeling, and the shadows indicated by means of blacking. "The least beautiful woman," he observes, "has bones, muscles, skin, and some sort of color. Here there is nothing."[4]

Thus is Olympia's scandal figured: she is a negation of the feminine, a stumbling block to the male viewer's desire, a disobedient body that offers no flattering consolation in fantasy. The subject of scandal is the lack in the representation. That lack is somehow made sensible in the image but does not simply coincide with the realistic portrayal of prostitution. If it did, the painting would have established a point of view from which it could be understood, the topic of prostitution being an established component of the discourse on woman in 1865.[5] I propose to argue that this lack is related to the mirror effect whereby Olympia reflects back to the male viewer the desire motivating his gaze. The scandal has something to do with a lack which that desire cannot face.

One of the most powerful traditions in Manet criticism takes precisely the notions of lack and absence to be the founding principles of his art. Surprisingly, Zola was the founder of this critical school. In a long article published in January 1867, Zola, who had met frequently with Manet in the previous months, defended his friend against critical hostility by explaining that Manet's subject matter was merely a pretext for his painting. *Olympia*, which Zola calls the painter's masterpiece, is to be read not in terms of a particular anecdotal content—Olympia in herself is of no interest, "this everyday girl, whom you might encounter on the sidewalk"—but in terms of a particular formal arrangement of chromatic tonalities and juxtaposed masses. Thus the bouquet of flowers was included, Zola imagines, because Manet needed "some bright and luminous patches," the negress and cat because he needed "some black patches." Meaning is of no import. "What does all that mean?" Zola asks. "You [that is, Manet] do not know, and neither do I."[6]

Zola's approach appropriates the scandalous principle of lack—the subject itself is lacking, is suppressed—in order to stress the way Manet's painting reflects not the viewer's desire but that of painting itself. The lack in the representation constitutes that representation as pure painting, Zola argues, and that purity erases whatever might be threatening to the male viewer in the content of the image.

Georges Bataille, in his book on Manet published in 1955, repeats this erasure in still more radical terms. He quotes Valéry's eloquent description of *Olympia* only to contest its accuracy. "The naked and cold Olympia, monster of banal love," writes Valéry, "inspires a sacred horror. . . . [She is] the Impure *par excellence*, whose function requires the untroubled and candid ignorance of all modesty. Bestial Vestal devoted to absolute nudity, she makes one dream of all that hides itself and is preserved of primitive barbarism and ritual animality in the ways and workings of big city prostitution."[7] Bataille admits that this conception may possibly constitute what he calls the *text* of the painting, but he insists that "the text is *effaced by the painting. And what the painting signifies is not the text but the effacement. It is to the extent that Manet did not want to say what Valéry says—to the extent that, on the contrary, he suppressed (pulverized) meaning—that this woman is there; in her provocative exactitude, she is nothing; her nudity (corresponding, it is true, to that of the body) is the silence that emerges from her as from a stranded ship, a vacant ship: what she is is the 'sacred horror' of her presence—of a presence whose simplicity is that of absence."[8]

One recognizes in this passage a strategy and vocabulary that has had widespread critical success in recent years: the text as effacement, the suppression of meaning, the articulation of silence and absence. What is perhaps less easily recognizable, given, precisely, the familiarity of the terminology, is its violence, a violence specifically addressed in this case against "all that hides itself and is preserved" ("tout qui se cache et se conserve," Valéry's suggestive phrase) in a primitive and aggressive female sexuality. That shockingly impure sexuality is reduced by Bataille to *rien*; Olympia as subject is pulverized; the power of her nudity is emptied of physical reference; her body is incongruously compared to a stranded boat; and her disturbing erotic presence is considered significant only insofar as it is effaced. Bataille himself acknowledges the violence involved in these operations, but he attributes them not to the murderous desire operating in his own fascinated gaze but to the destructive operation of the painting itself. "*Olympia* as a whole cannot easily be distinguished from a crime or from the spectacle of death," he writes.[9] This crime, I would argue, is Bataille's wish-fulfilling fantasy: he *wants* to imagine Olympia dead, for as he maintains in a later book, *Death and Sensuality*, the final sense of eroticism for him is death, is silence, is the violent transgression of the other's individuality, and that other is quintessentially woman, woman as object of desire, as prostitute, prostitution being, he says, "the logical consequence of the feminine attitude."[10]

So Bataille in reading the text of *Olympia* as the effacement of woman's desire is figuring her as the object of his own defacing erotic drive. The attraction of theory for Bataille—and this must account to some extent for his appeal as a theoretician—is the annihilation of the female difference. When he writes "What prevails when we look at *Olympia* is the feeling of a suppression,"[11] the suppression he attributes to the painting is a function of his own need to dominate and master. Bataille is intent on revealing *Olympia*'s scandalous secret, thereby destroying her trap, but instead he falls right in: the painting lures him into an awareness of suppression that he attempts in turn to suppress, his sense of mastery being the deluded reflection of Olympia's controlling gaze.

How is this remarkable control achieved? No critic has answered this question better than T. J. Clark, who brilliantly analyzes the various ways in which the painting frustrates the spectator's attempt to fix and appropriate Olympia's gaze. What Huysmans called the

"irritating enigma"[12] of that gaze functions as the focus of other un-
certainties in the picture. "It is a gaze," Clark writes, "which gives
nothing away, as the reader attempts to interpret its blatancy; a look
direct yet guarded, poised very precisely between address and resistance."[13] The effect of that undecidable poise is reinforced by the
unusual positioning of Olympia's body within the frame: reclining
on two mattresses and two immense puffed-up pillows, she is placed
just too high to offer the viewer easy access; yet she does not look
down at him either. The pillows are tilted at a sharp downward angle
that is strangely out of relation with the head-on perspective from
which the mattress is viewed. The result of these conflicting modes
of presentation is, in Clark's words, "stalemate, a kind of baulked
invitation, in which the spectator is given no established place for
viewing and identification, nor offered the tokens of exclusion and
resistance"[14] (as he is, for instance, by Courbet, who had portrayed
in *The Bather* of 1853 a grossly overweight bourgeoise turning her
fleshy back to the viewer).

Clark goes on to note that Olympia's body is constructed in two
inconsistent graphic modes. On the one hand is the emphatically
linear outline of her form and the hard-edged breaks and intersec-
tions that appear to sever her body into distinct pieces, the black
ribbon being, of course, the most striking instrument of this dis-
articulation. On the other hand, coexisting with this representation
of a *corps morcelé* is a kind of soft, fluid bodily territory where tran-
sitions are not clearly defined, as in the elusive contour of the right
breast and the whole area spreading in an almost uniform tonality
from that breast down to the thigh. Thus Olympia is at once muti-
lated and whole, her bodily parts at once dislocated and fused. Her
stature is similarly uncertain: the monumentality of the image leads
the viewer to think of her as imposing, while her scale in relation to
the bed, the black servant, and the flowers produces on the contrary
a sense of almost childlike proportions.

It is through these and other such modes of instability and equiv-
ocation that *Olympia* captivates its viewer. The viewer recognizes
numerous signs of femininity in the representation, but they refuse
to coalesce into a clearly readable meaning. Certain aspects of Olympia's body suggest yielding compliance, others defiant resistance. She
appears small and easily dominated, but also imperious and coldly
disdainful. The ambiguity of her name accentuates this troubling indeterminacy. There is, of course, a classical echo—Mount Olympus,
abode of the gods—but also a purely modern one: "Olympe" is listed
in Parent-Duchâtelet's 1836 study of prostitution in Paris as one of

the *noms de guerre* frequently assumed by upper-class prostitutes[15] (Dumas gives the name "Olympe" to the heartless, venal courtesan, Marguerite's rival, in *La Dame aux camélias*). But the most interesting hypothetical model, precisely because it thematizes the play of indeterminacy, is the mechanical doll named Olympia in E. T. A. Hoffmann's story "The Sandman," the text on which Freud based his analysis of the uncanny. The captivating doll is at once human and nonhuman, alive and dead, whole yet dismemberable, female yet not. It is associated, in obvious ways, with childhood, whence originate, according to Freud, the primitive beliefs whose recurrence after repression creates the effect of uncanniness.

What repressed primitive belief might Manet's painting be felt to evoke? In his mocking commentary on *Olympia*, one of the early hack critics of the 1865 salon made a connection that may provide us with a clue to this question. The journalist denounces Olympia as "some form or other blown up like a grotesque in indiarubber," and goes on to call her "a sort of monkey making fun of the pose and the movement of the arm of Titian's Venus, with a hand shamelessly flexed."[16] Viewing Olympia as a kind of doll, this writer is led to evoke the placement and articulation of the hand covering her sex. He does so via an allusion to Titian's *Venus of Urbino* (figure 2), a reference that is now a commonplace of art history but that he was the only critic to notice in 1865. Not that this commonplace, I should hasten to add, unambiguously clarifies Manet's intentions, since it is impossible to decide if Olympia is to be understood as the goddess of love in a new guise, an ironic subversion of that classical myth, or, as Theodore Reff maintains, a modern counterpart of the wealthy courtesan commonly thought to have been Titian's model.[17]

But back to that hand, very differently construed in the two paintings, though occupying in both the central focus of the composition. The hand of Titian's Venus folds inward, fading from view as it elides with her sex. The gesture carries a certain autoerotic suggestion, but that suggestion, as I read it, in no way excludes the male viewer, serving rather as an invitation, a sign of willing receptivity. Venus's look goes out toward the spectator, includes him, and brings his gaze back to the central point of her pliant sexuality, precisely marked by the vertical line of the screen behind her.

In contrast, Olympia's hand, in Reff's phrase, "conveys at once greater inhibition and a more deliberate provocativeness."[18] Her hand covers the entire pubic area in a gesture that, compared to Venus's relaxed, sensuous pose, seems self-conscious and tense. It is this deliberate gesture of concealment, in conjunction with Olympia's

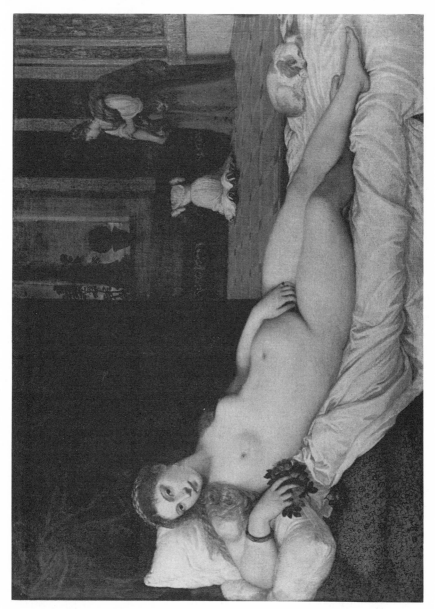

Fɪɢ. 2. Titian, *The Venus of Urbino*, 1538. Galleria degli Uffizi, Florence.

ambiguous gaze, "poised . . . between address and resistance," that appears provocative and even, to pursue our earlier line of argument, uncanny. The viewer seems to be challenged to ask: what is being concealed? What is being suppressed? As if he didn't know, you may object. But perhaps at the level of primitive belief that the uncanny evokes he is not so sure. Perhaps the subject that Zola and Bataille were so anxious to suppress is what threatens to emerge were this repressive hand removed. But let us look more closely: perhaps this repression has not been entirely successful and something is even now in the process of emerging—are not those fingers penislike, and did not Freud maintain that "a multiplication of penis symbols signifies castration"?[19]

As Laura Mulvey has argued in an influential article, "Woman as icon displayed for the gaze and enjoyment of men, the active controllers of the look, always threatens to evoke the anxiety [that icon] originally signified, [that is, woman's] lack of a penis, implying a threat of castration and hence unpleasure."[20] This, I believe, is the fantasized lack that generates Olympia's figuration as scandal. In a formulation that sounds perfectly Freudian, Mallarmé said of Manet's work that "it surprised us all as something long hidden but suddenly revealed."[21] *Olympia* traps the male viewer by making him unconsciously aware of an anxiety about sexual difference that he thought he had mastered but that now returns. This return is all the more unsettling in that its vehicle is an image of woman as publicly available commodity, displayed for male consumption. Valéry's phrase about "tout qui se cache et se conserve" in urban prostitution is telling indeed. What Olympia hides her representation preserves. The displacements of the hidden can be traced in the painting to the fleecy shock of fringe hanging over the side of the bed, and, even more scandalously, to the black cat, slang equivalent then as now of the female sexual organ. The caricaturists of 1865, who, to a man, gave the curved tail of Manet's feline a tumescent erection (see figures 3, 4), seem to have sensed the central ambiguity in the painting's sexual imagery: this *catin*'s pussy is potentially phallic.[22]

Finally, there are the flowers carried by the black servant. If the colorful bouquet functions as a desexualized displacement of Olympia's genitals, the connotations of the black female counteract this function. When a critic using the pseudonym Geronte referred to Olympia in 1865 as "that Hottentot Venus with a black cat,"[23] he was assimilating Olympia to her maid and underlining the meaning of the maid through the debased feline association. In an article bearing specifically on Manet's painting, Sander Gilman has shown that the

Fig. 3. Cham, *Manet, The Birth of the Little Cabinet-Maker (ébéniste)*.
Wood engraving in *Le Charivari*, May 14, 1865.

Fig. 4. Bertall, *The Cat's Tail, or the Coal Lady from Batignolles*.
Wood engraving in *L'Illustration*, June 3, 1865.

Hottentot women exhibited in France in the early part of the century, whose hypertrophied genitalia and protruding buttocks were considered anatomical marks of their atavistic physiology and primitive lasciviousness, were thought to typify the pathological sexuality of black women in general.[24] If a black woman was paired with a white female in a nineteenth-century representation, Gilman argues, the black figure's emblematic role was to suggest her white counterpart's primitive concupiscence and sexual degeneracy, a suggestion to which Geronte evidently responded. The link was all the easier to make given Olympia's identity as a prostitute, the prostitute's deviant sexuality being associated popularly with an atavistic return to an unbridled eroticism. Moreover, a tradition existed dating back to the eighteenth century of paintings in which black servants displayed their mistress's intimate charms to the spectator, a voyeuristic tradition whose connotations of prostitution became increasingly overt in the nineteenth century. So the black maid is not, as Zola and the formalists would have it, simply a darkly colored counterpart to Olympia's whiteness. In 1865 she may well have aroused in many male viewers the fantasy of a dark, threatening, anomalous sexuality lurking just underneath Olympia's hand.

The maid is in many ways as difficult to interpret as Olympia herself. Her very existence enters into the irresolvable problematic of Olympia's class. We wonder just how common this prostitute may be if she can afford to hire such an exotic servant. The maid's look at her mistress enters into the equally irresolvable problematic of Olympia's gaze. Blatantly ignoring her presence, Olympia cuts off communication with her attendant much as her stare cuts off communication with her spectator outside the frame. Thus the spectator is, to a degree, represented in the painting by the maid, who deferentially offers flowers but whose gift is ignored. Furthermore, the maid's gesture is itself an enactment of agency: she is, we surmise, offering the bouquet in the name of a male admirer. She is a deputy, or stand-in, a servant two-fold, of Olympia and of Olympia's client. This double subservience is an essential aspect of the maid's meaning, and the male viewer's sense of being represented by a glance emanating from a position defined through race and sex as one of servitude and mediation contributes to his discomfort with the image.

My point about the displaced signs of Olympia's sexual identity is that none of them resolves the castration threat associated with that uncanny identity. Fetishism is a strategy to gain control over the uncanny by embodying in a single object two incompatible propositions. Olympia herself is a perfect example of such an object. As we have seen, her body is represented as both violently severed and smoothly unified, decapitated by the ribbon around her neck yet composed of a single mass of yellowish color, lacking the phallus yet furnished with five digital substitutes. But I am not suggesting that Olympia functions as a fetish for the male viewer. My point is that she reflects back to him the fetishizing desire in his gaze, forcing him to respond to the scandalous lack she represents in his unconscious.

The painting initiates this subversive reflection by constructing its beholder as male. It is evidently to a male viewer that Olympia offers her availability as "a token of triumph over the threat of castration and a protection against it" (Freud).[25] She appears to be displayed as an erotic spectacle signifying passive submission to male desire. She seduces her viewer by seeming to confirm his mastery, reinforcing his illusion of narcissistic wholeness by presenting herself iconically as a magnifying mirror of his phallic power. But this tricky mirror is a trap. Instead of hiding its operation, the mirror reveals its distortions disseminated throughout the representational field.

Olympia thus activates and exposes the dynamics of the production of woman as fetish object in patriarchal consumer society. Manet's painting suggests empathetically that such a production constitutes female sexuality as prostitution. The painter expresses his empathy by saturating his picture of Olympia with elements constructed so that they mirror back to the male viewer his fetishistic mode of appropriating woman. This is why the critics of 1865, faced with Olympia's challenge, repeatedly evoked cadaver fantasies: the painting offered them no avenues of escape from their fearful association of female sexuality with castration, disease, and death. *Olympia* overtly displays the failure of the mechanisms whereby this fear is mastered, a refusal of patriarchal positioning. It translates the body into representational codes whose noncoincidence prevents visual resolutions; it performs displacements that reveal internal incompatibilities requiring further displacements. The viewer witnesses woman constructed as fetish object for capitalist consumption, but that consumption loses its appeal to the degree that the constructive machinery is exposed and the principle of lack driving the machine regains its original fantasmatic content.

Zola and Bataille attempt to block this potential return of the repressed by projecting the lack in *Olympia*'s representation back onto the canvas, where they effectively neutralize its sexual meaning. A similar strategy today might claim that the painting's multiple displacements activate a libidinal economy that generates pleasure through the very mobility of its psychic investments. Such an analysis would suppose a viewing of *Olympia* that transcends male anxiety and causes a certain euphoria through the liberating effect of the picture's semiotic irresolutions. Although this response may account for some of the "esthetic" pleasure the picture affords, the psychosexual origins of this pleasure are fundamentally no different from those sustaining the Zola/Bataille formalist approach. The essential motivating drive in both cases is the denial of female desire and subjectivity and the reduction of woman to inert fetish. Whereas Manet's empathetic art makes the viewer uneasily aware of the violence involved in this reduction—the black servant, emblem of woman as slave, contributes to this awareness—the formalist reading invites the reader/viewer to enjoy the spectacle of the prostitute's corpse.

What, then, of the position of the female viewer? According to my analysis, her position is constructed so as to problematize for the male *his* insecurity about sexual difference. How may a woman respond to being placed in this position? The question is complex, and I can do no more than allude to its importance here. The problem of describing the dynamics of the female gaze when it emanates from a position constructed as male—which, given the assumptions underlying representational practices for centuries, is nearly always the case—is one of the primary concerns of current feminist thinking about sexuality in the field of vision. As regards *Olympia*, a historical inquiry into viewer response could not easily be extended to female spectators, since, as far as I know, no woman recorded her impressions of Manet's painting in 1865. And this situation is typical. A history of the female gaze would be extremely difficult to document. Our present perspective does, however, allow us to theorize the dynamics of female viewing in ways that recognize both the conditions that inform woman's internalization of a male gaze and her strategies to subvert the operations of that gaze. For example, my analysis of the way *Olympia* destabilizes the male agency of the look could be associated with the notion, elaborated by certain feminist psychoanalytic and film theorists, of femininity as a deliberate masquerade, a kind of flaunting of the conventional signs of the feminine in order to prevent appropriation of the self as a stable image of masculine desire.[26] Olympia could well be perceived as performing such a masquerade, as if she were demonstrating the diverse modes of offering her body to public view while identifying herself with none of them, refusing to be present in any single version of her image. It may be this refusal that some female viewers of today appreciate most in Olympia's representation. Perhaps these viewers identify with Olympia's defiant look and through its medium gaze back at the discomfited male spectator whose desire it confounds. Such an identification would involve an appropriation by women of the processes of semiotic slippage and gender instability invented by the male masters of modernism to control their sexual anxiety.

NOTES

1. Charles Baudelaire, *Fusées*, in *Oeuvres complètes*, ed. Y.-G. LeDantec (Paris: Bibliothèque de la Pléiade, 1961), p. 1247.
2. John Berger, *Ways of Seeing* (London: Penguin Books, 1972), p. 56.
3. Timothy J. Clark, "Preliminaries to a Possible Treatment of 'Olympia' in 1865," *Screen* 21, no. 1 (Spring 1980), 20. This study forms the basis for Clark's long chapter on *Olympia* in *The Painting of Modern Life: Paris in the Art of Manet and His Followers* (New York: Knopf, 1985), which appeared shortly after my article was written. I am deeply indebted to Clark's stimulating work.
4. Théophile Gautier in *Le Moniteur universel*, June 24, 1985. Reprinted in *Tableaux à la plume* (Paris, 1880). Quoted in Clark's *The Painting of Modern Life*, p. 285, n. 24. For the critical response to Manet's painting, see also Theodore Reff, *Manet: Olympia* (New York: Viking Press, 1977), pp. 16–41.
5. However, as Clark points out, the discourse on prostitution performed its own repression: the *courtisane* was acceptable for representation as a figure of desire and modernity whereas the venal low-class prostitute was too threatening to be admissable as a subject for art (see *The Painting of Modern Life*, pp. 102–11).
6. Emile Zola, "Edouard Manet," in *Oeuvres complètes*, vol. 12, ed. Henri Mitterand (Paris: Cercle du livre précieux, 1969), p. 839.
7. Paul Valéry, "Triomphe de Manet" in *Oeuvres*, vol. 2, ed. Jean Hytier (Paris: Bibliothèque de la Pléiade, 1960), p. 1329.
8. Georges Bataille, *Manet* (Geneva: Skira, 1983), p. 62.
9. Ibid., p. 69.
10. Georges Bataille, *Death and Sensuality: A Study of Eroticism and the Taboo* (New York: Ballantine, 1969), p. 126.
11. Bataille, *Manet*, p. 63.
12. Quoted from Joris Karl Huysmans's annotated copy of the catalogue of an 1884 Manet exposition in Reff, *Manet: Olympia*, p. 28.
13. Clark, "Preliminaries," p. 34. Walter Benjamin finds a similar kind of gaze to be prevalent in Baudelaire's poetry, a gaze that fascinates to the extent that it is encumbered by distance. "The deeper the remoteness

which a glance has to overcome," writes Benjamin, "the stronger will be the spell that is apt to emanate from the gaze. In eyes that look at us with a mirrorlike blankness the remoteness remains complete. It is precisely for this reason that such eyes know nothing of distance" (*Illuminations* [New York: Harcourt, Brace and World, 1968], p. 192). Benjamin goes on to associate such a glance with the self-protective wariness of the prostitute.

14. Ibid.
15. A.-J.-B. Parent-Duchâtelet, *La Prostitution dans la ville de Paris*, vol. 1 (Paris: J.-B. Baillière, 1836), p. 132.
16. Quoted in Clark, "Preliminaries," p. 26.
17. Reff, *Manet: Olympia*, pp. 49–61.
18. Ibid., p. 58.
19. Sigmund Freud, "Medusa's Head" (1922, 1940), in *The Standard Edition of the Complete Psychological Works of Sigmund Freud* (hereafter *S.E.*), ed. and trans. James Strachey et al., 24 vols. (London: Hogarth Press, 1953–74), vol. 23, p. 273. In *The Painting of Modern Life* (p. 135), Clark moves tentatively in the direction I am suggesting here, observing that Olympia's hand may have enraged the critics "because it failed to enact the lack of the phallus (which is not to say it quite signified the opposite)."
20. Laura Mulvey, "Visual Pleasure and Narrative Cinema," *Screen* 16, no. 3 (1975), 13.
21. Stéphane Mallarmé, "The Impressionists and Edouard Manet," *Art Monthly Review*, Sept. 30, 1876.
22. That the cat suggests a threatening ambiguity about woman's sexual identity is also Werner Hofmann's thesis in *The Earthly Paradise: Art in the Nineteenth Century* (New York: Braziller, 1961), pp. 350–51. Hofmann sees the picture as dividing a sphinx figure into human and animal parts, the Sphinx being, as in Baudelaire's poem "La Beauté," "éternel et muet ainsi que la matière." It may be partly as a kind of hommage to Baudelaire that Manet included the cat in the painting.
23. Quoted in Clark, *The Painting of Modern Life*, p. 289, n. 70.
24. Sander Gilman, *Difference and Pathology: Stereotypes of Sexuality, Race, and Madness* (Ithaca: Cornell University Press, 1985), pp. 76–108.
25. Freud, "Fetishism" (1927), *S.E.*, 21:154.
26. See Michèle Montrelay, "Inquiry into Femininity," *m/f* 1 (1978), 83–101; and Mary Ann Doane, "Film and the Masquerade: Theorising the Female Spectator," *Screen* 23 (Sept.–Oct. 1982), 74–87.

Marlene Dietrich, *The Blue Angel*, and Female Performance

In recent years, feminist critics of the classical narrative cinema have attempted to rethink and reformulate the widely held view that the seductive pleasures of the cinema are rooted in voyeurism and fetishism, and structured by the polarities of the active, male look versus the passive, female object. It has been pointed out frequently enough that Laura Mulvey's famous formulation of the man as "bearer of the look," woman its object, assumes a male spectator.[1] Accordingly, increasing attention has been devoted to the vantage point of the female spectator, and to the ways in which a consideration of female spectatorship might then complicate, problematize, or otherwise put into question cinematic seduction understood as the regime of rigid gender polarity and heterosexual desire. Analysis of female spectatorship raises questions concerning how the cinematic apparatus addresses the sexual differentiation of spectators, and how spectators respond to films in ways that may well be unauthorized, but nonetheless meaningful, in terms other than those prescribed by the institutions of narrative cinema.

A promising direction for such explorations of the multiplicity of spectator positions, as opposed to the monolithic position of the spectator implied by the scenario of castration anxiety, is analysis of stars, of actors and actresses and the myths generated about them.[2] Recent studies of stars and the phenomenon of stardom have suggested the insufficiency of a number of critical and theoretical models in film studies. However different they may be in other ways, both traditional studies of the film *auteur* and more recent psychoanalytically based theories of the cinematic apparatus, for instance, share a definition of the cinema as reducible to a single, homogeneous entity, be it the film director or the cinematic apparatus. Analysis of stars has emphasized, by contrast, the shifting and sometimes contradictory levels at work in the creation of a "star image," challenging the definition of actors as mere vehicles for a director's vision, and challenging as well the notion of the "ideal spectator" as constructed and contained by the institutions of the cinema. Examination of the appeal of stars offers the possibility, then, of an understanding of cinematic seduction attuned to the contradictory movements of desire, and to scenarios of pleasure that exceed narrative formulas—whether the formula in question be the naive articulation of an author's vision, or the more complex (but equally reductive) reenactment of castration anxiety.

Richard Dyer states that "star images function crucially in relation to contradictions within and between ideologies, which they seek variously to manage or resolve. In exceptional cases, it has been argued that certain stars, far from managing contradictions, either expose them or embody an alternative or oppositional ideological position (itself usually contradictory) to dominant ideology."[3] Along those lines, Andrew Britton's study of Katharine Hepburn begins with the following affirmation: "The significance of the great female stars of the Hollywood cinema for feminist cultural studies lies in the contradictions they generate within narrative structures which are committed overall to the reaffirmation of bourgeois-patriarchal norms."[4]

Marlene Dietrich is a particularly appropriate example of the difficulties and complexities of a feminist reading of the female star.[5] Her sexual ambiguity has been noted more than once, both in the sense of her androgynous beauty, underscored by her appearances in drag, and of her transgression of heterosexual boundaries (for instance, the famous scene in *Morocco* where Dietrich kisses a female member of the audience).[6] Moreover, Dietrich's presence on screen virtually always implies a detachment, a sense of cool irony, even though her film roles often lead to an affirmation of sacrificial love and devotion. The myth of Dietrich as it has developed both on and off screen is without question full of contradictions. Her relationship with director Josef Von Sternberg remains the most famous example of the myth of the Hollywood director as Svengali, the actress as Trilby. Little in Dietrich's career leads us to believe that theirs was a collaboration of equals, even though it was Dietrich who emerged the more successful when their collaboration ended. Dietrich was also reputed to be—particularly later in her film career—an extremely difficult star who demanded control over her image. Alfred Hitchcock, who worked with her in *Stage Fright* (1950) said: "Miss Dietrich is a professional. A professional actress, a professional dress designer, a professional cameraman."[7] Similarly, the image of Dietrich that circulated through the popular press, and fan magazines in particular, focused constantly on the glamor queen who was really a *hausfrau* and a devoted mother, suggesting her contradictory status as an image, one that required regulation by recourse to stereotypical myths of woman-as-mother.

Central to many recent analyses of the female star is the notion of resistance, a subtle undermining of the very notion of woman as object of spectacle, with attendant implications for the film spectator for whom such ironic detachment may well be the basis for another kind of cinematic pleasure.[8] The notion of resistance is certainly a useful reminder that patriarchal discourse is neither a monolithic system nor a totally successful one in its objectification of the female body. However, the concept of resistance, if it is indeed useful in understanding the female star in relationship to female spectatorship, requires further elaboration. If a female character "resists" the power and authority of the male gaze, that resistance may well be nothing more than a temporary distraction, a brief interlude that serves to reinforce the conquest of the female body. Thus, using that resistance to read a film against the grain may be somewhat self-defeating. In other words, and as many critics have suggested, resistance may be a function of the classical cinema, and not an exception in absolute contradiction with narrative and visual momentum.[9]

Dietrich is often described as an example of a resisting image, and it has been suggested that many of her films are riven with contradictions.[10] *Blonde Venus* (1932) has received particular attention in this context, for the image of Dietrich as the title character Helen Faraday strains credibility. She is presented as a sexually enticing performer and as a mother who returns to the stage only to save her husband's life. That the film never manages successfully to integrate these two roles into a convincing whole has been taken as suggestive of a critique of women's position in patriarchy.[11] In a more general way, Dietrich has been cited as an example of an "exceptional" female star who consistently gets away with a return of the look, with, that is, an ironic commentary on the mechanics of performance and particularly on the sexual politics of the look. Dietrich's performance numbers are virtually always marked by a tone that ranges anywhere from subtle mockery to downright sarcasm. As a result of this attitude, so firmly identified with the Dietrich persona, even those performances which seem to entail a cutting down to size of the Dietrich legend (such as *Destry Rides Again* [1939]) are never quite successful. For if one could argue that Dietrich's ironic presence is contained and thus recuperated by the narrative structures of individual films, one might argue as well that her cool detachment has its own kind of recuperative value.

The Blue Angel (1930) marks the first collaboration between Josef Von Sternberg and Marlene Dietrich, a collaboration which is credited with having brought Dietrich international stardom. Dietrich portrays Lola Lola, a seductive nightclub singer who embodies many of the characteristics which would become central to the myth of Marlene Dietrich: she is self-absorbed, disdainful of men, inexplicably mysterious, and above all, unquestionably and irresistibly desirable. Thus *The Blue Angel* deserves particular attention not only as a central text in the creation of the Dietrich persona, but also as its founding myth. For Lola Lola is not unlike the actress to whom Von Sternberg was attracted, as he tells us in his autobiography, certainly for her face and her figure, but primarily for her "cold disdain" and "indifference."[12] *The Blue Angel* serves, then, as an appropriate vantage point from which to consider Marlene Dietrich and the phenomenon of resistance as constituting a seductive appeal of the cinema in its own right.

The story of *The Blue Angel* is well known. A professor is humiliated and degraded by his fatal attraction to the cabaret performer Lola Lola. Every description, even a rudimentary plot summary, however simple and straightforward, is also a reading. Numerous accounts of *The Blue Angel* begin with an apparently innocent summary of the film. Thus John Baxter describes the film as follows: "Emmanuel Rath, professor of English at a provincial high school, pursues a group of his pupils to a sleazy night club called 'The Blue Angel,' is infatuated with the cabaret singer Lola, gives up his career to marry her, and becomes a stooge in the troupe. Years later, the combination of Lola taking a new lover and his appearance on stage in the town where he once taught drives Rath insane, and he runs to his old school room, dying with his arms around the desk that was a symbol of his standing."[13]

The significant terms in Baxter's description are Rath's "infatuation," and the fact that he "gives up" his career, while Lola later "takes" a new lover. For such terms assume that Rath is an innocent creature who is corrupted by Lola. This reading may well be encouraged and authorized by the film, but it is just that—a reading. Similar readings are evident in the ways other critics describe significant details or the overall tone of the film. Alexander Walker says of Lola that she "regards the spectacle her victim is making of himself cooly and egoistically."[14] Donald Spoto describes the tone of "social and moral meanness" in the film that is located—"of course" —in the person of Lola Lola.[15] What is assumed, then, about *The Blue Angel* is that however complex or ambiguous the film may be in other ways, it tells nonetheless a straightforward story of a man who is humiliated by a woman.

That there may be something askew in such descriptions of the film is suggested pointedly by Angela Carter: "[Rath's] marriage to Lola-Lola looks less like the surrender to a fatal passion than a grab at the chance of a lifelong meal ticket. How anybody has ever been able to see this film as the tragedy of an upright citizen of Toytown ruined by the baleful influences of a floozy is quite beyond me." Carter's reading of *The Blue Angel* takes as its point of departure another point of view, that of Lola herself, whom she describes as the "attractive, unimaginative cabaret singer, who marries a boring old fart in a fit of weakness, lives to regret it but is too soft-hearted to actually throw him out until his sulks, tantrums and idleness become intolerable."[16] This is a point of view which insists, as well, on the position of a *female* spectator, for whom *The Blue Angel* is another film entirely than the one described by Baxter, Walker, and Spoto.

While there is by now an impressive tradition in feminist criticism of reading "against the grain," Carter's remarks suggest to me much more than a counter-reading of *The Blue Angel*. I would argue, rather, that *The Blue Angel* is structured by a tension between different modes of performance, and that the image of Marlene Dietrich that emerges in this film cannot be reduced to the simple duality of the male look versus the female object of the look. Nor would I argue, as some critics have, that Dietrich subverts that duality by "returning the look"—a dubious subversion in any case, since such a return of the gaze affirms the duality, and defines the female gaze as a reactive intervention.[17] If Dietrich has a resistant function at all, it is in articulating a mode of performance that is appealing and seductive precisely because it has a marginal place within the phallocentric logic of the gaze.

Professor Rath is a teacher whose authority over his male students is compromised by their fascination with Lola Lola. They look at photographs of her during class, and Rath discovers that even his prized pupil has photographs of this wanton female. Thus Herr Rath's first visit to the Blue Angel, the seedy nightclub where Lola performs, is motivated by a desire to affirm his authority by preventing the students from frequenting the club. When Professor Rath makes his way to the Blue Angel for the first time, his journey is one fraught with obstacles, suggesting the enormous psychic and social distance between his world and that of the cabaret. With its excessive movements, its seeming disorder and anarchy, its proliferation of bodies and smoke and grotesque symbols of lust, the nightclub seems a far cry from the orderly and authoritarian universe of the professor's classroom.

Professor Rath's teaching skills are based on intimidation and mimicry. When a student recites Hamlet's soliloquy, he stumbles on "that is the question," unable to pronounce properly the "th" sound. Indeed, mimicry is something of a problem for Professor Rath, for his student's inability, or refusal, to perfect an English sound both reflects his own failure to impart an image of perfection and assures his position of authority. Likewise within the Blue Angel, mimicry is everywhere on display. Lola herself is a parody of certain images of female decadence and sexual attraction, recalling nineteenth-century *femmes fatales* as well as Wedekind's Lulu and Berlin cabarets of the 1920s.[18] She is a pastiche, a collection of allusions, exemplifying Roland Barthes's suggestion that "beauty cannot assert itself save in the form of a citation."[19]

Within the nightclub, though, mimicry has no pretense of authority. The first image that we see of the interior of the Blue Angel presents a spectacle that is in every way opposed to the spectacle of Rath's classroom, where there is clear demarcation of the boundaries between performer and onlookers, teacher and students. Lola is onstage, singing, surrounded by other women in the performing troupe onstage with her. Lola drinks from another woman's glass, and casually wipes her mouth with a piece of her costume. Scenery is changed in full view of the audience; the mechanics of performance are just as much part of the spectacle as the finished product. Lola is a curious object of attention, for distraction seems to be a fundamental principle of the cabaret: waiters shout orders over her song, and the stage is so full of women and stage props that it is difficult to center one's attention on her. Indeed, the close-up, the centering device par excellence in the cinema, is rarely used in the film, and during the first scenes in the Blue Angel, what few close-ups there are, are used for what seem initially to be quite inappropriate objects. A cardboard cherub, part of the stage scenery, is seen in close-up, foreshadowing the role that Rath will soon acquire; and another close-up shows a very large woman who rolls her eyes in a mockery of sexual seduction. The close-up is used, in other words, to foreground and caricature performer and onlooker alike.

Most strikingly, of course, the cabaret is populated by women, of all shapes and sizes, both onstage and in the audience. In Rath's classroom, a female chorus is heard when Rath opens the windows while his class writes a composition. But whereas Rath can shut out those female voices at will simply by closing the window, the image of Lola, secretly circulating amongst his students, is not so easily contained. In the cabaret, the female voice and the female body presented in such a fragmented way in the classroom come together with a vengeance. Lola sings off-key and she parades around in a variety of silly costumes, all of which parody the conventions of femininity, from the half-skirt which covers only Lola's front to the cutaway skirt which reveals her underwear and garters; from the excess of frilly stereotypes to the combination of male and female attire. And the female chorus remains, now a chorus most vehemently of the flesh as well as the voice.

The women who surround Lola onstage have from the outset an ambivalent status. It has been suggested that Von Sternberg surrounded Lola with "horses" to better accentuate Lola's charms.[20] For the women onstage are of different shapes and sizes, but they are all plump. Donald Spoto remarks that Lola herself is plump, "but she's surrounded by so many who are downright fat that we don't notice."[21] Interestingly enough, however, there is little within the film to mark this differentiation between Lola and the "horses." To be sure, she is the featured performer, but when another woman carries on her song while Lola changes clothes, or when extremely plump women are seen onstage, there is nothing in the reaction of the audience within the film to suggest that these women are somehow less attractive for their abundance of flesh. I would argue that at the beginning of the film, there is in fact little differentiation between the women performers. Put another way, there is more connection between the women of the Blue Angel than there is opposition, a connection defined by the open mockery and satire of the objectification of the female body. There is no hierarchy in the club comparable, say, to that of the classroom. The first glimpse that we have of the nightclub is remarkably suggestive of the carnivalesque mode described by Bakhtin: an abundance of flesh, a mockery of established conventions of taste and art, and a preoccupation with the body, and in particular with the lower regions of the body (emphasized by virtually all of Dietrich's costumes).[22]

If I envision the female bodies onstage as something other than so many props to set off Lola, it is to suggest that there is more to *The Blue Angel* than the story of Professor Rath's fatal discovery of his libido. There is another downfall in *The Blue Angel* which may not have quite the dramatic contours of the professor's humiliation, but which is crucial to a reading of performance in the film. This downfall is the disintegration of the carnivalesque world of the cabaret, a disintegration which is initiated, in narrative terms, by the scrutiny of the professor. For however much he appears to lose virtually every sense of bourgeois reason once he has become "contaminated" by the sheer erotic energy of Lola and her surroundings, Professor Rath nonetheless continues to exercise supreme narrative authority. The activation of his desires provides the necessary complications and oppositions to make a story.

However confused the professor is when he ventures into this alien world, his presence does initiate a significant change. When Rath first enters the nightclub, he becomes entangled in a fishnet and is suddenly caught unaware by a spotlight which the women turn on members of their audience. Rath may well be confused and befuddled by his suddenly being thrust into the limelight, but his position as a spectator within the film soon neutralizes the frenzied excesses of the performance initially associated with the Blue Angel. For if the professor is flung into the recesses of his own desires, a parallel reversal occurs in Lola. The professor makes a second visit to the nightclub, ostensibly to return Lola's underwear, which a student had mischievously placed in the professor's pocket. Kiepert (the manager of the performing troupe) and the proprietor of the club have arranged a rendezvous between Lola and a customer. Lola refuses the advances of the customer, and Rath creates a disturbance by insisting that the man leave Lola alone. Suddenly, it becomes clear that Lola has a desire for bourgeois respectability just as repressed as Rath's sexual desires. For Lola looks somewhat stunned when she says "Someone fighting over me? That hasn't happened for a long time!"

In parallel to this revelation of another side to Lola is the emergence of another kind of spectacle, one which provides a sharp contrast to the carnivalesque performance characteristic of the first scenes in the nightclub. For when Kiepert seats Rath in the honored loge in the cabaret, during Lola's performance of "Falling in Love Again," a conventional shot–reverse shot, moving from (male) spectator to (female) performer, isolates the man who is falling in love and the woman who emanates her desirability. To be sure, there are disturbances in this neat symmetry: Lola is still surrounded by women performers, even if she is much more centered than in previous performances, and Rath's schoolboy giggles betray a male spectator who possesses little of the authority that we have come to associate with the subject of the look. Images of the clown—described by Siegfried Kracauer as a "silent witness" in the film[23]—and a female statue strain the symmetry of the scene, but do not upset it. The traces of the carnivalesque atmosphere remain, in other words, but they have been repressed and marginalized.

It could be argued that the principal male subject of *The Blue Angel* is Kiepert, the manager of the performance, the master of ceremonies who stages the encounter between Lola and Rath. That the central struggle in *The Blue Angel* is between Rath and Kiepert becomes increasingly evident in the film, particularly near the conclusion, when it is Kiepert who humiliates Rath onstage. The final performance number of the film, when Kiepert puts Rath in the role of student and orders him to crow, is a parody of Rath's teaching techniques. The scene suggests that mimicry has come full circle in the film, from Rath's classroom to the stage of the Blue Angel. However, there is an enormous difference between the parody that concludes the film and leads to Rath's death, and the parody that characterizes the nightclub earlier in the film. Amongst the women, and between the women and the audience, there is little of the deadly humiliation that emerges when a spectacle is created from the power struggle between two men. And it is precisely that struggle which affirms a principle of male sovereignty.

The role of Guste, a secondary female character, is significant in this respect. For when we first see the cabaret, Guste is one of many women onstage. She is the performer who continues Lola's song while Lola changes clothes; and she later scolds Rath mockingly when she discovers him holding Lola's underwear. Only when Rath comes to the Blue Angel with the intention of proposing marriage to Lola is Guste revealed to be Kiepert's wife. From that point on she becomes a cliché, a nagging wife. Previously Guste was associated with the ebullient and straightforward sexuality of the women in the cabaret; once Rath proposes, and once bourgeois order is imposed, she becomes nothing more than the stereotype of a conventional wife. The shift in representation of Guste thus reflects the changing mode of performance in the film, but with an interesting twist. Guste does not become the object of the male gaze in any typical sense, but her transformation in the film is determined by an equally phallocentric principle of narrative representation. Initially defined in terms of her identity as part of the community of women who appear onstage, Guste is suddenly removed from the world of performance proper. She then acquires a narrative function only by virtue of her relationship to Kiepert. Her heterosexual identity, and her connection to the manager of the performance, become visible only when the opposing worlds of Rath and Lola intersect.

After the marriage of Rath and Lola, the performances change even more drastically, for Lola performs virtually solo. Gone is the group of women sitting onstage, with the suggestions of the erasure of boundaries between spectator and performer; instead, Lola appears in the foreground of the image, accompanied by an orchestra or by a group of chorines—the visual equivalent of the chorus of voices heard early in the film in Rath's classroom. In Lola's final number, a rendition of "Falling in Love Again" which functions as an ironic commentary on Rath's final return to the schoolroom, she is isolated in a medium closeup, with virtually no background material. Lola's performance is now a mirror image of what Rath attempted to impose on his classroom, for she has become a perfectly containable image of a tart, a man-eater, a seductress and destroyer of men. To be sure, Lola is from the outset a superb mimic of the conventions of sexual desire, but her mode of imitation is playful and irreducible to the clichés of seductress that are produced in the course of the film. What *The Blue Angel* demonstrates, then, is the creation of an image of woman to the measure of male fantasy.

If Rath's attraction to Lola is fatal, then so too is Lola's attraction to Rath. Lola may emerge at the conclusion of the film as a conventional vamp, but the price paid for her victory—if indeed it can be called a victory—is her representability within the confines of patriarchal discourse. What *The Blue Angel* traces then, in the reciprocal seductions of the male bourgeois and the female performer, is the transformation of one kind of performance into another: the transformation of a world of transgressed boundaries between spectator and performer, male and female, thin and fat, into woman defined, purely and simply, as object of the male gaze. In this sense, I would agree with Laura Mulvey's assertion that Sternberg produces the "ultimate fetish, taking it to the point where the powerful look of the male protagonist (characteristic of traditional narrative film) is broken in favour of the image in direct erotic rapport with the spectator."[24] However, what makes *The Blue Angel* interesting in these terms is not simply the *fact* of that "direct erotic rapport," but the way in which it is produced and manufactured in the course of the film.

What *The Blue Angel* offers, then, is the exposition of two conflicting modes of performance, and two conflicting modes of subjectivity—the one a dissolution of the boundaries between self and other, the other an affirmation of them. But two questions remain as to the position of this carnivalesque mode of performance. The first is a narrative question: is this mode of performance evoked as a fleetingly glimpsed other world, as the embodiment of everything the professor fears and loathes? Is this carnival of female bodies and voices nothing more than the projection of male desire, the reverse image of the idealized woman? Or, rather, does *The Blue Angel* suggest another point of view, a position other than that of Rath or Kiepert or the presumably eager fetishist in the audience? The second, related question concerns the implications of a feminist reading of performance in terms beyond this particular film. As Mary Russo puts it, "In what sense can women really produce or make spectacles out of themselves?"[25]

Gender identification in the cinema does not mean that female viewers identify automatically with women, and male viewers with men. While *The Blue Angel* seems to insist upon spectatorship as a complex and contradictory entity, it is presented in the film as a male-centered entity, where issues of pleasure and humiliation, activity and passivity, looking and being looked at, are posed from a uniquely male vantage point. Indeed, Peter Baxter's reading of *The Blue Angel* through the naked thighs of Marlene Dietrich suggests quite convincingly that "[a]round the sight of the female organ, and the threat of castration, the whole network of the fragmented and partially evident text spreads out."[26] Such a reading may expose the repressed fantasy of the text, but begins—as any reading must—with a vantage point, a narrative position, within the text. If *The Blue Angel* focuses so obsessively on a male point of view, how do the conflicting modes of performance acquire a separate point of view of their own?

The Blue Angel articulates male desire through a series of stages, from a group of schoolboys who gape and gaze at photographs of Lola Lola, to the professor's foray into the cabaret where he himself becomes a spectator of Lola's charms. For all its obsession with Lola's fatal powers of attraction to men, however, *The Blue Angel* introduces Lola not through the eyes of men, but through the reaction of a woman. The film opens on a crowded village street. A woman worker opens the metal grill of a shop window, and throws a bucket of water on the window. Displayed in the window is a poster of Lola Lola, her hips thrust forward in the provocative pose for which Dietrich is famous, with a cherub clinging to her leg. The woman proceeds to clean the window, seemingly impervious to what lies behind it. When she catches sight of Lola's legs, however, she pauses, and imitates Lola's pose.

The first male response we see to Lola Lola in the film is the reaction of the young men in Professor Rath's class who ogle photographs of her and blow on them. That these responses to the images of Lola are to be the narrative and symbolic matrix of the film is suggested from the way in which they are represented, and the difference between those actions and the actions which open the film. For the photographs are kept from the view of the film spectator until Professor Rath later discovers them in the notebooks of his prized pupil. The narrative strategies of delay and secrecy are thus marshalled in relationship to the male look and the female object of the look. In contrast, the image of the cleaning woman briefly imitating Lola's pose is flat, obvious, and transparent: there is no mystery here, and nothing worthy of narrative density or complexity. The surface separating the image of Lola from the cleaning woman, the shop window streaked with water, suggests some distance. But the gesture of imitation that this surface inspires pales in comparison with the ogling eyes and, more significant, the pursed lips of the schoolboys who energetically blow the feathers concealing Lola's crotch. The female spectator thus identified in *The Blue Angel* is characterized by what Mary Ann Doane calls her "inability to fetishize."[27]

The cleaning woman suggests the two interrelated ways in which the relationship of women to the screen image has been defined in contemporary film theory. On the one hand, the female spectator is identified with the object of the male gaze; hence the position of the female spectator is a negative position, that is, one defined only by her absence. Female spectatorship, defined in this way, is predicated on the assumption of the cinema as the acting out of male desire; hence the dilemma, as Sylvia Bovenschen puts it, is that "woman could either betray her sex and identify with the masculine point of view, or, in a state of accepted passivity, she could be masochistic/narcissistic and identify with the object of the masculine representation."[28] On the other hand, female spectatorship has been defined as emanating from the role of women as consumers; hence the function of film as a "living display window."[29] These two aspects of female spectatorship are in no way contradictory; indeed, the one functions as the visible support for the other. For what else do women consume, if not images of themselves made to the measure of male desire? And if the movie screen is indeed a display window, then the idealized figure reflected back to the female spectator is part of a fantasy in which she plays a role only as object and as consumer—never as subject.

The resulting role assigned to the female spectator is precisely what we see in the opening of *The Blue Angel:* mimicry. Mimicry is, as Luce Irigaray reminds us, the path "historically assigned to the feminine."[30] For the cleaning woman, consuming the image and identifying with it are one and the same process; they allow a momentary break in a routine, but one which the film will not pursue in any systematic way. But what, then, of the female spectator watching *The Blue Angel*? Recent discussions of female spectatorship have moved away from the denial of female spectatorship implicit in the polarities of the active male look versus the passive female image, and have emphasized the multiple positions of identification and desire implicit in female spectatorship. As Teresa de Lauretis points out, "The analogy that links identification-with-the-look to masculinity and identification-with-the-image to femininity breaks down precisely when we think of a spectator alternating between the two. Neither can be abandoned for the other, even for a moment; no image can be identified, or identified with, apart from the look that inscribes it as image, and vice versa. If the female subject were indeed related to the film in this manner, its division would be irreparable, unsuturable; no identification or meaning would be possible."[31]

Given the importance of mimicry in *The Blue Angel*, from the male students' inability (or refusal) to mimic their teacher's English sounds, to the profusion of parody and imitation that contributes both to the creation of the figure of Lola Lola and to the mode of performance associated with the nightclub, it would be mistaken, I think, to consider it as nothing more than the reified and objectified relationship of woman to the image. For what this film opens up is another space, another definition of mimicry: the playful, ironic imitation of the conventions of femininity and masculinity.

A risk encountered in the work of those who have used Bakhtin's explorations—indeed, a risk present in Bakhtin's own work—is the assumption that the mode of carnival is by very definition radical, posited from outside the dominant order rather than from within it, or at the very least, posited as the discourse of those who are excluded from power and from dominant discourse. Such enthusiastic celebration of the carnival obscures the extent to which the carnival may exist as a safety valve, as a controlled eruption that guarantees the maintenance of the existing order.[32]

In feminist terms, flirtation with the carnivalesque is equally risky. Equating the carnivalesque with female resistance to the patriarchal order may be a celebration of precisely those qualities that define women as irrelevant in patriarchal terms. Hence Juliet Mitchell, for instance, responds to the notion of the carnival as "the area of the feminine": "I don't think so. It is just what the patriarchal universe defines as the feminine, the intuitive, the religious, the mystical, the playful, all those things that have been assigned to women—the heterogeneous, the notion that women's sexuality is much more one of a whole body, not so genital, not so phallic. It is not that the carnival cannot be disruptive of the law; but it disrupts only within the terms of that law."[33] The risk, then, is ascribing a resistant function to an element that may function quite well within the logic of patriarchal discourse. While I agree that conflating the feminine with any of a number of murky regions, from the carnival to the preoedipal, is a potentially conservative gesture, it is equally problematic, not to mention conservative, to define discourse as so dominated by a single, overarching structure that there are only either/or propositions—either one is within dominant discourse and therefore recuperated, or outside of discourse and therefore incoherent. A figure like Dietrich is both contained by patriarchal representation and resistant to it; this "both/and," rather than "either/or," constitutes the very possibility of a feminist reading of performance.

If *The Blue Angel* has a special place in the mythology of Marlene Dietrich, it is in part because the film articulates a narrative and visual structure which would be associated with Dietrich for virtually all of her career. As I have suggested, there are competing levels to that structure, so that it is not so much incorrect, as incomplete, to describe Dietrich uniquely in terms of her image as a *femme fatale*—that is, uniquely in terms of her status as object of the (male) look. The conflicting modes of performance represented in *The Blue Angel* suggest conflicting narratives and conflicting points of view. While it is tempting to label these narratives as "male" and "female," that temptation is better resisted, even though the difference established by the film at the outset between the cleaning woman and the boys in Rath's classroom suggests that there are indeed two distinct ways of looking at an image of the female body, two distinct desires—mimicry and possession. However, that difference is undone by the film, for what separates the conflicting modes of performance are radically different conceptions of address and of representation: a carnivalesque mode of performance where dualities are broken down, and a hierarchical mode of performance where they are reasserted most forcefully. To be sure, the space which links the cleaning woman to the carnivalesque performance of the nightclub is closed down in the film, swept away by the momentum of a conflict and collision of desires the most appropriate representation of which is the final rendition of Lola singing "Falling in Love Again." But *The Blue Angel* is but one chapter in another narrative, another story, which is the myth of Marlene Dietrich.

Indeed, I would argue that the Dietrich image is fashioned precisely on the kind of structure articulated in *The Blue Angel:* the representation of a woman's body and of female performance as contained by certain stereotypes of the *femme fatale,* and yet resistant to them. If "resistance" is, then, an appropriate word to describe the Dietrich image, it is not because Dietrich returns the male look, but rather because that process of resistance is fully a part of the narrative and visual imagery that comprise the Dietrich persona. Feminist critics have perhaps accepted too blithely the proposition that cinematic discourse is fully and totally under the sway of patriarchal dominion. Sylvia Bovenschen reminds us that "an element of female resistance, if only a passive one, has always contributed to artistic production."[34] Dietrich embodies that element of female resistance with a vengeance.

Discussions of Dietrich, whether as a *femme fatale* or as a principle of resistance, tend to concentrate on the seven films made with Josef Von Sternberg. While these films may well be the most stunning demonstrations of the Dietrich persona, they form nonetheless only one part of Dietrich's career. Dietrich continued to play the part of the sexually attractive woman long beyond the age when other actresses would have been relegated to the euphemistic category of character roles. As Mary Russo suggests, the aging female body is a particularly strong point of displacement in theories of the carnival, and I would argue that in the later films of Dietrich's career, this remarkable actress functions consistently to "destabilize idealizations of female beauty" and to "realign the mechanisms of desire."[35]

Witness for the Prosecution (1958) is a particularly appropriate conclusion to this discussion of Dietrich and performance. Based on Agatha Christie's play, Billy Wilder's film version becomes, among other things, a retelling of *The Blue Angel.* Dietrich plays the role of Christine Vole, the wife of a man who has been convicted of murdering an older, wealthy woman. In flashback, Leonard Vole tells of how he and Christine met in Germany immediately after World War II. Christine worked in a nightclub called "The Blue Lantern," and a poster outside the club is virtually identical to the one seen in *The Blue Angel.* The spectacle inside the club is a quotation of the earlier film, but with some significant changes. Christine stands on a small stage, singing, playing her accordion(!), and wearing a man's jacket and pants (thus evoking many other Dietrich films in which she is dressed in male attire). The crowded club is populated only by men, and two men are designated in close-ups: Leonard himself, and another man, a worker, who operates the spotlight. A riot breaks out and the police are called when the men, eager to see those legs advertised in the poster outside the club, rip Christine's pant leg. Leonard avoids the police, returns later, and begins a relationship with Christine. The "Blue Angel" that is evoked here is, perhaps not surprisingly, a particularly sanitized version of the first glimpse of the nightclub that is offered in the 1930 film. Here, there is certainly none of the topsy-turvy, frenetic performance that characterizes the cabaret, but rather, an image that corresponds to what is produced at the conclusion of Von Sternberg's film. For in this nightclub, Dietrich is unquestionably the object of the male look, suggested not only by the uniquely male audience, and by Leonard's designation as a privileged spectator, but also by the man with the spotlight. In *The Blue Angel*, we recall, it is the women onstage who turn the spotlight on the members of the audience.

Light has an important function in *Witness for the Prosecution* as a revelation of truth. Leonard Vole is presented initially in the film as innocent, particularly when Sir Wilfred, the lawyer who defends him (played by Charles Laughton) gives him a somewhat eccentric truth test: Sir Wilfred positions his monocle in such a way that sunlight shines directly and uncomfortably in his potential client's eyes. Leonard Vole blinks only momentarily, and then continues to speak, unflinchingly. By contrast, when Sir Wilfred applies the same test to Christine Vole, she fails miserably: quite uncomfortably, she shields her eyes from the light, moves to the window and closes the curtain. Christine Vole "fails" the truth test, although she also refuses to play.

That is, she refuses to play by their rules—"their" being a curious collection of men, certainly, but also the English. ("What hypocrites you are in this country," Christine says when a lawyer suggests that Leonard was like a son or a nephew to the murdered woman.) What is revealed in *Witness for the Prosecution* is that Christine and Leonard are both playing parts, but unexpected parts: Leonard's façade of innocence and naivete conceals a heartless, selfish murderer, whereas Christine's cool, icy exterior conceals a woman who is desperately in love with her husband and wants to save him at any cost, even though she knows he is guilty.

Christine Vole puts on a masterful performance, then, but the disruptive effects of that performance are quickly displaced at the conclusion of the film when Christine's expert performance is revealed to be motivated by a single cause: her desperate, pathetic devotion to a man who couldn't care less for her. And yet, I would argue that this trick ending, quite apart from questions of effectiveness, needs to be seen in relationship to another revelation in the film. Christine's trump card is her disguise as a lower-class woman who presents Sir Wilfred with a set of letters ostensibly written by Christine, and which establish definitively her perjurious testimony. Whether one guesses that this is Dietrich at this point or is surprised by the revelation at the end of the film seems to me entirely beside the point. For this grotesque female figure is the other side of Christine Vole, the other side of the Dietrich persona: her bulky flesh, her dress, her affected accent, her scarred face, all suggest the female mimicry characteristic of performance in *The Blue Angel*.

Witness for the Prosecution may present a version of the cabaret that represses virtually every sign of the carnivalesque performance in *The Blue Angel*, but the association between Dietrich and that other mode of performance erupts elsewhere, in the adoption of the disguise. The emergence of Dietrich in disguise speaks her affinity with another female body, with another kind of performance, in which mimicry and impersonation threaten to upset that theater of patriarchal law and order, the courtroom. The threat is dispelled in the narrative resolution of *Witness for the Prosecution*, as it is at the conclusion of *The Blue Angel*. But for those not so readily seduced by the dominant visual and narrative momentum of the classical cinema, Marlene Dietrich powerfully embodies the possibility of other desires and other modes of performance.

NOTES

1. Laura Mulvey, "Visual Pleasure and Narrative Cinema," *Screen* 16, no. 3 (1975), 11.
2. See Andrew Britton, *Cary Grant: Comedy and Male Desire* (Newcastle, England: Tyneside Cinema, 1983); and idem, *Katharine Hepburn: The Thirties and After* (Newcastle, England: Tyneside Cinema, 1984); Richard Dyer, *Stars* (London: British Film Institute, 1979); Miriam Hansen, "Pleasure, Ambivalence, Identification: Valentino and Female Spectatorship," *Cinema Journal* 25, no. 4 (1986), 6–32; and the special issue of *Wide Angle* (6, no. 4 [1985]) on "Actors and Acting."
3. Dyer, *Stars*, p. 38.
4. Britton, *Katharine Hepburn*, p. 1.
5. In his introduction to *Katharine Hepburn*, Andrew Britton says: "With the exception of Sternberg's Dietrich, who clearly constitutes a special case, Katharine Hepburn is the only star of the classical cinema

who embodies contradictions (about the nature and status of women) in a way which not only resists their satisfactory resolution in a stable, affirmable ideological coherence, but which also continually threatens to produce an *oppositional* coherence which is registered by the films as a serious ideological threat" (p. 1).

6. See Rebecca Bell-Metereau's discussion of Dietrich in *Hollywood Androgyny* (New York: Columbia University Press, 1985), pp. 103–10.

7. Cited in Alexander Walker, *Dietrich* (London: Thames and Hudson, 1984), p. 174.

8. In *Women and Film: Both Sides of the Camera* (New York: Methuen, 1983), E. Ann Kaplan says that "the female spectator may read the masculinized female image as a *resisting* image in a way that no male spectator would suspect" (p. 50). Annette Kuhn, in *Women's Pictures* (London: Routledge and Kegan Paul, 1982), describes how, given the masculine forms of address in mainstream cinema, women may be "peculiarly able to stand at a distance from the ideological operations of dominant cinema, in that the marginal place they occupy in relation to its address may be conducive to the formation of a critical perspective" (p. 64).

9. Describing the work of theorists such as Raymond Bellour, Thierry Kuntzel, and Stephen Heath, Constance Penley says that "the contradictions and gaps that the feminists had been positivistically ascribing to the attempt to stage a feminine discourse in a patriarchal form or to the specific difficulty that the woman's image entails, were for the male theorists no more than necessary components of the classical film's illusionistic economy." See " 'A Certain Refusal of Difference': Feminism and Film Theory," in *Art after Modernism: Rethinking Representation*, ed. Brian Wallis (New York: New Museum of Contemporary Art, 1984), p. 377.

10. For example, Julia Lesage writes that Dietrich "is used in Von Sternberg's films to defy patriarchy even though she is reabsorbed into the male plot structure." See "Women and Film: A Discussion of Feminist Aesthetics," *New German Critique* no. 13 (1978), 90.

11. See Kaplan, *Women and Film*, pp. 49–59; Bill Nichols, *Ideology and the Image* (Bloomington: Indiana University Press, 1981), chap. 4; and Robin Wood, "Venus de Marlene," *Film Comment* 14 (1978), 58–63.

12. Josef Von Sternberg, *Fun in a Chinese Laundry* (New York: Macmillan, 1965), p. 231.

13. John Baxter, *The Cinema of Josef Von Sternberg* (New York: A. S. Barnes and Co.), p. 70.

14. Walker, *Dietrich*, p. 59.

15. Donald Spoto, *Falling in Love Again: Marlene Dietrich* (Boston: Little, Brown and Co.), p. 26.

16. Angela Carter, *Nothing Sacred* (London: Virago, 1985), p. 122.

17. Although Gaylyn Studlar has proposed a theory of cinematic identifi-

cation, based on Gilles Deleuze's reading of masochism, as an alternative to the voyeuristic-fetishistic model, she nonetheless describes Dietrich's function in the very terms of the model in question: "The Von Sternberg/Dietrich heroine is the object of male desire, but she is not the passive object of a controlling look. Dietrich looks back. . . . The female subverts the power of the male gaze. . . . Von Sternberg's films emphasize the active aspect of the female's gaze and the passive element in the male's look." See "Visual Pleasure and the Masochistic Aesthetic," *Journal of Film and Video* 37 (1985), 21–22.

18. See Herman Weinberg, ed., *Josef Von Sternberg* (New York: E. P. Dutton, 1967), pp. 84–85; and Baxter, *Cinema of Josef Von Sternberg*, pp. 68–69, for a discussion of the sources for Lola Lola.

19. Roland Barthes, *S/Z*, trans. Richard Miller (New York: Hill and Wang, 1974), p. 33.

20. Ado Kyrou, "Sternberg and the Marlene Myth," in Weinberg, ed., *Josef Von Sternberg*, p. 194.

21. Spoto, *Falling in Love Again*, p. 26.

22. Mikhail Bakhtin, *Rabelais and His World*, trans. Helen Iswolsky (Bloomington: Indiana University Press, 1984).

23. Siegfried Kracauer, *From Caligari to Hitler* (Princeton: Princeton University Press, 1967), p. 218.

24. Mulvey, "Visual Pleasure and Narrative Cinema," p. 14.

25. Mary Russo, "Female Grotesques: Carnival and Theory," in *Feminist Studies/Critical Studies*, ed. Teresa de Lauretis (Bloomington: Indiana University Press, 1986), p. 217.

26. Peter Baxter, "On the Naked Thighs of Miss Dietrich," *Wide Angle* 2 (1978), 23.

27. Mary Ann Doane, "Film and the Masquerade: Theorising the Female Spectator," *Screen* 23 (1982), 80.

28. Sylvia Bovenschen, "Is There a Feminine Aesthetic?" *New German Critique*, no. 10 (1977), 127.

29. Charles Eckert, "The Carole Lombard in Macy's Window," *Quarterly Review of Film Studies* 3, no. 1 (1978), 4.

30. Luce Irigaray, *This Sex Which Is Not One*, trans. Catherine Porter (Ithaca, New York: Cornell University Press, 1985), p. 76.

31. Teresa de Lauretis, *Alice Doesn't: Feminism, Semiotics, Cinema* (Bloomington: Indiana University Press, 1984), p. 143.

32. For an excellent discussion of the status of the carnival in theory and criticism, see Peter Stallybrass and Allon White, *The Politics and Poetics of Transgression* (Ithaca: Cornell University Press, 1986).

33. Juliet Mitchell, *Women: The Longest Revolution* (New York: Pantheon, 1984), p. 291.

34. Bovenschen, "Is There a Feminine Aesthetic?" p. 125.

35. Russo, "Female Grotesques," p. 221.

Seductive Spaces:
Private Fascinations and Public
Fantasies in Popular Cinema

A cop stealthily enters the tract-house bedroom of his occasional lover, a young blonde woman whose parole he oversees. Her observance of parole consists in passing him information and sleeping with him upon demand. This familiar pornographic formula (where seduction is tinged with sadism in the imposed authority of the police, and linked to the forced prostitution of an innocently wide-eyed victim) is enacted in a scene that renders the male body as spectacle. While the woman remains in the bed where she has just awakened, the cop, back-lit by dawn light through the window which frames him, performs a rapid strip-tease that ends in a pose, arms folded, legs apart—an aggressive full frontal display reminiscent of male nude magazines. This almost parodic rehearsal of a stylized porn scenario is one of the two moments of heterosexual sex that punctuate William Freidkin's *To Live and Die in L.A.* (1985).

The second of these moments centers on Rick Masters, the adversary of Richie Chance, the cop of the first scene. Masters is shown making love with his girlfriend, while they watch videotapes of themselves making love. Our gaze is directed by Masters's away from the current sexual scene to the image, just as he is immobilized by fascination with it. It is as if this scene figured the concentration of all erotic energy in the gaze, a gaze captivated by a pornographic home movie; that is, as if the image of sex were more seductive and engaging than the fictional real sex.

American Gigolo (Paul Schrader, 1980) constructs its version of male sexual display in a similar way. The initial seduction sequence between the gigolo and the woman with whom he has fallen in love consists of an even distribution of medium close-ups of portions of both bodies, but ends by framing the male body against a window running the length of the screen, and casting bars of light across the nude. Central to the character's construction as image, this scene prefigures his appearance behind bars when he is wrongly imprisoned for murder, or "framed." Indeed, the whole film enacts the process of framing the gigolo, its narrative designed to show why, as one character puts it, "you were frameable."

My interest in juxtaposing these two films arises from their shared interest in framing the male body as spectacle. Such a construction of masculinity as image, as body to be displayed, is relatively rare in its inversion of traditional cinematic codings of sexual difference. But the context of these different versions of masculinity is crucial. Both films are charged with a homoerotic subtext, just as they are haunted by sexual ambivalence and the threat of castration or feminization: *American Gigolo*'s Julian Kaye (who is always called by the feminized diminutive, Julie) struggles to avoid returning to the world of male prostitution, while *To Live and Die*'s principal antagonists are locked in a cycle of homosocial aggression. Further, the narrative scenes of seduction are peripheral to the most powerful seductive circuits of these films, both of which are intensely fascinated with seduction and simulation. This fascination focuses on displacements and dissolutions of boundaries, between the real and its simulacra, between the art object and the object of consumption, between the authentic and the counterfeit.

Sexual difference here becomes only one problem arrayed in a network of insufficiently established differences, which the films set out to order. These questions of differentiation are organized in spaces coded to represent culture, high art, and good taste, which are established by contrast to the menace of the common, the vulgar, the popular, and the lower class. These ambivalent cinematic constructions of sexual difference thus coincide with aesthetic ambivalence, with instability of value in the circulation of objects and the mapping of space. Construction of male body as spectacle here seems to depend on its articulation as part of a captivating consumer space.

In their constructions of space, *To Live and Die* and *American Gigolo* reproduce the spaces and fascinations of the postmodern urban scene. It's not incidental, it seems to me, that both films were shot in Los Angeles, a city that has been constructed as the "capitol of postmodernism," in part because its version of urban landscape seems to embody the theoretical features of postmodernism. Its heterogeneous ethnicity is dispersed in a fragmented topography, where spaces seem not to communicate, much less interlock, because one can circulate through them only by driving. The city, then, appears as centerless, depthless, a vast extension of scenery, framed by a windshield, viewed at distance, and at high speed. Further, as a major production site for cinema and television, Los Angeles is ideally suited to figure effects of endless reproducibility; the city is pure image endlessly reproducing itself.[1]

Since *To Live and Die*'s narrative stages a confrontation between the artist and the law (in the figures of Masters, the neoexpressionist painter and counterfeiter, and Chance, the maniacally macho treasury agent), in which the character who has the most style and taste is the most seductive, the film rehearses certain preoccupations of postmodernist theories of representational strategy. By presenting the artist as a transgressive figure with a strong resemblance to the media-mythologized neoexpressionists of the contemporary art scene and casting him within a popular cultural vehicle—a fairly formulaic detective thriller—it forces the emergence of a confrontation between high culture and consumer culture, a displacement of boundaries that is articulated around the figure of counterfeit and simulation. Part of the seductiveness of such a popular culture object may be that it shares our theoretical preoccupations, that it theorizes on the same ground as so-called high culture and its criticism.

One of the discourses with which this seductive apparatus engages most fully is psychoanalysis. Much of the most rigorous and provocative work on cinematic seduction today is psychoanalytically based and feminist. In the work of such theorists as Christian Metz, Stephen Heath, Laura Mulvey, Mary Ann Doane, and Teresa de Lauretis, to name only a few, analysis of cinematic seduction depends on exploring the workings of scopophilia and fetishism, elaborating a theory of imaginary mechanisms and narcissistic investments— identification, desire, and aggression.[2] This psychoanalytic grounding is fundamental to the most powerful analyses of subject construction in ideology. It has consequently become crucial to studies of the spectator as ideological subject, one who is sutured into spectator positions, as into discursive ideological positions.[3] While psychoanalysis is the discourse most apt to examine the ideological and unconscious effects of cinema, and therefore to allow us to analyze the construction of subjectivity by and for the image, psychoanalytic approaches to fantasy structure mobilized in film tend to cast the cinematic apparatus within a frame limited to and by the individual subject. This tendency may be related to their concern with confronting pleasure and aggression, both of which seem most easily accessible within the frame of individual subjectivity.

The difficulty of analyzing pleasure has to do with its profound ambiguity. Colin Mercer argues that "this [is] probably because it also implies the unspoken figure to which it applies—the individual pleasure is about individual taste and preferences. More than any other notion (except perhaps those of taste or choice), it entails individual sovereignty. This is the 'unsaid' of pleasure, its presupposition when mobilized in any discourse (collective pleasures are always a bit tacky)."[4] Even on the individual level, pleasure is unstable, elusive, subject to loss in analysis. To try to "socialize" pleasure seems to risk dispersing it completely. However, it seems that psychoanalytic approaches to filmic pleasure and seduction are all too often seduced by their own theoretical apparatus, too readily confined to their own frame—an individual, if abstract, subject. They are further seduced by cinematic objects which enact most successfully, that is, most powerfully and subtly, the configurations of scopophilia and fetishism that psychoanalytic criticism has so vigorously studied. (For example, why are there many more studies on Hitchcock than, say, Coppola or Spielberg? The most widely circulated cultural objects are often left aside).

However, the operations of the cinematic apparatus are social, and the subject they construct and seduce is a social one. Cinema does not work, then, only upon the subjective imaginary. Rather, we must consider it as a "ceaseless working up of social imaginaries," in Jean-Louis Comolli's phrase.[5] Consequently, we must focus on the framing mechanisms that condition representational practices (including distribution and circulation, the institutions governing consumption), and on the forms of address that locate a spectator *for* these representations. Framing mechanisms are the threshold of complex exchanges that continually dissolve and reconstitute these imaginary zones of public and private and that rework boundaries between high and popular culture.

Even while offering the pleasures and the lure of an illusory, highly privatized space, cinematic experience is, in many ways, the most eminently social form of consumption. Thus we must work on the contradictions common to the subject constructed through cinematic forms of address, and to the apparatus itself; on the crucial ideological formation that splits public from private. Cinematic production and consumption, reciprocally conditioning as they are, are embedded in social power formations. Produced within cultural exchange and circulation, images also construct the conditions of their reception, the positions the spectator occupies or invests. The spectator's act of filmic consumption involves accepting its forms of address, but it also entails producing its legibility, and negotiating its disjunctions, the elaborate exchanges among its semiotic systems (i.e., the image work: the camera montage and editing; the sound: voice and music, background effects, the narrative).

However, as a discourse generated in a social field, the film itself incorporates, or consumes, messages, collective representations. Consumer as well as producer of discourses and images, cinema works the way popular culture in general does, according to Laura Kipnis, "by *transforming* elements at large in the culture—not through inventing or imposing arbitrary materials on a stunned and passive populace."[6] To stress the work of transformation this way is to argue for considering popular culture and cinema as a process that operates in a circuit of exchanges, and to leave room for the possibility of ambivalence, resistances, and contradictions within it. This is the space of oppositional discourses and culture which may be available, may be activated, or may be repressed in the fabric of apparently dominant-order film.

Once we decide to consider popular culture and its cinema not as imposed from without on a passive public, but as responsive to certain collective demands or desires, however vaguely articulated, we are in a better position to study both social fantasies and the strategies designed to activate and regulate them. This is why Simon Frith argues for replacing the terms "popular" and "mass" culture with the term "capitalist" culture: "culture defined, that is, not in terms of production and consumption of commodities (though this is involved), but as the way in which people deal with/symbolise/articulate/share/resist the *experience* of capitalism (including, but not exclusively, the ideological experience of capitalism)."[7] He seeks to eliminate the hierarchical and static suggestions of "mass culture" (stressing the consumers' subjection to producers), and to render historically specific the *form* of mass culture: in capitalism it is a culture in a state of permanent crisis.

We need to analyze a cinema that responds to, reads, and maps collective fantasies, utopian and anxious, a cinema that is always reading us—reading our social configurations of power and desire, pleasure and violence. This is part of film's allure: as we read it, it also reads us. But if cinema mobilizes and channels pleasure, violence, and resistances, it often does so only to capture or manage them. Popular cinema's machine of pleasure announces itself as gratuitous, as socially and politically irresponsible, luxuriously abundant in simulacra, asserting the comforting reproducibility of reality—at a distance, and in consumable form. This is a cinema that claims legibility without work, code without pertinent message, that claims to produce nothing, but rather, to reproduce the entirely consumable, already-read.[8]

To analyze cinema as a social machine entails understanding seduction, in general, not as a privatized exchange, but as part of social libidinal channelling and mapping. Seduction here cannot be confined to sexual exchange that is thematized in images of sexual activity, or of the body, or in narrated thematics of desire. Seduction does not just lead toward; it always leads away from something as well. I am interested in those moments and details that we may be seduced into *not* seeing.

In the postmodern moment, mass culture increasingly operates through strategies it shares with experimental art. Dana Polan argues that it tends to work with "montage that produces collision of messages that continually destabilize and negate each other."[9] Confronted with this kind of practice, we can only posit a spectator who goes to cinema precisely for a loss of reality, continually to reactivate that loss in simulation effects. This is a spectator who uses the apparatus, with all its reality effects, to give him/herself away to a lure, but one which is already understood as such, understood as spectacle, in a kind of self-seduction.

I want to argue that *To Live and Die* and *American Gigolo* are films that invite us to abandon ourselves to just such a fascination, an absorption in simulation effects. But these effects interrupt and reroute narrative and gaze all at once, and activate seduction quite self-consciously upon editing and shot composition. Indeed, their exhilaration within effects of simulation is their critical edge, precisely because these effects are both thematized and performed. Simulation and fakery are central narrative issues, which are also quite explicitly and self-consciously staged in the work of the camera —in its production of space and spectator positions for that space.

The three opening sequences of *To Live and Die* embed the totality of its plot and mark out the multilayered space in which it will unfold. An aerial shot of the Los Angeles skyline resolves into a sharper image with the digital time reading printed across it: December 20, 1410 hours (in a standard cue of police timekeeping that will punctuate the film throughout). Under Wang Chung's sound track, a presidential motorcade leads into the action sequence which will introduce one of the film's two antagonists. Before they appear, the first voice of the film sets its terms. Ronald Reagan's voice is heard off camera, speaking about death and taxes, terms which emerge in the film's central nexus, where not only money, but the Treasury Department, is connected to murder. The next sequence mobilizes (literally and figuratively) Richie Chance, the treasury agent, and his older partner/mentor, whose subsequent murder will launch Chance's relentless pursuit of Rick Masters, the counterfeiter. (The punning similarity of first names insists that the contest we will witness pits chance against mastery.) In this sequence, however, the adversary is, in a completely unaccountable turn, an Arab terrorist, wrapped in sticks of dynamite, who plunges to his death from the hotel roof, shouting a parody of terrorist discourse: "Death to Israel and America and all enemies of Islam." In a gratuitous glancing gesture toward the topical, we are given a construction of an enemy other whose behavior is motivated only by insanity, while the really unaccountable violence is that which is played out through the rest of the film.[10]

The cut to the next sequence fixes on the Los Angeles skyline again, obscured and transformed through dusky light. This sequence involves rapid cross cutting between images of paintings in the contemporary neoexpressionist style of Schnabel and Salle, and sections of Los Angeles—mostly industrial sites, like oil tanks, and a movie set—a sort of map of Los Angeles's "production sites." At the same time, this is the credit sequence. The sort of montage effects commonly seen under credits now appear to interrupt the film, but also to establish a space beyond the narrative instance we've just seen, and to indicate, across the disjunctions of their tense, jumpy editing, a context. But narrative context is precisely the film's most unstable area, one that it constantly renegotiates and obscures or dissolves. The most prominent series of images here is that of transactions—money changing hands, moving from one anonymous hand to another. Interestingly, what emerges from this anonymity is, first, a kind of racial mapping: black men exchange money, black and hispanic men exchange money, then a black man and a white man, a black woman and a white man, a white woman and black men, a black man and a white man. If this film is to be about money circulating, we must assume that it will circulate across race and gender; money will structure racial and sexual exchanges. This circuit of exchanges, however, closes with a photograph of Masters, the artist-counterfeiter, "master" and source of these circulating effects. Not surprisingly, but amusingly enough, the name which crosses the screen at this point is Freidkin's own.

This last image is matched with a shot of Masters in his studio, surrounded by his paintings. The next shot shows a canvas unrolled against a wall. After a cut to a close-up of Masters's gaze at his own work, we see him light a corner of it with his cigarette lighter and watch it go up in flames. If these two sequences begin to articulate money and art across Masters's image, they also anticipate his end —when he is immolated in his studio. That is, in the end, Masters becomes his image, in two ways: he burns up like this first painting, and he persists as an image on the videotapes that his girlfriend takes away with her at the end of the film.

Masters is also figured as the gaze of mastery—frequently shown in medium close-up, facing off, aggressively or sexually, with another character, or regarding his own images (and here the ambiguity of the possessive is apt: this figure conflates production and reproduction bound together in his own narcissism), and finally appearing in the mirror, surveying his girlfriend or his adversaries. Often, we can't locate him; he is most present as image projected or reflected.

But Masters's mastery also figures several kinds of power which are staged as intersecting, and which produce a certain spatial trajectory. His power is located on the axis of art and culture, accompanied by connoisseurship, as well as on that of economics, and finally on that of sexualized violence and aggression. His economic power, reflected in his glimmering museum-home, with its network of electronic apparatus, is supported by his engagement with the technology of reproduction. For the artist here is a counterfeiter; we watch, with the fascinated camera, as the process of mechanical reproduction of twenty-dollar bills unfolds. This is a long sequence which presents the "hand of the artist" in immense detail, as it produces a plate and prints and colors the bills, with particularly captivating close-ups of the mixing of luxurious gobs of paint —red, black, green, and white together. Here the postmodern injoking of the film's discourse operates on several levels: Masters is an *enfant terrible* neoexpressionist whose artistic talent translates directly into cash. Of course, the cash is fake, just as he is. This sequence also plays on a fascination with surface detail, and upon the infinite extension of serial reproduction.

Counterfeit money, the reproduced image of a mass-produced image, is valuable only if exchanged. It must circulate, and keep on circulating, if it is to remain undetected, if it is to continue to convert directly into real money. Now, on the first level of legibility, the film is about the collapse of the simulacrum and the real, a proposition which it repeatedly asserts. Chance and his new partner want to pose as potential customers in order to entrap Masters, so they have to become outlaws in order to get enough real money for the deposit that will both permit delivery of the counterfeit and convince Masters of the authenticity of their pose. They will authenticate themselves with real money. On the other hand, the film here carries its almost parodically excessive libertarian discourse to the limit; since the government won't put up the money for their venture, Chance has to steal it. As his partner points out, they've had to steal thirty thousand dollars of real money, taxpayer's money at that, to buy counterfeit. So it is the simulacrum that turns the law into an outlaw. There is no difference between the pose and the reality: to impersonate outlaws, they must become outlaws. Further, given both Chance's ardent pursuit of Masters and Chance's replacement at the end of the film by his partner, who "takes over his life," continuing his work, adopting his traits, and becoming the lover of his parolee charge, it seems that the law somehow desires the simulacrum, is itself a simulacrum.

But if counterfeit must circulate endlessly in order to maintain its value, Masters, too, is constantly circulating. His passage from one social space to another, one milieu to another, defines the spacing of the film. At once classless and classy, Masters moves from the underworld gym, where he is surrounded by thugs, to his girlfriend's trendy nightclub dance performances, to the offices of lawyers like Grimes and Waxman, glassed-in display cases—the one showcasing the Los Angeles skyline, the other presenting an art collection.

Similarly, *American Gigolo*'s primary appeal is in its class transcendence, an effect that is continually threatened by its relation to gender and to sexual inversion. *American Gigolo* is explicitly structured around the male body as a feminized display, exchange object, in the figure of a male prostitute. The story of the gigolo's being falsely accused of the rape and murder of a client entails the unraveling of his pose, and his position in the world, where he circulates in high-class circles—hotels, clubs, art galleries—and the implicit threat of a social fall back into the world of the streets and gay discos. At the same time that the character is cast in a feminine pose (in his work as a prostitute who circulates among wealthy female clients, in his feminized name, changed from Julian to Julie, and in his ritualistic relation to costuming and display), his efforts to avoid being framed for the crime engage a vigorous effort to ward off feminization. Because he resists domination by female procurers, he falls out of the relay of power and influence that could protect him from false accusation. Indeed, it is his momentary lapse, in agreeing to substitute on a job for Leon, his former employer, that sets him up for the accusation. Ultimately, however, the real threat appears to come from homosexuality, which is precisely equated with feminization as a loss of power, and with a fall from his social network back into the world of the freaky and kinky, male tricks. This is the fate to be desperately warded off, a homophobic anxiety worked out on the figure of Leon, the gay black pimp who arranges for the evidence against Julie in order to protect the real killer, his own lover.

It is money or its simulacrum (counterfeit in *To Live and Die*, and style in *Gigolo*, and connoisseurship in both films) that negotiates among spaces, weaves them together, cuts a path through them, and finally, equalizes them. Similarly, in a narrative universe where everyone is corrupt, where no character sustains a positive affective charge for the spectator, it is the one with the best taste and the most style who wins. That is, even though Chance's partner survives him and Masters, basically by becoming a replica of Chance, Masters survives Chance, who gets his head blown off. In *Gigolo*, the character with the best taste is the good guy. This is apparent in one of Julie's dialogues with the police detective who is investigating him. Julie offers to show the detective how to dress for success with women, but in the frame of a discussion which puts him "above the law," on the side of women. As he puts it, "Men make the laws, and they're not always right; sometimes they're stupid or jealous."

In a stunning moment of competing tastes in *To Live and Die*, Masters confronts Max Waxman, a yuppie lawyer who has tried to cheat him. When Masters is ordering Waxman to open his safe, and is temporarily distracted, Waxman hits him with a statue. After retaliating by shooting the lawyer in the crotch, Masters evaluates the statue: "Eighteenth-century Cameroon? Your taste is in your ass," before shooting the lethal shot, to the face this time. Leaving aside for the moment the sadistic cast to this homoerotic imagery, and the camera's adoption of the viewpoint of the victim, which is a recurrent motif, for now I want to focus on the issue of taste. Waxman is an unequal contender in this masculine cycle of aggression, because his taste is bad.

American Gigolo's Julian is also coded as a connoisseur; in one sequence he accompanies a date to Sotheby's and advises her on purchases. Interestingly enough, *American Gigolo* is similar to *To Live and Die* in its production of scenes which link aesthetics and aggression. At the final confrontation between Julie and Leon, Leon's apartment is presented as garishly and vulgarly decorated (in contrast to Julie's tastefully sparse, gray-walled, track-lighted home). Further, Leon is seated on a couch in front of a painting that dominates the screen, and which represents a series of men's buttocks, thus emphasizing his deviance. It is as if he were incriminated by his taste in art.

However, the question of bad taste (and indeed, of poor taste, given the relentless relay of anal erotic innuendos in *To Live and Die*) is encoded, played out, in a montage and mise-en-scène that foreground style, and indeed, a collision of styles. Just as the credit sequence recalls rock video editing and relation to sound, a later sequence contains shots which resemble contemporary beer commercials. When Chance enters a bar, the camera is angled as if from the point of view of one seated at the bar, and the joking exchange of camaraderie takes place in a scene where the frame's horizon line is dominated by an array of Miller beer bottles and glasses. It is those objects which are the focus of the scene. A later scene of tense exchange between Chance and his partner is also compositionally structured by beer bottles, again with the camera at bar level. (Whatever Miller paid for this kind of representation, surely the film's explicit reproduction of beer commercial motifs is in excess of advertising). But it is precisely this kind of juxtaposition of codes, the commercial with the artistic, that may constitute the film's critical edge.

Otherwise, why use a cameraman like Robby Muller (formerly best known for his work with Wim Wenders), whose camera specializes in a density of texture and a startling and highly contrasted shot composition, a lingering attention to detail that seems here to mark European art film style? Something similar is at work in *American Gigolo*'s shots of Julie preparing for a weekend trip. As he lays out jackets, shirts, and ties side by side, the camera's slow tracking along his vast bed, the temporary display surface, presents the object in medium close-up. In a shot that stresses seriality in the composition of outfits, the clothing is monumentalized in a way that suggests advertising and retail store appeals to consumer desire. Here, too, the particularity of the camera style is significant. John Bailey's European-influenced shot composition both monumentalizes objects and breaks down their environment into the density and resistance of individual detail in such a way as to emphasize a fetishistic relation to objects.

However much the distinct photographic style may be read as yet another of the excesses with which these films are fascinated, the still-life-like compositions here seem to have another function as well. They lay out a superabundance of objects, a luxury in detail that implies a fetishization. As Hal Foster describes aesthetic fetishism, it is linked to coding: "It is the purity and uniformity of our system of object-signs that fascinates. This clue, together with the fact that what we consume in the code is the difference of object-

signs, suggests that fetishism is involved. . . . Like the narcissism of
the child, the perfection of the code excludes us, seduces us—precisely because it seems to offer 'another side or beyond' to castration
and to labor."[11]

Using cinematographers who display highly individualized, sig-
nature styles, both films rather aggressively mix modes to suggest
an equivalency—in this case, given the narrative frame, an equivalency established on the commercial level. These films operate most
critically through their display of the shared ground of art and advertising. Indeed, they seem bound to demonstrate Laura Kipnis's assertion that "in post-modernism, the artistic subject produced in high
art, in mass culture, in advertising and consumption *is* the bourgeois
subject."[12]

The questions that are central to this analysis, then, involve
constructions of space, where space is saturated with value and embedded in power relations. Within these cinematic spaces, seductive
effects emerge out of our implication as both producers and consumers of space, since the film's real effects are focused by a simulation
of postmodern living spaces—both urban and domestic landscapes,
in which the home is a museumlike cloister sealed off from the menace of the under- or overterritorialized urban landscape. Our seduction occurs through our relation to those spaces. Figuratively, space
presents itself as a screen for our projections, or a surface reflecting
our desire. At the same time, our gaze circulates through it, unim-
peded by its boundaries and divisions. Finally, because the space is
a display space, offering itself to our visual exploration, we may feel
that it acquires depth through our look; that our look produces it.[13]

To Live and Die seems to embrace and reproduce the postmodern breakdown of spatial boundaries in its sacrifice of the scene to
extended, endlessly unfolding spaces of simulation and spectacle in
a kind of hyperspace,[14] where the terms "public" and "private" no
longer make sense. According to Jean Baudrillard, such a breakdown
depends on the loss of spectacle in the public, and the loss of secrecy
in the private domain. Our contemporary architecture, he argues,
is "not a public scene, or a true public space, but gigantic spaces
of circulation, ventilation and ephemeral connections." Concomitantly, private space must collapse in the loss of distinction between
interior and exterior, and with it, what Baudrillard calls "the sovereignty of a symbolic space which was also that of the subject."[15]

Yet, however much *To Live and Die* both reproduces and celebrates this exhilarating or vertiginous circulation in and of spaces,

its fantasmatic cartography of the city reconstructs a set of spatial divisions which map the power relations of our culture. Museum-like home and business spaces may be indistinguishable from each other, but they are radically different from the homes in the industrial side of Los Angeles, in the shadow of oil tanks, like that inhabited by Chance's sexual slave, and from the black neighborhood of Masters's associate, Jeff. Spatial position is also charged with anxiety about social position in *American Gigolo*. Julie does business in a space that is utterly homogeneous with his domestic enclave, between country club, Sotheby's, clients' homes, and luxury hotels. His terror of falling out of his social zone is filmically inscribed as a spatial anxiety: the fear of slipping back into the space of the gay disco and the street leading to it. His increasing panic as his arrest becomes imminent is expressed in his systematic disordering of his domestic space, and in the dizzying car ride through neon-lit streets. The play of light on the car windshield produces a disorienting effect replicated by the flashing and rotating colored lights in the gay disco where he meets Leon. Space remains implicitly social, and class and race relations are spatialized in a particularly intense fashion. The seductiveness of certain spaces depends upon and is haunted by another space which they hold off, evacuate—this is the space that remains firmly grounded in social power relations.

The spaces of fetishization, of glistening surface, of display and collection (the lawyer's office, Masters's studio, Julie's apartment)—the consumer space par excellence—taken in the frame of the films' overall developments, seem to participate in a rhetoric of spatialization, where history and social formation become matters of space. It is as if spatial division and the accumulation of objects it permits entailed an accumulation and containment of history as well, space calculated to function as a museum does.

Such composed spaces tend to negate the gaze, to produce mortifying immobilization of the gaze, along with a negation of traces of use or production.[16] In *American Gigolo*, this effect is foregrounded. Julie is an object on display in a space filled with consumer display objects, like his paintings and ceramics. He is consistently presented as an element in still life, framed in one of the mirrors that structure his apartment, displayed by the window frame, and later consumed by the surface. His body is marked by graphic details, like the slats of light; he is shown flattened against a poster, and finally, in the nightclub scene, a cylindrically coiled pulsating neon sign shows behind his head, and appears about to suck him in, to consume him.

Our gaze, then, is fascinated by a sealed space which excludes us, and which reduces all objects—including human ones—to the same status.

Such fetishization parallels a technical fetishization in camera work on the compositional level, and in certain excesses. In *American Gigolo*, what I am calling excesses are a kind of gratuitous and luxurious abundance of detail, a fixation on surfaces. This is evident in the opening shot of Julie driving down the highway to the sound of Blondie's "Call Me." The editing matches the rhythmic pace of the music, dissecting the car into parts, first focusing on the gleaming wheels, on the door, before pulling back to show the whole object. Such excess figures also in Julie's later random drives around Los Angeles in search of Leon, in the disorienting play of lights in the street and across the car's reflecting surfaces. Finally, the mixture of anxiety and pleasure produced by the camera's detailed exploration of Julie's wrecked apartment seems to participate in the same economy of excess and fetishism. On two occasions, once when the police search the apartment, and once when Julie himself searches it and his car for evidence he fears has been planted there, the camera works out a destruction of objects and aesthetic order. The combination of anxiety and pleasure here, I think, is related to our posture as consuming subjects—the appeal of the objects simultaneously produces aesthetic pleasure and a desire to possess. That combination of appeals can channel easily into both anxiety about aesthetic disturbance and aggressive pleasure in the destruction of a desired space which excludes us.

One of *To Live and Die*'s examples of similar excess is the exceptionally long and virtuoso chase scene for which the film is noted. Grounded in gratuitous anxiety, this sequence presents a chase through a dry riverbed and through a truck loading yard, with camera racing head-on toward enormous tractor-trailers, to culminate in a race against the flow of dense freeway traffic. We see it from a point of view within the car, and later shot from above, pulling away in relief, as we gleefully watch the havoc on the freeway. An explicit excess, based on commuter traffic anxiety, this sequence rehearses the pleasure of seeing traffic entirely disrupted, while one is not involved. Such a sequence participates in a certain rhetoric of expenditure which structures the film; here it is articulated in terms of cost, tricks, affect, and anxiety. However, this move is also meanspirited in its focus of affect on simple, everyday commuter anxiety and stress. Ultimately, the sequence stresses virtuoso performance, the staged quality of the spectacle, and serves to reencode other instances of excessive violence and aggression as equally random and nonpertinent, playful, or incidental occasions for affective discharge.

If *To Live and Die*'s vertiginous circulation is emblematized in a credit sequence of financial transactions and their social map, its later chase sequence is designed to stage an excessive expenditure. The chase produces a rhythmic anxiety, or unpleasure and release/pleasure mechanism built around the figure of circulation—the car appears to go anywhere, to circulate even against the flow of traffic. Two kinds of flow collide. But this excess, mapped as expenditure (financial and affective), is picked up on another relay, channeled through a circuit of violent masculine homoerotic/homophobic exchanges, which operate both visually and verbally. Verbal violence operates in reciprocal challenge and insult, in phrases organized by an anal erotic aggressive subtext. Indeed, this form of aggressivity is the zone of most intense narrative affectivity—the only zone of consistent affect, where the term "to fuck" becomes "to fuck over."

In its aggressive rhetoric and its theme of horrific violence between men (Chance has his brains blown out; he is shot in the face like Waxman, who is also shot in the groin; Masters intimidates the black character, Jeff, by sitting on him and putting a revolver in his mouth; Carl, the prisoner Chance wants to use as an informer, escapes by kicking him first in the groin and then in the face), the film represents an almost parodically hypermasculinized genre. In Mary Ann Doane's assessment, "feminine" genres, like the love story, and "masculine" genres, like Westerns and detective films, are constructed upon an opposition between emotionalism and violence. She writes, "Theories of scopophilia, the imaginary relation of spectator to film, and the mirror phase all suggest that aggressivity is an inevitable component of the imaginary relation in the cinema. In the Western and detective film aggressivity or violence is internalized as narrative content."[17] In so-called women's films, she argues, "the violence is displaced onto affect." By its very excessive violence, *To Live and Die* manages to maintain both levels of intensity; it thematizes violence and it produces bursts of affect channeled as spectator horror. It is as if the film sadistically exposed the aggressive component in cinematic fascination, just as it cleverly plays on castration anxiety: male characters accuse each other of "having no balls"; fights involve an attack, a kick, jab, or shot, to the groin.

Homoerotic suggestions repeatedly emerge in an endless relay of jokes about asses, anality, and even in the early gift exchange between Chance and his mentor—giving the older man a fishing rod as a retirement gift, Chance allows as how "it's been burning a hole in my truck." In the epithets shouted during the chase scene, or between Chance and his series of adversaries, the film is a barrage of anal sadistic slang.

But why? This film sets up an endless circulation effect, a circulation of affect among figures who are all enemies. The one exception to this rule is Chance's first partner, the only one to whom he is not antagonistic, and whose murder launches the central pursuit of the film. But this character, a father-mentor on the point of his retirement, is figured as somewhat out of style, archaic, unprepared for the new rules of the game, for the new kind of criminality Masters embodies. After his death, all characters are equally bad or perverse and menacing; there is no stable point of identification in a continual escalation of reciprocal aggression. At stake is a construction of masculinity. This male hysteria is designed to ward off feminization, but in the process it exposes the homoerotics of mimetic rivalry, which so frequently structures classic Hollywood narratives of equal adversaries. Sexual difference is remapped in this film—erotic heterosexual attractions are doubled by homoerotic ones (in various triangles: Chance and Bukovitch and the parolee; Masters, his girlfriend and Waxman; and in the peculiar parallel between Masters's physical position and framing in relation to his girlfriend at the moment of a kiss, and his aggressive confrontations with Chance). Further, the film's logic suggests that the winner is the one who gets to say "fuck you" last.[18] I don't mean this lightly, because it is the case that all the male characters systematically say this to each other in moments of rage. On this reading, the triumph belongs to Masters's girlfriend and her lesbian lover, since they ride off together in the end, in Masters's car, with his money. Indeed, part of the vicious thrust of the film is displaced onto the lesbian couple, as the most corrupt and most affectless.

In a central moment, Masters meets his girlfriend just after a dance performance. The dancers, all masked and short-haired, are entirely androgynous. The next shot shows the dressing room and Masters looking into the camera as he is approached by a tall, broad-shouldered figure, shot from the back in medium close-up. As they kiss, the camera turns slowly to the side of the heads and we discover that the partner is a woman. This seems to be the moment of the film's most aggressive assertion of its seductive powers: a "fuck you" to the audience. This is the moment of our awareness that the film can dupe us, mislead us. It is as if the film asserted: This is not what you think you expected to see, but what you *really* wanted to see. It is also the scene where the girlfriend's relation to her woman lover is first established, in a relay of gazes over Masters's shoulder and through dressing room mirrors—as if they have already mastered him. Notably, the homosexual charge in the kiss is immediately displaced and reconfigured upon the women.

But why all this violence in connection with homoerotics? It seems that one could argue, as Tania Modleski does concerning the pleasures of horror films, that horrific violence may be pleasurable if certain anxieties and fantasies are managed and contained at some other level of the film's operation. She wonders what sort of pleasure or stable position of mastery spectators obtain from films that seem only to rehearse a random "lust for destruction," within a narrative that presents interchangeable and unsympathetic "villains and victims," without offering the satisfaction of a logically coherent narrative closure. She concludes that "the mastery these popular texts no longer permit through effecting closure or eliciting narcissistic identification is often reasserted through projecting the experience of submission and defenselessness onto the female body."[19]

This is a particularly useful reading for *To Live and Die*, where the homoerotic violence seems to repress and reveal a subterranean homophobia (an anxiety about displacement or reconfigurations of power and sexual difference). Male homosocial bonding, to use Eve Sedgwick's term, depends on keeping its distance, through repression and violence, from male homosexuality; hence it depends, in its historical construction, upon homophobia. The thrust of the dancers' dressing room scene is to reinsert the reassuring woman, to rehearse homophobia and hold off homosexual panic.

As Sedgwick argues: "To draw the 'homosocial' back into the orbit of 'desire' of the potentially erotic, then, is to hypothesize the potential unbrokenness of a continuum between the homosocial and the homosexual—a continuum whose visibility, for men in our society, is radically disrupted."[20] The intense aggressive energy of this film, then, is, as it were, powered or fueled by homosexual panic, which can be read in the repeated connection of homoerotics to insult.

But this particular configuration of male homosocial agonistics and the violent affect it is designed to rehearse places the spectator in a masochistic position, as the gaze of the victim caught up in a paranoiac universe—in the titillating fear of being taken unawares. In this regard, Gaylyn Studlar's recent essay, "Masochism and the Perverse Pleasures of the Cinema," is particularly interesting. Studlar argues that the emphasis on voyeurism and sadistic scopophilia in

most feminist film theory causes it to ignore the strength of masochistic impulses in spectator seduction. In contrast, she suggests
we examine pleasure as generated from submission as well as from
control. "Spectatorial pleasure," she writes, "is a limited one like the
infantile, extragenital sexual pleasure that defines the masochist."
Further, she continues, "the spectator's narcissistic omnipotence is
like the narcissistic, infantile omnipotence of the masochist, who
ultimately cannot control the active partner."[21] This argument not
only provides a means of examining more than one type of spectator
pleasure, but it accounts for a more complex reading of the play of
identification and desire in spectator seduction, such that a spectator could both desire to control and desire to submit, just as it allows
for a masculine spectator position based in both desire for and identification with the woman as image. But it also allows us to analyze
the pleasure and seductive effects of a film like *To Live and Die*,
where the spectator is agitated by violence, and where there is no
stable point of identification, but rather a steady rhythm of reciprocal
aggression.

Aggression, here, however, also works out a distribution of power
along racial lines. In one of the most brutal scenes of the film, a
scene that partakes of the same excess as the chase scene, an excessive implausibility, a racial anxiety seems to be at work. Masters
enters the black neighborhood (shown in ample detail as a neighborhood) for the second time, because Jeff, a black man who distributes
counterfeit, has failed to fulfill his promise to have Masters's courier
assassinated in prison before he can inform on him. Accompanied by
only one other white man, he defeats five black men in Jeff's home,
that is, "on their own turf," even though these men are armed with
knives and all display martial arts training, which Masters doesn't
use. Thus, the narrative rehearses particular white fantasies, of dark
nights in black neighborhoods, and manages them with Masters's
brutal conquest of Jeff. This is a fantasy of rape, articulated when
Masters places a pistol in Jeff's mouth while saying, "You'll have to
suck on this until you shit that money," where the anal reference
effects a fantasmatic displacement. Now this is coded as a minor
scene, one of narrative peripeteia, a pretext for more violent excesses
in the filmic economy of expenditure. Yet in the context of the film's
fantasmatic relays, the circulation through spaces, it constructs a
territory off-limits, a space to be partitioned off, a threat put to rest.
This, then, is the social side which is made to appear and disappear; the space where simulacra can't circulate. Masters wants his
money back so he can burn it, because, as he says, "it's no good to me

after they've handled it." It has circulated in the wrong space, miscirculated in that other space, a space of labor, industry, and poverty which must be held off. It would seem that what Modleski describes as the pleasure of reasserted mastery appears here as an identification with space, or spatial boundaries. Spectator desire and identification come to be focused upon spaces, constructed scenes, which separate Masters's zone from that of the black men, upon whose bodies the film inscribes submission and defeat.

Beneath and beyond the narrative movements they offer, these two films concern the conquest of space by money, an operation reproduced in the filmic spectacle, where simulation wards off social referentiality. Yet if we refuse to disavow the referential level, we see another picture altogether. And we must refuse this disavowal, for the films' fictional production of nonpertinent differences, their reduction of social power differences to equivalent effects in spectacle, *depends* fundamentally upon maintaining at least a trace, a residue, of referential charge. That is, part of the narrative titillation resides in the display of real social differences, the lived power distributions and antagonisms which structure contemporary social life. But these social differences are presented as elements in an array of diverse details, proliferating differences in texture and intensity that structure the spectacle or that motivate narrative disjunctions, obstacles, and shifts. The point is that these are not just *any* details; they are manifestly particular social pressure points that these films regulate and manage.

Such work upon social difference within representations is characterized by Judith Williamson as fundamental to cultural domination and ideological reproduction: "These differences represented within, which our culture so liberally offers, are to a great extent reconstructions of captured external differences. Our culture, deeply rooted in imperialism, needs to destroy genuine difference, to capture what is beyond its reach; at the same time, it needs constructs of difference in order to signify itself at all."[22] That is, our cultural objects tend to occlude the specificity and significance of differences, making them appear as arbitrary and nonsignifying, by presenting them as part of a totality of random differences.

In these films, the spectacle achieves its regulation of social contradictions not by direct confrontation, but rather, by distraction. If we can ignore the social referentiality here, it is because we are seduced: we look aside, look elsewhere, give ourselves to spectacle produced on the ground of these differences. It is in this sense that these films participate in the cultural dominance that reduces differences in power distributed according to gender, race, class, and sexuality to a play of equivalent differences. At the same time, these differences, rendered as spectacle, do constitute a reconstruction of social antagonisms and the anxiety they generate for members of the dominant or privileged groups. The seductive effects of spatial circulation, of style and surface, as well as of narrative affect—love story and sentiment in *Gigolo* and violent outbursts in *To Live and Die*— relegate the films' rehearsal and management of white middle-class heterosexual anxieties to a peripheral position. Almost out of frame, but everywhere glimpsed as part of the frame, like the black shoe-shine man in *Gigolo* whose head protrudes into the frame as Julie discusses the law with Detective Sunday, men of color and homosexuals emerge only as recipients of a certain amount of violence continually routed toward them. It is because this aggression is not the primary filmic focus, but rather appears as a byproduct, a residue of the simulation machine, that it is so seductive, so effective. No spectator is obliged to take entirely seriously his or her pleasure or relief in these outbursts; they are only vaguely noticed, peripheral, incidental, immaterial, and substitutable.

But these films produce a series of confusing and conflicting messages around these sites as well. They manage to set up homosexuality and blackness as sometimes competing, sometimes merging, sometimes conflicting figures. For instance, in Leon, the black homosexual pimp of *Gigolo*, homosexuality begins to overcome and neutralize racial difference: he is sinister and he ultimately dies because of his effort to protect his blonde boy lover. In *To Live and Die*, there is yet another turn of the screw: the homoeroticization of violence against Jeff switches the channels of violence and rage. The homoerotic subtext to this scene displaces responsibility for the violence onto homosexual desire; homophobic charges are worked out across a black character as victim, with the residual effect of pitting the two groups against each other. These effects are possible because both films exhibit and circulate differences among which there are no stable oppositions or positions; everyone is corrupt, confused, and perverted, or "turned aside."

Because these films depend upon collisions of categories, of differences, and upon perpetual exchangeability, in which all figures are corrupt and perverse, seduced and seductive, then the seductive effects upon the spectator are related to circulation and collision. These representations reduce social and cultural points of resistance to mere frictions, a stimulation of spectator affect with no referential charge. If they mix their messages as they mix editing styles, they

produce spectator pleasure in the reassurance that there are no positions to take, only postures; that there are no contradictions, only
frictions and collisions. Our pleasure, then, and our seduction, may
arise from submission to a lack of positioning. The global message
of the spectacle may boil down to something quite simple: there are
no positions and no possibility of resistance. This is Dana Polan's
contention about the function of postmodern culture to induce an
exhilarating sense of impotence: "More than ever, mass culture can
come to encourage a powerlessness . . . powerlessness in post-modern
mass culture now comes from a situation in which the montage of
elements calls into question each and every position one might care
to adopt."[23] In the particular context of these films, this reading is
coherent with what Hal Foster describes as the particular quality of
fascination in a "society of spectacle"—fascination is expressed "as
loss, as unreality," in simulation, where "signs . . . precede and posit
the real."[24] The dominant seductive effect here is an exhilarating
dislocation, a loss of referentiality.

Can we not reframe both these films *and* the postmodern aesthetic which they reprocess? The films feed upon and feed into a
set of collective fantasies and desires which they rework in the cinematic frame. Their work is social; they are one site of subject construction in a social field constituted of many such sites. One of
these sites is certainly theoretical discourse and its critical interventions.

If we see it as another point of subject construction, is not the
theoretical apparatus of postmodernism, in its own fascination with
loss of reality, itself all too seductive? Does it not seduce us by its
very denial of referentiality, its rendering of social contradictions as
equivalent and nonmeaningful disjunctions in a fragmented play of
heterogeneous elements? Such a discourse would seem to leave us
captivated by analysis of our own autoseductions, at the expense of
examining our insertion as historical and cultural subjects in a social
field.

In this regard, postmodern theoretical discourse resembles these
films, whose appeal works through captivation by surfaces and staging of intense affect, producing two narcissistic pleasures. That narcissistic investment in pleasure permits the films' incorporation of
social antagonisms as mere props for spectacular scenes. Staging us
as spectators, these films construct us as consumers, consumers of
social conflict as well as of stylish spaces. If we buy this, we accept
the comfortable notion that social conflict can be reduced to a consumable and containable form, as an exciting spectacle. Once staged

as spectacle, such political and social antagonisms can be excavated, exhausted, just as the figures who represent them are made to disappear. Finally, the scene is an old and familiar one, for as aggressive as straight white men are toward each other in these films, it is always a straight white male who focuses the scene, who commands the space.

NOTES

1. For a good discussion of the particular features of Los Angeles's urban space and architecture, as well as an example of the privilege accorded to it by postmodern theoretical writing, see Fredric Jameson, "Postmodernism and the Cultural Logic of Late Capitalism," *New Left Review* 146 (1984), 80–84.

2. See, for example, Christian Metz, *The Imaginary Signifier* (Bloomington: Indiana University Press, 1982); Stephen Heath, *Questions of Cinema* (Bloomington: Indiana University Press, 1981); Mary Ann Doane, *The Desire to Desire: The Woman's Film of the 1940's* (Bloomington: Indiana University Press, 1987); E. Ann Kaplan, *Women and Film: Both Sides of the Camera* (New York: Methuen, 1983); Teresa de Lauretis, *Alice Doesn't* (Bloomington: Indiana University Press, 1984); Teresa de Lauretis and Stephen Heath, eds., *The Cinematic Apparatus* (New York: St. Martin's Press, 1980); Laura Mulvey, "Visual Pleasure and Narrative Cinema," *Screen* 16, no. 3 (1975).

3. See, in particular, the work of the journal *Screen*; Stephen Heath, *Questions of Cinema*; Bill Nichols, *Ideology and the Image* (Bloomington: Indiana University Press, 1981); Kaja Silverman, *The Subject of Semiotics* (New York: Oxford University Press, 1983).

4. Colin Mercer, "A Poverty of Desire," in *Formations of Pleasure* (London: Routledge and Kegan Paul, 1983), pp. 95–96.

5. Jean-Louis Comolli, "Machines of the Visible," in de Lauretis and Heath, eds., *Cinematic Apparatus*, p. 121.

6. Laura Kipnis, " 'Re-functioning' Reconsidered: Towards a Left Popular Culture," in *High Theory/Low Culture: Analysing Popular Television and Film*, ed. Colin MacCabe (New York: St. Martin's Press, 1986), p. 31.

7. Simon Frith, "Hearing Secret Harmonies," in MacCabe, ed., *High Theory/Low Culture*, p. 55.

8. Jean Baudrillard examines the postmodern fetishism of the code in a passage that links it to consumption, whereby we read for the "already-read," the message reduced to a function of the code. He writes: "The role of the message is no longer information, but testing and polling, and finally control ('contra-role,' in the sense that your answers are already inscribed in the 'role,' on the anticipated registers of the code). Montage and codification demand, in effect, that the receiver construe and decode by observing the same procedure whereby the work was assembled. The

reading of the message is then only a perpetual examination of the code" (*Simulations* [New York: Semiotext(e), 1983], pp. 119–20).

9. Dana Polan, "Brief Encounters: Mass Culture and the Evacuation of Sense," in *Studies in Entertainment: Critical Approaches to Mass Culture*, ed. Tania Modelski (Bloomington: Indiana University Press, 1986), p. 182.

10. This moment has become a common one in recent popular film (I think of the narratively incomprehensible appearance of fantasmatic hybrids, Palestinian-Libyan terrorists, in *Back to the Future*, for instance). In *To Live and Die*, this embedded figure of American foreign policy anxiety also allows the film the occasion to blow the Third World off the screen, so to speak, leaving only its resonances with the "domestic" Third World, the black characters.

11. Hal Foster, *Recodings: Art, Spectacle, Cultural Politics* (Port Townsend, Wash.: Bay Press, 1985), p. 175.

12. Kipnis, "Re-functioning Reconsidered," p. 27.

13. Such a combination of codes of consumption seems to be increasingly a feature of cinematic pleasure. One remarkable example is the recent *Year of the Dragon* (Cimino, 1985), in which a loft apartment becomes one primary site of intrigue. Particularly detailed examination of its space is ratified and reasserted in the final credits, where the name of the loft designer is noted.

14. See Jameson, "Post-modernism and the Cultural Logic of Late Capitalism," pp. 80–81.

15. Jean Baudrillard, "The Ecstasy of Communication," in *The Anti-Aesthetic*, ed. Hal Foster (Port Townsend, Wash.: Bay Press, 1983), p. 130.

16. This effect participates in what Baudrillard designates as the "hyperreal" produced by simulation: "the collapse of the real into hyperrealism, in the minute duplication of the real, preferably on the basis of another reproductive medium—advertising, photography, etc. . . . From medium to medium the real is volatilized . . . it becomes the real for the real, fetish of the lost object—no longer object of representation, but ecstasy of denegation and of its own ritual extermination" (*Simulations*, pp. 141–42). If our relation to objects becomes entirely fetishistic through this process, at the same time, the fetishistic channeling of our gaze immobilizes it, freezes it in fascination, mortifies or annihilates it. If simulation destroys the *object* of representation, it simultaneously negates the *subject* of representation.

17. Doane, *The Desire to Desire*, p. 95.

18. I thank Jeffrey Nunakawa for this deft formulation of the problem; it very economically engages with the film's vicious logic.

19. Tania Modleski, "The Terror of Pleasure," in Modleski, ed., *Studies in Entertainment*, p. 163.

20. Eve Sedgwick, *Between Men: English Literature and Male Homosocial Desire* (New York: Columbia University Press, 1985), pp. 1–2.

21. Gaylyn Studlar, "Masochism and the Perverse Pleasures of the Cinema,"

in *Movies and Methods*, vol. 2, ed. Bill Nichols (Berkeley: University of California Press, 1985), pp. 612–13.

22. Judith Williamson, "Woman Is an Island: Femininity and Colonization," in Modelski, ed., *Studies in Entertainment*, pp. 100–101.

23. Polan, "Brief Encounters," p. 183.

24. Foster, *Recodings*, p. 90.

PART TWO

Seduction at the Origin
of Psychoanalysis

Hysteria and the Seduction of Theory

Psychoanalytic theory was initially shaped as a response to hysteria. I want to examine some of the effects of that early relationship between hysteria and psychoanalysis and explicate the role seduction plays in the peculiar dynamics of desire, shaping the relationships among the psychoanalyst, the hysteric, and psychoanalytic theory. I shall show, in particular, how Freud's early seduction theory of hysteria led, in turn, to his seduction by oedipal theory.

Freud made a radical change in previous conceptualizations of hysteria. In the early part of the nineteenth century, hysteria was characterized as a disease according to the prevailing medical model of mental disorder: it was considered to be a separate entity distinguishable not only from other diseases, but also and most especially from its opposite, health, represented specifically by psychiatry and its practitioners. Discourse on hysteria, that is, the theories describing and explaining it, thus existed in a domain radically separate from the disease itself. The discourse could serve, therefore, not only as an arm in the conquering of the disease but also as an example of its own healthiness.

In many respects, Freud's first theory of hysteria, called the seduction theory, remained within the medical disease model: he considered hysteria to be "caused" by a specific, locatable event, a trauma, something similar in its effects to a train wreck, one of the other traumatic events commonly considered to cause hysterical neurosis at the time.[1] The medical disease model is evident in Freud's early writings on hysteria, especially in "The Neuro-psychoses of Defence" (1894), where he insists that the hysteric is characteristically in good health up to the time of the onset of the disease.

In these early studies, Freud often discusses the traumatic events causing hysteria—always sexual in nature according to him—and describes them as "attacks" (*Angriffen*) and "abuse" (*Abusus*). Strangely, though, while mentioning a whole host of possible perpetrators of these sexual attacks, often within the family, including brothers and other relatives, Freud never mentions fathers and never uses the word "incest." In *Studies on Hysteria*, he reveals in footnotes added in 1924 (pp. 134 and 170) that in two of the cases reported there—Katharina and Rosalia H.—he had shifted responsibility for the sexual attack from the real perpetrator, the father, to a fictive uncle. As Jeffrey Masson has argued, although Freud asserted that this disguise by displacement was the result of "discretion" on his part, given the medical context of his publication, his explanation is hardly persuasive.[2]

The incestuous nature of the sexual trauma at the root of hysteria, especially the culpability of the father, seems to have troubled Freud deeply. With a certain horrified disbelief, he worries in his letters to Wilhelm Fliess about the possibility that his own father (recently dead) was a "pervert"[3] and refers to his own "over-affectionate" dream of his daughter Mathilde.[4] In Freud's published writings about the aetiology of hysteria, his discomfiture is tellingly, one might say symptomatically, revealed/hidden by the increasingly common substitution of the word "seduction" (*Verführung*) for the terms "attack" and "abuse."[5] An ambiguous term, "seduction," which, in its contemporary usage could imply the use of persuasion in the sexual corruption of another individual, thus comes to stand for and eventually replace the more explicit terms Freud had previously used to denote what he himself had described as the "positively revolting sexual injuries (*Schädigungen*)" inflicted on young children.[6] Freud's use of the word "seduction" to refer to his trauma theory of the causation of hysteria became so systematic in his writings that later commentators designated this theory as the "seduction theory."[7]

The shift in Freud's vocabulary from words denoting injury to one implying persuasion and even possible assent can be seen as part of a widespread social pattern which minimizes the sexual exploitation of women by men. In English common law, for instance, in cases where a female minor was induced to sexual intercourse, the *father* was the plaintiff in the case. In cases of father-daughter incest, the father was, therefore, at least in theory, infringing only his own rights.

The paradoxical obverse of this tendency to minimize or even conceal the real sexual victimization of women consistently shows up in Freud's writing about hysteria in the form of a mythology of the

female hysteric and the male doctor. Although Freud observed numerous male hysterics in Charcot's clinic in Paris when he studied
there in 1885–86, and although he defended the notion of male hysteria to his colleagues in Vienna who challenged him on this point
upon his return,[8] all of the case histories of hysteria Freud presented
in his writings concerned women patients. In addition, Freud's notion that the pathogenic element in seduction was the child's *passivity*, a mode of reactivity he was later to equate with femininity,
contributed to the feminization of the hysterical patient.[9]

Although Freud ended up abandoning his initial perception of
the roots of hysterical pathology in the sexual abuse of children,
especially of young girls by their fathers, and although there was
nothing in his new theory that precluded men—including himself
—from being hysterics, he continued throughout his life generally
to maintain and perpetuate the old paradigm of hysteria along its
traditional gender lines. In fact, as I will discuss later in this essay,
Freud's theoretical manipulation of hysteria depends precisely on
the fantasy of a feminine patient and a masculine authority figure.

Freud's legacy has tended to persist in modern psychoanalysis
in spite of efforts to resist the traditionally gendered paradigm, and
in spite of the patent contradictions reality has come to offer in the
form of increasingly numerous women psychiatrists and psychoanalysts and of hysterical patients who are male. This model of hysteria
and theory in which the patient occupies the female position and
the doctor the male has been recently renewed in France, a renewal
which, as I will show later, demonstrates how deeply rooted the fear
of the unruly (hysterical) female is and how urgent the need to contain her in male law.

When Freud first announced his abandonment of the seduction
theory in his letter of September 21, 1897, to Fliess,[10] he, as so many
doctors before him, decided his hysterics had not been telling the
truth. Their stories of seduction were, he said, products of their own
unconscious fantasies. Rather than being traceable to a real event, or
series of events, in which sexual abuse was present, hysteria was now
construed as a pathological variant of a universal desire of female
children for their fathers. It is interesting to note that when fathers,
as a result of this shift, no longer play the role of sexual pervert but
of something coming close to a victim,[11] they reemerge from the protective covering of avuncular substitutes into direct representation
in Freud's texts.[12]

This change in the status of fathers—now redeemed—is accompanied by another displacement: when Freud rejects the theory of

seduction, seduction reappears in the operation of theory itself. What had been veiled in the first theory by Freud's textual displacement of the father and by the secondary substitution of the ambiguous "seduction" for words denoting active abuse, now reemerges in the construction of theory itself. Freud expresses relief and celebration in his letter to Fliess announcing the shift from the seduction theory.[13] Performing its function as an alleviator of the anxiety provoked by the idea of the guilt of the father, Freud's new theory can be seen as a symptom at once symbolically reenacting and concealing the abuse of young women.

First, the seduction, or, more properly, the violation of young girls that is denied in the new approach, reappears in symbolic form as part of the act of theorizing. In the Dora case, for instance, Freud states that he knows that if he had asked his hysterical patients if they were willing to have their case histories written up and published, they would certainly have said no.[14] He has ignored this anticipated negative, he says, in the "higher" interest of science. Thus his theorizing in print about hysteria can be seen as a transformed repetition of the acts of invasion first denied by the use of the word "seduction," and secondarily suppressed by the rejection of the seduction theory itself. The hysteric is exhibited against her will in the name of theory (etymologically linked to the verb "to show") by a man to his colleagues, thus becoming an object of exchange between them.

On another level, Freud's rejection of the seduction theory marks a transformation of the status of theoretical discourse by its break with the medical disease model of mental illness. When Freud shifted the supposed aetiology of hysteria to unconscious fantasies and showed that, in effect, all discourse is impelled and shaped by the unconscious, the disease and the writing about it could no longer be demarcated by a fixed frontier. Hysteria and psychoanalytic theory now fall, rather, onto a sliding scale in such a way that the discourse of the analyst and the discourse of the hysteric can never be decisively distinguished one from the other. This shift in the status of theory paradoxically opens up a new possibility in the relationship of the analyst to his writing: it makes theory a possible locus of the analyst's intellectual seduction.

In order to write about hysteria, in order to objectify and show the overall patterns present in a case history to his colleagues, Freud must not only violate the will of his patient, converting Dora, for instance, from a subject to an object of his will, he has also to remove himself from the domain of subjectivity in order to establish a reliable boundary between himself and his patient. In order to create a scientific theory, that is, a reliable account separate from the disorder itself, the analyst must act as if his own unconscious were not speaking in the theory. Freud and his followers find themselves thus in the paradoxical position of having to deny a capital element of their theory in order to enunciate it. In this respect, the writing of psychoanalytic theory represents a *seduction of the analyst*, who, in the original etymological sense of the word, is drawn away, turned aside, from the truth of his own perceptions.

Just as hysteria served as the original model relating neurosis to theoretical discourse, it may presently serve as the occasion for us to analyze the seductive function of theory in psychoanalysis. In its long history hysteria has often been the focus of professional disputes in medical and religious organizations.[15] In France at the present time, hysteria operates as the issue against which many psychoanalysts and psychoanalytically oriented psychiatrists are measuring both their profession and themselves. Interestingly enough, the central issues in their discussions are precisely the relationship between doctor and patient that I have been discussing and the challenge that hysteria represents to analytic knowledge.

In these discussions, hysteria is characterized as the disorder that puts in question objective knowledge, and in particular, the knowledge of the analyst.[16] As the phenomenon that marks a limit to science, the major issue hysteria poses to the analyst as a theorist is the question of who, between the analyst and the hysteric, knows what.

The hysteric—who, in line with Freud's revised theory, has now traded places and become a seducer, not the seduced—serves as a focal point for the current French reevaluation of the doctor/patient relationship. The bad conscience of analysis, what was repressed— the subjectivity of the doctor—is now resurfacing. But the metaphorizing, in current theory, of the hysteric/analyst dyad as a couple, even when it permits a franker discussion of countertransference issues in the treatment of hysteria than had been the case in the past, reproduces at the same time the old partition of gender roles, reactivating the paradigm of hysteria as a heterosexual love story.

The interpretation of the hysteric/analyst couple as a gendered paradigm is still carried on, as it was by Freud, only from the point of view of the analyst, who always has the last word.[17] Although couching their comments in different terms than those of their nineteenth-century predecessors, many contemporary analysts writing about hysteria in France still assume that the position of the analyst as

knower and interpreter is male; and they typify hysterics as occupying a female position, characterizing them as difficult patients
who elicit reactions of hostility, impatience, anger, exasperation, and
sometimes love.[18] In general, whether yielding to anger or to desire,
the analyst, represented as playing the male role in this romance,
appears to feel undone by the hysteric, who perpetually attempts to
dislodge him from his place as an authority.

One thing that makes the hysteric so difficult both as a patient
and as an element of theory, is the fact that her seductiveness is false;
she won't follow through. She is what the French call an *allumeuse*,
firing men up only to say "no" in the end.[19] Since the feminine version of seduction, different from the male, persuasive model earlier
used by Freud, includes posing oneself *as an object of desire for
another*, the falsity of the hysteric's seduction lies precisely in her
posing limits to the self as an object. The seduction ends when the
hysteric insists on subjectivity, on her status as a subject. While this
insistence may take on the characteristics of caricature in the hysteric, her status as subject, however flamboyant and exaggerated, is
posed in an undeniable way.

This sequence of seductiveness and withdrawal seems to be particularly enraging to male analysts. Desire is first aroused according
to the normal procedures of female seduction by a woman posing
herself as an object; but then the desire is left unsatisfied by the hysteric's insistence on her status as subject, which includes, among
other things, the possibility of rejecting what was first demanded. In
these circumstances, analysts say they feel undone, impotent, or castrated, and their response is to master their anger and humiliation by
returning the hysteric to object status as an item in textual theory.
The act of theorizing therefore becomes an equivalent of phallic display.[20] This phallic display is destined, however, not for the woman,
but rather for the analyst's colleagues, who, even when there are
women among them, are always addressed as male.

In reaction to the humiliation suffered at the hands of a capricious hysteric, the analyst retreats to a group conventionally defined
as male in order to seek the recognition and admiration he failed to
get from the hysteric. In this context, the writing of theory becomes
a *regressive* move, a journey back from the realm of oedipal desire
on whose threshold the hysteric has also stumbled, to the domain
of narcissistic relationships where the analyst can be mirrored and
affirmed by his counterparts.

The function of theory as a belief system which provides an
anticipatory defence against the hysteric's refusal of seduction be-

comes clear. Following the lead of their compatriot, the historian Michel Foucault, French analysts themselves have begun systematically to examine the general defensive function of theory that may shape their encounter with the patient by a constant, unconscious filtering of perceptions and reactions.[21] The possibility that the analyst's theoretical persuasions may act as a permanent, nonanalyzed element of the doctor/patient relationship poses a serious challenge to the neutrality of the analytic process. Countertransference issues have long been widely discussed, but the perception that theory operates as a permanent defensive filter is presently leading some analysts to muse that the whole field of practice may be tainted, precisely by the theoretical allegiances of the analyst.[22] These recent examinations in France of the countertransference aspects of theory point up what often remains unacknowledged—the degree to which patients may be made into objects in practice even before they are turned into objects in and by theory.

In the heterosexual paradigm of doctor/patient relationships, the hysteric challenges the desire of the analyst not only on a sexual level, but, as we have just seen, on the level of theory as well, exposing to our analysis the implication of one in the other. By insisting on her status as subject, the hysteric incites the analyst to act out the defensive function of theory, thus opening to view how theory itself can function as an acting out of regressive, narcissistic wishes. Where the female hysteric/male doctor paradigm is in play, analytic knowledge plays a protective role for the analyst, safeguarding him against the traumatic effects of a devastating encounter with a female subject of desire. But if theory operates as a symptom, then the unacceptable knowledge that was originally denied in and by that symptom risks returning to consciousness.

What precisely is the denied knowledge protectively replaced by psychoanalytic theories of hysteria? Is the theory simply an angry revenge for rejection, as we have intimated, or is it something else? Here we enter a territory where analysts usually do not speak of themselves, at least to outsiders, and where I, as a female subject excluded in and by their theory, can propose only conjectures.

My hypotheses are based on Freud's "Dora" case. One of the elements in that case which remained unanalyzed by Freud and which has not attracted comment in the many commentaries the case history has provoked, is precisely the question of Dora's sexual knowledge. Her knowledge, especially of sexual techniques, considered shocking and inappropriate by most of the actors in her drama, seems, on the contrary, to intrigue Freud. The explanation for the fascination and scandal her knowledge evokes seems, indeed, too obvious—that young women in the Vienna of that time were not supposed to *know* anything, although, one might add, they seem to have been expected to *do* a lot; or at least that is what one might surmise from Herr K.'s attempt to seduce Dora when she was fourteen and from Freud's apparent condoning of that act. Although young women were expected to yield to male sexual pressure and persuasion— Dora's negative reactions were for Freud an indication of pathology— young women weren't supposed to know anything about sex. In other words, actual sexual activity on the part of young women seemed less dystonic with Viennese ideals of femininity than knowledge of the act. This paradox remains unanalyzed in Freud's case history.

The sexual knowledge and awareness of children plays, however, an important role in the theoretical formulation which eventually took the place of Freud's rejected seduction theory of hysteria. In his letters to Fliess, two weeks after his announcement of the abandonment of the seduction theory of hysteria Freud first evokes the story of Oedipus.[23] What is strange in Freud's shift from the seduction theory to the theoretical assertion of sexual drives in young children is the uncanny substitution that takes place: at the center of the seduction theory is a young girl seduced by the father; at the center of the oedipus complex, there is a young boy constructing erotic fantasies about his mother. In the new, substitute theoretical formulation, then, the little boy takes the place of the victimized girl.

Aside from the shape of the story dictated by the Greek myth, one may speculate that other considerations determined Freud's shift to a male protagonist. Indeed, according to Freud's own laws of symptom formation, one may assume that there was for him a particular rightness in this substitutability of the one for the other. The similarity of situation making possible the substitution of the boy in oedipal theory for the girl in seduction theory gives us a clue to what Freud might have been denying when he decided to disbelieve his early hysterical patients. Beyond resistance to the sadistic role of the (his) father and his own potentially sadistic role as analyst lies the substitutability of the boy for the girl, or, more precisely, the recognition that the boy has always already occupied at some time a female position.

What was denied along with the stories of childhood sexual abuse and then returns symptomatically in the second theory is the (for Freud) devastating knowledge that a boy—perhaps he himself— might experience sexual seduction in the passive mode of a female; that, to state it more radically, a boy might be treated like a girl.

The theory of childhood sexual fantasies which supplants the seduction theory very precisely protects against this indeterminacy of the sexes by positing a law of heterosexuality: the boy will necessarily desire his mother, the girl her father.

Having identified the regularization of the sexes and their position in the triangle of desire as it is formulated in oedipal theory, we can now go back and reinterpret the repressed version of these dynamics at work not only in the treatment of patients but in Freud's construction of psychoanalytic theory itself. The pattern of female seductiveness in hysteria, castration fears on the part of the analyst, and the analyst's retreat for reassurance to idealized, older male figures, which I have analyzed above, all suggest that the trio of hysteric/analyst/colleague constitutes a version of the officially formulated oedipal triangle. And if we can read the theory of the oedipal complex as a repression of male hysteria (fear of feminization), we can see that in the triangle of hysteric/analyst/colleague, the underlying positions and roles of the genders are not as clear as they originally appeared in Freud's theory, but are, rather, hopelessly blurred and shifty. Without the protection of his oedipal theory, the analyst would stand in the original place of the hysteric, with the hysteric combining the roles of mother, *allumeuse,* and castrating father. Armed with psychoanalytic discourse, on the other hand, the analyst turns to male colleagues who play the role of idealized father-comforter. What we see at work behind the oedipal theory is a more anxious, more unruly complex where gender roles are reversible if not undecidable, where sex is not frustrated but, on the contrary, overwhelming, and where narcissistic identifications dominate.[24]

The revelation of the repressed origins of the oedipus complex in hysteria and the elucidation of oedipal elements in its treatment not only permit us to uncover some hitherto hidden dimensions of the theory, but also to interpret the knowledge of the hysteric as an analytic question and not simply an issue of the mores of turn-of-the-century Vienna. Freud's fascination with Dora's knowledge emerges as a symptom-formation, covering a paradoxical and anxious view of femaleness both as powerlessness and as total power. In this view, the female is both castrated and a phallic mother. If Dora knows something the analyst does not, the analyst may feel castrated. If the sexual autonomy of the hysteric were to be recognized, her desire would appear as contingent rather than necessary. Dora's knowledge subverts Freud's theory of female desire as necessarily being directed not only toward men in general, but toward specific men (the father, the analyst). Autonomy of female desire would remove the hysteric from the purview of this psychoanalytic law, turning seduction into a chancy, capricious exchange marking the limit of theory's power to master.

In Freud's seduction theory of hysteria, "seduction" was a cover for rape and incest in which fathers played the guilty role. In the second theory, fathers were relieved of their guilt by the law of female fantasies of seduction. Freud traded responsibility on one level for mastery on another, for in the second theory, men may be objects of desire, but analysts are also and foremost the knowers of that desire. In the first instance, "seduction" denied the blatant exercise of sexual power by fathers with respect to their young daughters; in the second, daughters were made the initiators of illicit desire in fantasies of oedipal seduction, but subjected simultaneously to the power of the father by the regularization of their desire in the laws of theory. Denied in these instances is first, fear of being feminized by seduction, and second, fear of losing control of knowledge, with concomitant fear of the sexual autonomy and power of women. Freud's response to both these fears is to wish that the sexes be clearly separate and that their natures be determined by necessity. Freud's (protected) male position is defined at this time by his insistence on constructing a *scientific* theory of hysteria, in other words, a theory that is not hysterical but which contains hysteria within knowable laws.

Autonomy of female desire, on the one hand, and the engagement of psychoanalysis self-reflexively in its own processes, on the other, subvert the framework of the theories we have been examining. The seduction theory and the theory of the oedipus complex can be turned topsy-turvy, exploded from within. As Madelon Sprengnether has argued, in Freud's theory of the oedipus complex, the father's role as rival is a defensive formation representing the wish for a *law* of separation.[25] But the father's presence as an intervention between mother and son is an unnecessary psychological law, because if one recognizes maternal subjectivity, one sees that the mother *may or may not* desire her son; the presence of the father is not required to prevent the fulfillment of oedipal desire. The father's intervening presence implies an independent guarantee of the difference and separation of the sexes, a difference hysteria strives to question.

The theory of the oedipal complex was a replacement for the initial seduction theory of hysteria, but in a way different from Freud's explanation of the shift. While Freud apparently established a rule-

bound triangle in which the places of the different genders were separate and predetermined, the replacement of the (hysteric) daughter
by the son suggests, as we have seen, a hidden agenda that makes
of the oedipus complex a substitution of another kind—a wish fulfillment that the indeterminacy of the sexes and the autonomy of
women revealed in hysteria not be true. It is both a dream of seduction and a seductive dream, the fulfillment of the son's wish that his
mother always desire him and only him, and that, were it not for the
castrating father, oedipal desire could be fulfilled.

The mother's subjectivity, denied in Freud's formulation of the
oedipus complex, and the unacceptable, humiliating recognition that
the mother's desire for her son is uncertain, unreliable, puts phallic
analytic power at risk, making the doctor a feminized, passive re-
spondent not to a fear of castration by the father, but rather to an
uncapturable female desire. This is the fascinating, forbidden knowledge the hysteric dramatizes and the analyst attempts to repress and
control in the construction of theory.

One can see why psychoanalytic theory in general, and the theory
of the oedipus complex in particular, is so seductive: *it represents
the dream of desire subject to law* in which the places of the sexes
are clearly defined, women are always available, and heterosexuality
is natural. One French analyst recently said that theory is *la jouis-
sance*.[26] If psychoanalytic theory presents a fantasy of desire subject
to law, if, like a seductive woman who never asserts herself as a
subject, desire can be made to seem accessible to possession, then
theory can indeed be bliss, as deliciously irresistible as the dream of
a woman who will never say "no."

As long as the construction of psychoanalytic theory promotes
separation—of the sexes, of knowledge and desire—it will always be
at odds with itself, self-seductive, undoing its own truth. As long
as the disease model persists in the practice of theory and analysts
claim to be separate from what they see as pathology, the unconscious will operate in that theory like a seductive woman, the *mise
en abyme* of the original hysterical oedipal daughter. But insofar as
the law of separation can be seen as a symptom in psychoanalysis,
as Freud's defence against the humiliation of being feminized by a
powerful woman, the seduction of and by theory is itself contingent,
not necessary. The construction of psychoanalytic theory need not
be subjected, then, to the daughter's seduction or the father's law;[27]
it need not fall into the alternatives of being either hysterical or perverse, but may be, rather, the locus of another kind of connection,

a seduction—in yet another sense of the word *seducere* where the prefix "se" is at once reflexive and diacritical—leading back to a self which is already a marker of difference.

NOTES

1. Sigmund Freud (with J. Breuer), *Studies in Hysteria* (1893–95), in *The Standard Edition of the Complete Psychological Works of Sigmund Freud* (hereafter *S.E.*), ed. and trans. James Strachey et al., 24 vols. (London: Hogarth Press, 1953–74), vol. 2. Also "Further Remarks on the Neuro-psychoses of Defence" (1896), *S.E.*, 3:157–85; and "The Aetiology of Hysteria" (1896), *S.E.*, 3:187–221.
2. Jeffrey Moussaieff Masson, *The Assault on Truth: Freud's Suppression of the Seduction Theory* (New York: Farrar, Straus and Giroux, 1984).
3. Sigmund Freud, Letter of Sept. 21, 1897, to Wilhelm Fliess, in *S.E.*, 1:259.
4. Freud, Letter of May 31, 1897, to Fliess, in *S.E.*, 1:253–54.
5. See "Unpublished Documents," *S.E.*, vol. 1; "Three Essays on the Theory of Sexuality," *S.E.*, 7:123–245; and "My Views on the Part Played by Sexuality in the Aetiology of the Neuroses," *S.E.*, 7:269–79.
6. Freud, "Further Remarks on the Neuro-psychoses of Defence," *S.E.*, 3:164.
7. See Masson, *Assault on Truth*, and Alexander Schusdek, "Freud's Seduction Theory: A Reconstruction," *Journal of the History of the Behavioral Sciences* 2:159–66.
8. Frank Sulloway, *Freud, Biologist of the Mind: Beyond the Psychoanalytic Legend* (New York: Basic Books, 1979), pp. 36–41.
9. Freud, "The Aetiology of Hysteria," *S.E.*, 3:214–15; and "My Views on the Part Played by Sexuality in the Aetiology of the Neuroses," *S.E.*, 7:276–77.
10. In *S.E.*, 1:249–60.
11. See the article, praised by Freud, of Karl Abraham, "The Early Experiencing of Sexual Traumas as a Form of Sexual Activity" (1907), in *Selected Papers of Karl Abraham*, trans. Douglas Bryan and Alix Strachey (1927; reprint ed., London, 1948), pp. 47–63.
12. Freud, "An Autobiographical Study" (1925), in *S.E.*, 20:33–34.
13. "If I were depressed, confused, or exhausted, doubts of this kind would no doubt have to be interpreted as signs of weakness. Since I am in the opposite state, I must . . . be proud that after going so deep I am still capable of such criticism. . . . It is remarkable, too, that there has been an absence of any feeling of shame, for which, after all, there might be occasion . . . I have more of the feeling of a victory than of a defeat." Freud, Letter of Sept. 21, 1897, in *S.E.*, 1:260.
14. "Fragment of an Analysis of a Case of Hysteria," *S.E.*, 7:8.
15. Etienne Trillat, *Histoire de l'hystérie* (Paris: Seghers, 1986).

16. See Lucien Israël, *L'Hystérique, le sexe et le médecin* (Paris: Masson, 1980); Charles Melman, *Nouvelles études sur l'hystérie* (Paris: Clims-Denoël, 1984); and Gérard Wajeman, *Le Maître et l'hystérique* (Paris: Navarin, 1982).

17. Z. B. A. Ramadan and A. J. B. M. de Almeida, "Phénoménologie du 'Cas Anna O' et les pôles du langage," *Evolution psychiatrique*, 43 (1978), 325–35.

18. Lucien Israël, *L'Hystérique*.

19. Etienne Trillat, *Histoire*, p. 272.

20. M. Godard et al., "L'Agressivité: Un aspect trop oublié de l'hystérie," *Actualités psychiatriques*, no. 4 (1981), 28–30; Lucien Israël, "Les Victimes de l'hystérie," *Congrès de Lausanne* (Paris: Masson, 1965).

21. See Luce Irigaray, *Parler n'est jamais neutre* (Paris: Editions de Minuit, 1985); François Roustang, . . . *Elle ne le lâche plus* (Paris: Editions de Minuit, 1980); and Etienne Trillat, *Histoire*.

22. Bernard Jolivet, "Théories pratiques" (Paper presented at colloquium, *Hystérie et obsession*, Paris, 1986).

23. Letter, Freud to Fliess, Oct. 15, 1897, *S.E.*, 1:265.

24. See Jacques Lacan's reading of the oedipal complex in the Rat Man case in "The Neurotic's Individual Myth," *Psychoanalytic Quarterly* 48 (1979), 405–25.

25. Madelon Sprengnether has made this point on several occasions, including the Modern Language Association convention in 1987. See her forthcoming book on Freud, *The Spectral Mother* (Cornell University Press). My argument about the defensive function of Freud's suppression of maternal subjectivity and my hope for a theory of the mother who is a marker of difference is indebted to Sprengnether's formulations.

26. Pierre Martin, "Vengeance contre le temps et son il était" (Paper presented at colloquium, *Hystérie et obsession*, Paris, 1986).

27. In *The Daughter's Seduction: Feminism and Psychoanalysis* (Ithaca: Cornell University Press, 1982) Jane Gallop discusses the seductive relationship between psychoanalysis and its feminist daughters. In many ways, Jacques Lacan represents the ideal practitioner of psychoanalytic theory as I outline it in the conclusion of this essay except for the fact that, once again, woman is theorized as the locus of unknowing.

Freud and Fliess:
Homophobia and Seduction

When I first read *The Complete Letters of Sigmund Freud to Wilhelm Fliess: 1887–1904*, edited by Jeffrey Moussaieff Masson,[1] what was most apparent—and surprising—to me about them was that they are love letters. Careful rereadings have not changed my first impression. Yet most who write about the letters ignore or submerge the erotic energy that pervades them. Many writers on Freud see the relationship between Freud and Fliess as involving the kind of transference that occurs between analysand and analyst, but tend not to discuss the erotic components that such a relationship may involve.

Freud and Fliess met in 1887 and began a friendship and correspondence that continued past the turn of the century. They wrote frequently and saw each other often until they quarreled in 1900, when Fliess questioned the value of Freud's psychoanalytic research. Their friendship ended irreparably and their correspondence broke off in 1904, when Fliess accused Freud of transmitting his ideas on bisexuality, which he had revealed to Freud in confidence and had only partially published.[2] Sometime after the friendship between the two men had ended, Freud described it as a manifestation of homosexual longing, which he claimed he no longer felt; he wrote Sandor Ferenczi, his friend and colleague: "You not only noticed, but also understood, that I *no longer* have any need to uncover my personality completely, and you correctly traced this back to the traumatic reason for it. Since Fliess's case, with the overcoming of which you recently saw me occupied, that need has been extinguished. A part of homosexual cathexis has been withdrawn and made use of to enlarge my own ego. I have succeeded where the paranoiac fails."[3]

Masson quotes two other unpublished letters to Ferenczi written during the same period in which Freud again insists that he has overcome his homosexual attraction to Fliess. On October 17, 1910, he wrote: "You probably imagine that I have secrets quite other than those I have reserved for myself, or you believe that my secrets are connected with a special sorrow, whereas I feel capable of handling everything and am pleased with the greater independence that results from having overcome my homosexuality." Two months later he asserts, "I have now overcome Fliess, about whom you were so curious" (*Letters*, p. 4n).[4] To say that the relationship represents a homosexual attachment defines the sex of its object, but does not describe the quality of the relationship. In order to explore the nature of Freud's love for Fliess, I want to read Freud's text as I might a literary text or as Freud might "read" an analysand's discourse, though I acknowledge that there is some slippage in reading letters, literary texts, and patients.

From the time I began reading the letters, I heard repeated in Freud's correspondence with Fliess the voice of Shakespeare's *Sonnets*, a sequence of love poems, the majority written to a young man and the others addressed to a "dark lady." Both Shakespeare and Freud idealize the men to whom they write, continually praise them and profess their importance to the writers' personal and professional lives, extenuate their faults, and are abject and lonely when the friends are absent or when friendship pales. Dealing directly with the young man's physical beauty and attractiveness, Shakespeare's poems are at moments more frankly homoerotic than Freud's letters. But for both Freud and Shakespeare, male friendships were extremely important. Both evidently felt the pulls of bisexual attraction, which would undoubtedly be more usual, common, "normal" among Westerners generally except for the need to accommodate the demands of cultural repression. Shakespeare's homoerotic attractions may have been stronger than Freud's, or they may only appear to be so because the poetic mode in which the artist worked allowed him more freedom to express them. But as the two men reveal themselves in their writing, both have bisexual temperaments.

Shakespeare in fact served Freud as an important reference for understanding experience.[5] When Freud was discovering in his self-analysis his own love of his mother and jealousy of his father and framing his theory of the oedipus complex as part of a larger scheme of sexual development, he turned for example and definition first to *Oedipus Rex* and then to *Hamlet* (October 15, 1897). Freud may have been drawn to Shakespeare in part because he felt their emotional kinship. Both men may have been able to realize their creative powers as fully as they did partly because they were more able than most to let their "feminine" sides live.

Yet Freud and Shakespeare both shared their culture's fear of homosexuality. Shakespeare did not contemplate the possibility of a homosexual relationship sexually realized. For instance, he laments that by creating the youth male instead of female, "Nature" keeps them apart:

> And for a woman wert thou first created,
> Till Nature as she wrought thee fell a-doting,
> And by addition me of thee defeated,
> By adding one thing to my purpose nothing
>   But since she pricked thee out for women's pleasure,
>   Mine be thy love, and thy love's use their treasure.[6]

The most overtly homosexual character Shakespeare created was Antonio in *The Merchant of Venice*, and he gave him the lines, "I am a tainted wether of the flock, / Meetest for death" (4.1.113–15). Similarly, Freud was never comfortable with his homosexual feeling; as his letters to Ferenczi make clear, it was something to be "overcome." Freud came to see homosexuality in his system of thought as an unsuccessful outcome of the oedipal phase, a sign of immaturity.

Freud and Shakespeare, therefore, suspended their friendships with men between a crucial desire for intimacy and union and a need to keep those feelings at bay. It was within this space that Freud's friendship with Fliess unfolded. On the one hand, his love for Fliess served him as inspiration and gave him creative energy. On the other, his homophobia, his fear of homosexuality, was destructive. His need to deny and repress his feelings contributed to the depression and psychosomatic illnesses he suffered and caused him to adopt painful strategies to win Fliess's affection. Freud also displaced his erotic energies in ways that were harmful to himself and others. It was his relentless homophobia rather than his homosexual feelings that led Freud astray.

That Freud was drawn to Fliess seems natural. At the time he met Fliess, Freud was a lecturer in neuropathology at the University of Vienna and had established a neurological practice. Fliess was a successful ear, nose, and throat doctor in Berlin. Freud was thirty-one and Fliess was twenty-nine; both were from middle-class Jewish families. Freud had recently married, and Fliess would marry soon; both expected to have families and hoped and aimed for professional success. They enjoyed many of the same social, intellectual, and artistic pleasures. Similar educational backgrounds trained them in the humanities, and they were conversant in classical and modern literature. Instructed in the Helmholtz school of physics and physiology, they had almost identical scientific backgrounds.[7]

Their scientific interests were such that the two men could collaborate with and complement each other. Both were interested in neuroses: Fliess, locating them in an organic source; Freud, formulating a psychological basis. Freud describes Fliess as one who "can say what life is" and himself as one who "can say (almost) what the mind is" (December 22, 1897). When Fliess discovered that he could clear up a number of symptoms by administering cocaine to the nasal mucous membrane, he developed a notion of "nasal reflex neurosis," in which numerous symptoms were supposed to proceed from the nose. He asserted a special connection between nasal and genital areas in both men and women. He also developed a theory of periodicity, in which both women and men were affected by cycles: of twenty-eight days, the feminine period (related to women's menstrual cycles); and twenty-three days, the masculine period. According to Fliess, humans were influenced by both components and were, therefore, bisexual. Intimately connected to sexual processes, these periods determined the events of life, including birth, illness, and death. Fliess also speculated that similar periods influenced animals and other organisms. Freud's attraction to Fliess led him to entertain his theories with more sympathy and generosity than they merited and indeed than his contemporaries accorded them. To many, Fliess's theories seemed not only untenable, but even bizarre, as most commentators tend to regard them today.[8]

According to Jones, Fliess had two major advantages as colleague and friend over Joseph Breuer, Freud's closest intellectual companion before he met Fliess. Unlike Breuer, Fliess had made sexual problems the center of his work. Breuer was "reserved, cautious, averse to any generalization, realistic, and above all vacillating in his ambivalence"; whereas, Fliess "was extremely self-confident, outspoken, unhesitatingly gave the most daring sweep to his generalizations, and swam in the empyrean of his ideas with ease, grace, and infectious felicity." Fliess was generally thought to be a magnetic person; Jones describes him as a "brilliant and interesting talker on a variety of subjects."[9] As medical researchers, Freud and Fliess had unconventional interests and considerable energy for pursuing them. As Masson writes, "Both were interested in aspects of medical science that lay outside the customary channels of research. Both, for instance, visited Paris to work with Charcot. A love of scientific adventure and inquiry seemed to unite them professionally" (*Letters*, p. 2).

When Fliess came to study with specialists in Vienna in the fall of 1887, Breuer suggested that he attend Freud's lectures. Freud was evidently dazzled. His immediate attraction is apparent from the first words of his first letter to Fliess: "My letter of today admittedly is occasioned by business, but I must introduce it by confessing that I entertain hopes of continuing the relationship with you and that you have left a deep impression on me which could easily lead me to tell you outright in what category of men I place you" (November 24, 1887). Fliess evidently responded to Freud's enthusiasm with presents; Freud's reply suggests that he expects their mutually felt friendliness to continue:

> Your cordial letter and your magnificent gifts awakened the most pleasant memories for me, and the sentiment I discern behind both Christmas presents fills me with the expectation of a lively and mutually gratifying relationship between us in the future. I still do not know how I won you; the bit of speculative anatomy of the brain cannot have impressed your rigorous judgment for long. But I am very happy about it. So far I have always had the good fortune of finding my friends among the best of men, and I have always been particularly proud of this good fortune. So I thank you and ask you not to be surprised if at the moment I have nothing to offer in return for your charming present. (December 28, 1887)

They began to meet irregularly in August of 1890 and continued to do so for the next ten years. Freud obviously admired Fliess greatly and felt energized by his presence—"When I talked with you and saw that you thought well of me, I even used to think something of myself, and the picture of absolutely convincing energy that you offered was not without its effect on me" (August 1, 1890).

While Freud's friendship with Fliess was to be the most significant male friendship of his life, it takes its place beside others. Though Freud had many friends, he had particularly intense relationships with a few men who were both colleagues and personal friends. Before he met Fliess, his closest companions were Ernst von Fleischl-Marxow and Breuer, both of whom he had met at the University of Vienna in the Institute of Physiology. Freud tried to cure Fleischl of his addiction to morphia and nursed him during extreme stages of illness until his untimely death at forty-six.[10] Fourteen years older than Freud, and his mentor and collaborator on *Studies on*

Hysteria, Breuer was Freud's good friend for twenty years. Close relationships that followed his friendship with Fliess were mainly with men involved in the psychoanalytic movement and younger than Freud. They included Carl Jung, Karl Abraham, Sandor Ferenczi, Ernest Jones, and Oskar Pfister among others. Freud's friendships with Breuer, Jung, and Ferenczi were particularly intense and, like his companionship with Fliess, marked by difficult quarrels and bad endings.

Freud recognized the pattern in his life of passionate male friendships accompanied by intense dislike. Tracing it back to his childhood, he located it in his relationship to a brother who died in infancy and his nephew John, who because of his family constellation was a year older than Freud.[11] Writing Fliess about his discoveries during his self-analysis, he explained, "I greeted my one-year-younger brother (who died after a few months) with adverse wishes and genuine childhood jealousy; and . . . his death left the germ of [self-] reproaches in me. I have also long known the companion of my misdeeds between the ages of one and two years; it is my nephew, a year older than myself. . . . The two of us seem occasionally to have behaved cruelly to my niece, who was a year younger. This nephew and his younger brother have determined, then, what is neurotic, but also what is intense, in all my friendships" (October 3, 1897).

Looking back at his own development, Freud remarked in regard to his nephew: "My emotional life has always insisted that I should have an intimate friend and a hated enemy. I have always been able to provide myself afresh with both, and it has not infrequently happened that the ideal situation of childhood has been so completely reproduced that friend and enemy have come together in a single individual."[12] Perhaps suspecting this side of himself before he knew it clearly, he wrote to Fliess of his declining friendship with Breuer: "That everything one enjoys in life has to be paid for so dearly is decidedly not an admirable arrangement. Will the two of us experience the same thing with each other?" (March 1, 1896).

The intensity of Freud's male friendships is indicated by their provocation of jealousies. Freud evidently sensed that his relationship with Fleischl might appear to give his fiancée cause for jealousy, for he writes Martha: "I admire and love him with an intellectual passion, if you will allow such a phrase. His destruction will move me as the destruction of a sacred and famous temple would have affected an ancient Greek. I love him not so much as a human being, but as one of Creation's precious achievements. And you needn't be at all jealous."[13] Ida Fliess was apparently jealous of Freud's relationship with her husband. When the two men's friendship was in decline, Freud reminded Fliess of Breuer's warning to Ida, which she credited: "What is your wife doing other than working out in a dark compulsion the notion that Breuer once planted in her mind when he told her how lucky she was that I did not live in Berlin and could not interfere with her marriage" (August 7, 1901). Freud was apparently jealous of Fliess's intimacies with other men. He writes to Fliess about Felix Gattel, a former pupil who became Fliess's colleague in Berlin: "I don't know that you should tell him so many of your most intimate matters. Besides, I envy him for it" (September 27, 1898).

Freud continually insisted on the importance of male friendship, which offered him something companionship with women did not. "No one," he writes, "can replace for me the relationship with the friend which a special—possibly feminine—side demands" (May 7, 1900). After they had begun to fall out with each other, Freud writes Fliess, "I do not share your contempt for friendship between men, probably because I am to a high degree party to it. In my life, as you know, woman has never replaced the comrade, the friend" (August 7, 1901).

There are moments in the correspondence in which Freud engages Fliess in a relationship with him that excludes their wives or in which he shares with Fliess intimacies about Martha or his relationship with her that make clear what he means when he says, "woman has never replaced the comrade, the friend." When Freud sends Fliess his paper "The Etiology of the Neuroses," he warns him, "You will of course keep the manuscript away from your young wife" (February 8, 1893). Presumably, the forbidden material is the identification of masturbation as the cause of neurasthenia. It may also be the alternatives of Freud's conclusion: either sexual freedom or a society "doomed to fall victim to incurable neuroses, which reduce the enjoyment of life to a minimum, destroy marital relations, and bring hereditary ruin on the whole coming generation." In Freud's caution about keeping his manuscript away from Ida, there is a hint of teasing and even coyness, a kind of signal that this is a moment between men. On a more somber occasion, when Freud fears he has myocarditis and must face "uncertainty" and a "shortened life expectancy," he tells Fliess that Martha "is not a confidante of my death deliria" (April 19, 1894). Clearly there is an implication that men are of stronger stuff than women and may more comfortably and appropriately face sex and death together.

Though Freud is scrupulous about protecting Martha's privacy when it comes to publishing dreams or using illustrations in which she might be recognizable, he occasionally exposes her and matters pertaining to their private lives to Fliess.[14] When he postpones a visit to Fliess in order to accommodate Martha's wish to stay with him on Mount Rax, he explains, "I do not believe I can deny her this wish. You can imagine what is behind it; gratitude, a feeling of coming back to life again of the woman who for the time being does not have to expect a child for a year because we are now living in abstinence; and you know the reasons for this as well" (August 20, 1893). Not only does he explain their sexual relationship, but he also indicates that he has discussed their abstinence more fully with Fliess. On another occasion, he describes one of Martha's illnesses, including the details of her "breakdown of intestinal activity" (October 9, 1898).

We have no way of knowing what Martha Freud would have thought about Freud's revealing such personal matters to Fliess. Jones tells us an amazing story about Martha. When Nazi authorities forced their way into the Freud home, Martha, "as people do in an emergency, had responded to the occasion with the essence of her personality. In her most hospitable manner she invited the sentry at the door to be seated; as she said afterward, she found it unpleasant to see a stranger standing up in her home."[15] It is hard to imagine that a woman who was able to call on this kind of decorum and formality in such an extreme situation would have wanted her husband to discuss their sexual relationship or her bowels with his personal friend. Even though Fliess was a doctor, he was not Martha's doctor. Yet unlike Ida Fliess, Martha apparently did not disapprove of the friendship between the two men. Masson translates a passage on this theme from Marie Bonaparte's notebook: "Ida Fliess, moreover, 'a bad woman,' out of jealousy, did everything possible to sow discord between the two friends, whereas Martha Freud understood very well that Fliess was able to give her husband something beyond what she could" (Letters, p. 196, n. 1).[16]

What the letters suggest of Freud's relationship to Martha and his family is that Freud was respectful, concerned, interested, and at moments, amused by them. Jones has remarked that Freud was "peculiarly monogamous" and attributes this to his happy marriage. He comments that Martha "was assuredly the only woman in Freud's love life, and she always came first before all other mortals. While it is likely that the more passionate side of married life subsided with him earlier than it does with many men—indeed we know this in so many words—it was replaced by an unshakable devotion and a perfect harmony of understanding."[17]

At the same time, Freud had significant friendships with other women, the most important of whom was Minna Bernays, Martha's younger sister. They had been friends since Freud and Martha were engaged, when Minna was the fiancée of Ignaz Schönberg. Of the four, Freud once remarked that "two of them were thoroughly good people, Martha and Schönberg, and two were wild passionate people, not so good, Minna and himself: two who were adaptable and two who wanted their own way." After Schönberg died as a young man, Minna never married. She came to live in the Freud household late in 1896. A close companion for Freud, she occasionally went on short holidays with him. During the period of his correspondence with Fliess when he felt professionally isolated, he described Minna as the only other person besides Fliess with whom he could discuss his burgeoning and revolutionary ideas. Jones describes Minna as the most important of a series of "intellectual and rather masculine women" whose company Freud enjoyed—Emma Eckstein, Loe Kann, Lou Andreas-Salomé, Joan Riviere, and Marie Bonaparte. "Intellectual" probably meant "masculine" for Jones (as well as Freud); none of these women would seem to have been masculine in appearance.[18]

While Jones insists that there was no "sexual attraction" between Minna and Freud and that the other women had "no erotic attraction" for Freud, he cannot know this. Nor does he address the possibility of the sublimated eroticism that often pervades intellectual conversation and indeed is often its point. Others have claimed that Freud and Minna were probably in love with each other and, indeed, had an affair. Jung claimed that Minna told him that Freud was in love with her and that their relationship was "intimate."[19]

The picture that the letters to Fliess and Freud's biography create is of a man who had, on the one hand, intense, emotionally charged, and often tumultuous relationships with men; and on the other, a sustaining, harmonious marriage, though by mutual agreement it was evidently not sexual after the early years. Somewhere in the middle ground was a series of friendships with intellectual women, who participated in a society occupied mainly by men although they were, perforce, on the margins of that world and inevitably associated with the domestic realm in which Martha was located.

If Freud was not erotically drawn to these women, it may be because they fell into the category of assertive women. He once wrote, "A robust woman who in case of need can single-handed throw her husband and servants out of doors was never my ideal. . . . What I have always found attractive is someone delicate whom I could take care of."[20] Unlike his relationships with many of the men who were important to him, Freud's relationships with women were not fraught with difficulties and unhappy conclusions. Freud's sexual relationships parallel the more common and easily recognizable social pattern in which men align themselves with men and see women as other.[21] From early in his correspondence with Fliess, I think, Freud was aware that his attraction to Fliess threatened to disturb the overtly heterosexual route his life had taken up until that time.

Despite Freud's immediate and strong admiration for Fliess when they met in 1887, their correspondence did not blossom until 1892. Given the evident intensity of feeling, we might wonder why it took five years for the friendship to gather the momentum that the early letters and their meetings with each other would seem to anticipate. Though it is frequently noticed that Freud began to use the familiar *Du* with Fliess in his letter of June 28, 1892, several other signs of familiarity occurred around this moment. In addition to using the familiar pronoun, Freud began to write more frequently. Between 1887 and 1892, there were eleven letters altogether, about three a year. In 1892 there were nine. The number increased steadily each year, reaching thirty or more between 1894 and 1898, culminating in forty-four—almost a letter each week—in 1899, after which time they declined in number. In a letter dated May 25, 1892, written just before the June 28 letter, Freud used "Dearest friend," which he had used only once before; at first he addressed Fliess "Esteemed friend and colleague" and later "Dear friend." Beginning with the May 25 letter, he used "Dearest friend" almost exclusively until December 17, 1894, when he began to use first names. Occurring in the spring of 1892, these signs of familiarity coincided with Fliess's marriage to Ida Bondy.

The marriage obviously allowed Freud to become emotionally closer to Fliess. In the letter of May 25, Freud tells Fliess that he will be meeting Martha in Reichenau, where Fliess and Ida plan to spend their honeymoon, and proposes seeing Fliess to "congratulate" him. After the honeymoon, Freud uses *Du* for the first time: "I have had no opportunity other than in memory to refer back to the beautiful evening on which I saw you among yours next to your bride. . . . I happened upon you, the comforting thought welled up in me: he is now well taken care of and in good hands. This certainty also set the tone for my correspondence with you. You will not misunderstand it" (June 28, 1892). The presence of a wife put Fliess securely within heterosexual boundaries, making him safe for Freud's affection.

By suggesting that Fliess might "misunderstand" his tone, Freud recognized its exuberance. In other words, by saying that it might be misunderstood, he acknowledged that there was something in it to *be* misunderstood. He also implied that now he could say what he really felt because it would not be thought to suggest homosexual feeling on his part or, perhaps, encourage homosexual feeling on Fliess's. It is as though Freud found a way of acknowledging both to himself and to Fliess the strength of his feeling and at the same time curbed it. Having done this, he could continue the correspondence in a new vein. By setting up a situation that would allow him to express his feelings with the certainty that Fliess would not act in response to them or fear that Freud would do so, Freud might be seen to have created a relationship that would permit the kind of trans-ference that makes self-analysis possible. Stated in more human and recognizable terms, he began a flirtation. But the flirtation was not an overture; it was an end in itself. It allowed Freud to indulge his feelings and to deny how deeply they affected him.

There are several predominant themes in the letters. Freud uses the correspondence to explore and recount various professional matters. These include ideas and theories regarding psychoanalysis; discussions of papers and works in progress, such as *The Interpre-tation of Dreams*; his self-analysis; his relationships with various colleagues; and his responses to Fliess's work. Equally prominent are his expressions of affection for Fliess, his disappointment when they cannot meet, and his sadness at their separation. Finally, Freud describes his various illnesses and shows concern over Fliess's. In the interstices are news of Freud's family, relatives, and friends and responses to similar news from Fliess.

Throughout the correspondence Fliess serves Freud as inspira-tion as well as audience, and this aspect of their relationship is one of its features that has caused writers on Freud to find a similarity to transference, in which a psychoanalyst may serve as a sustaining presence for an analysand. While the friendship may serve Freud in that way, what I hear in the letters is the more familiar language of someone who is in love. When I first read the letters, Dante's Beatrice, Petrarch's Laura, Sidney's Stella came to mind. But Freud and Fliess are more like Shakespeare and the young man who is both muse and beloved for the poet, for their relationship is grounded in more down-to-earth longing and the pleasures and fears of love that is more real than imagined. Continual themes in the letters are Fliess as a source of creativity and good spirits for Freud; his absence, the cause of anxiety and pain:

I rarely have felt so low and down, almost melancholic; all my interests have lost their meaning. The letdown following the increasing loneliness after our long time together must have contributed. (March 13, 1895)

Altogether, I miss you very much. Am I really the same person who was overflowing with ideas and projects as long as you were within reach? When I sit down at the desk in the evening, I often do not know what I should work on. (March 28, 1895)

Your letter gave me such pleasure and caused me to regret anew what I feel is the great gap in my life—that I cannot reach you in any other way. (May 25, 1895)

The first leisure time in the New Year belongs to you—to clasp your hand across these few kilometers and to tell you how glad I was to have your recent news from the family room and study. That you have a son—and with him the prospect of other children; as long as the hope for him was still a distant one, I did not want to admit either to you or to myself what you would have missed. Your kind should not die out, my dear friend; the rest of us need people like you too much. How much I owe you: solace, understanding, stimulation in my loneliness, meaning to my life that I gained through you, and finally even health that no one else could have given back to me. It is primarily through your example that intellectually I gained the strength to trust my judgment, even when I am left alone—though not by you—and, like you, to face with lofty humility all the difficulties that the future may bring. For all that, accept my humble thanks! I know that you do not need me as much as I need you but I also know that I have a secure place in your affection. (January 1, 1896)

In the course of the correspondence, Freud reveals his affection for Fliess through expressions of longing, direct compliment, earnest declaration of Fliess's importance to him, and flattery, which is at times teasing. Freud's tone is not characteristic of his letters to other men, even to Jung, of whom he was particularly fond.

Freud began to use first names in the correspondence at the end of 1894, and his first letter of the new year in 1895 begins with "Dearest Wilhelm," his most common form of address during that year and a frequent salutation in 1896. After that, he drops "Dearest" and writes to "Dear Wilhelm." The pleasure and confidence he felt in the friendship with Fliess are reflected as well in his playful addresses in 1895: "Dear Magician" (April 26, 1895), "Hail, cherished Wilhelm!" (June 22, 1895), "Daimonie" (July 24, 1895), and "Carissimo Guglielmo" (August 28, 1895).[22] This period marks a time of particular closeness between Freud and Fliess.

The friendship was strong enough for Freud to want to name Anna Freud after Fliess had she been a boy, "If it had been a son, I would have sent you the news by telegram because he would have carried your name. Since it turned out to be a little daughter by the name of Anna, she is being introduced to you belatedly" (December 3, 1895). Freud's friendship with Breuer began to collapse during these years, and he undoubtedly felt nearer to Fliess on this account. After the summer of 1894 Freud and Breuer did not collaborate again, and their friendship declined seriously by the spring of 1896. Early in the year he wrote Fliess, "In spite of everything, I find it very painful that he has so completely removed himself from my life" (February 13, 1896).[23]

Although Ernst Kris has asserted that the "true motive" behind Freud and Fliess's relationship was not personal, but was rather their "common scientific interests,"[24] the letters confirm the significance of both impulses. The personal and intellectual fuse, each giving energy to the other:

> Since our congress I have felt unburdened scientifically, it is true, but from a personal point of view another one is an urgent necessity for me. (April 26, 1896)

> Received postcard and telegram and regret that the congress did not bring you what it brought me—pleasure and renewal. Since then I have been in a continual euphoria and have been working like a young man. (May 2, 1897)

> The truth is that we keep pace wonderfully in suffering, but less so in creativity. . . . In Aussee I know a wonderful wood full of ferns and mushrooms where you must reveal to me the secrets of the world of lower animals and the world of children. I have never before felt so stupidly expectant in the face of your disclosures. (June 22, 1897)

Freud's common reference to his meetings with Fliess as "congresses" emphasizes their intellectual motive since "congress" is the term Europeans generally give to professional meetings or conferences. According to Jones, Freud used the term "half jocularly, half sadly";[25] he evidently had mixed feelings in recognizing that much of the time he and Fliess were each other's only audience. Though the word for "congress" in German does not carry the meaning of "sexual congress," as it does in English, Freud may have used the term with a double meaning since he knew English. But he also calls his meetings with Fliess "idylls": "Can you clear that day for an idyll for the two of us . . . ?" (September 21, 1897).[26] This term suggests another kind of romanticization, stressing the personal, free-spirited, exuberant side of the meetings.

Freud continually discussed various physical ailments with Fliess, sometimes in great detail. In the course of the correspondence, Freud complained of heart pains, nasal difficulties, and headaches. Illness provided Freud an oblique way of expressing affection for Fliess and calling forth the same. It is clear from Freud's early letters to Fliess that he was reticent about expressing his feelings directly. In his first letter, quoted more fully above, he tells Fliess, "You have left a deep impression on me which could easily lead me to tell you outright in what category of men I place you" (November 24, 1887). Telling Fliess outright how deeply he was moved was an unusual act for Freud. Since there seemed to be a limit on the openness that was appropriate, Freud found another way to express and elicit caring. Illness allowed acceptable concern, tenderness, intimacy. When Freud once begins, "Dearest friend," he immediately remarks, "Dearest in truth, because I find it touching that you should so thoroughly go into my condition at a time when you are either very busy or not well or possibly both" (May 21, 1894). Acknowledging how stories of illness call forth affection, he writes Fliess, "You write nothing about the state of your health, apparently so as not to hurt me" (December 20, 1898).

Later in life, when Freud had cancer and underwent numerous painful and disfiguring operations, he was so patient in the face of suffering and stoic in confronting death that many remark on it. The disparity between that characterization of Freud and his image in these letters is striking. His desire to affect Fliess most probably accounts for the difference between his responses to illness in the letters and toward the end of his life. When he wrote to Fliess, he was obsessed with his symptoms and spoke of them often. He apparently recognized that he complained to Fliess a great deal; he once wrote him, "Then came your letter . . . but not a word about your own health. I have noted for some time that you bear suffering better and with more dignity than I" (May 21, 1894).

During this period, Freud began to have fears of dying. He wrote Fliess that though he had "no scientific basis" for it, he expected to "go on suffering from various complaints for another four to five to eight years with good and bad periods, and then between forty and fifty perish very abruptly from a rupture of the heart" (June 22, 1894). While heart pain would, of course, have made him worry, the specificity of his imaginings and his writing of them to Fliess suggest that he dwelt on them, indulged them. It is possible that he unconsciously felt guilty about his love for Fliess and imagined that he would be punished for it, even die for it. But imagined death also offered him a way of dealing with his forbidden attraction. He could not fulfill his love for Fliess; at the same time, he may have feared he could not live without it. At the least, his fantasies of dying became occasions for imagining a union with Fliess: "That I shall not leave this beautiful world without summoning you for a personal farewell has been settled in my mind ever since I began to feel ill" (April 25, 1894). A few months later he tells Fliess, "When I think of the many weeks when I felt uncertain about my life, my need to be with you again increases greatly" (August 7, 1894). Freud's elaborations of illness and prospective death and imaginings around them called up in him, and presumably in Fliess, an intensity of feeling similar to that which might have been evoked by a more fully realized love relationship. In other words, illness and imagined death provided a language of love.

Had Freud's repressed feelings found expression only in complaints of illness, little harm would have been done. But his physical symptoms themselves may have been a consequence of his denial of the strength of his feelings for Fliess. His physical heartache, for example, suggests the metaphorical heartache he may have been suffering. Freud considered the possibility that his symptoms were psychologically caused.[27] He tells Fliess that it would "embarrass" him "to suggest a hypochondriacal evaluation" of his heart pains (June 22, 1894).

Freud gives cues for reading his physical symptoms as stemming from psychological causes. He describes himself as having a "neurosis" (July 7, 1897) and speaks of his need to resolve his "hysteria" (October 3, 1897). He recognizes neurotic elements in his friendships, as we have seen. On one occasion, he interprets his need to travel as a hysterical symptom: "The secret of this restlessness is hysteria." He goes on to say that he is disappointed because he has come to feel that his work has less value than he had hoped; therefore, he explains his hysterical restlessness: "So I am running away from myself to gather as much energy and objectivity as is possible because, indeed, I cannot let the work go" (August 31, 1898). After undertaking his self-analysis, he concludes: "All this work has been very good for my own emotional life; I am apparently much more normal than I was four or five years ago" (March 2, 1899). The period in which he implies that he was less "normal" was a time when he suffered extreme cardiac symptoms and nasal distress, and feared he was dying. It was the same time that he had Fliess operate on his nose and engaged him to perform surgery on Emma Eckstein.

While Freud often accepts diagnoses of his various illnesses that confirm physical origins for them, most of the time he does not. On some occasions he clearly attributes his symptoms to his mental state: "Under the influence of analysis my cardiac symptoms are now very frequently replaced by gastrointestinal symptoms" (October 31, 1897). He continually presents his symptoms as interchangeable: "As always, the first week after our talks was a very productive one for me. Then followed a few desolate days with rotten mood and pain displaced from my head (or heart) to my legs. As of this morning, a complete clearing. I shall go on striving and erring" (January 4, 1898). "There exists the most touching substitute relationship between my migraine and my cardiac symptoms and the like. Since Reichenau I once again do not know whether I have a *cor* [heart trouble]; instead I have a running cold and a very unsteady head. Formerly it was the reverse" (June 9, 1898).

Freud's inability to locate the source of his various pains, to pin them down, suggests an elusive and perhaps mental source. Given that Fliess is always looking for concrete physical origins, attributing illnesses to "periods," Freud teases him about the instability of his body: "But I can do something you cannot do—replace headaches or cardiac pains with ridiculous back pains, which are deceptively like cardiac pains" (June 20, 1898). Recalling Freud's earlier image of Fliess as the one who "can say what life is" and himself as the one who "can say (almost) what the mind is" (December 22, 1897), Freud seems to be alluding to his faith in the power of the mental to determine the physical, in this case, his own symptoms. But he continually reports the course of his various distresses to Fliess as though he hopes to be able to believe Fliess's diagnoses of physical origins, which will inevitably come. While he invites Fliess's opinion, he makes clear that he expects to find a "meaning," i.e., a psychological cause or reason for his pains (November 19, 1899).

It is, of course, commonly accepted that heart pains and headaches are often signs of stress and other emotional difficulties. Nasal problems are less often seen as psychosomatic symptoms. But in Freud's case, they may have been. In at least one instance, he links his nasal trouble with other symptoms that he recognizes as psychosomatic. After citing some concurrences of others' illnesses with certain dates, which will give Fliess evidence for his notions of periodicity, he adds, "As for me, I note migraine, nasal secretion, and attacks of fears of dying, such as today, although Tilgner's car-

diac death is most likely more responsible for this than the date"
(April 16, 1896). (Victor Tilgner was a sculptor whose death had
special significance for Freud.)[28] Freud complained of his nose and
his heart early in his relationship with Fliess; later he more often
mentioned migraines and depression. Both he and Fliess had operations on their noses. Whatever inherent difficulty Freud may have
had with his nose, it was probably magnified by Fliess's interest in
it.[29] He continually described having a stopped-up nose and head and
copious discharges of pus. While he was speculating that Emma Eckstein suffered from hysterical bleeding from her nose, he suffered
from symptoms that might have been seen similarly.

Freud's nasal distress gave him an opportunity to put himself in
Fliess's care and to let Fliess minister to him in an intimate way.
After Fliess operated on Freud, cauterizing his nose, the two men
had their picture taken together. Sending Fliess the picture, Freud
comments, "Beautiful we are not (or no longer), but my pleasure
in having you close by my side after the operation clearly shows"
(March 4, 1895).[30] On another occasion, he tells Fliess that if his
nasal condition does not improve, he will have him cauterize him
again when they are together in Breslau for one of their congresses
(December 12, 1897). Given Fliess's conviction that the nose was related to many sexual problems, that operations on it could remedy
dismenorrhea or prevent masturbation, for example, it is noticeable
that no comments pass between the two men about their own noses
and sexuality, as a source of humor if nothing else. Indeed, there are
only two moments of levity on the subject of their noses. Once when
Freud is anticipating a visit to Berlin, he teases, "We can share quar-
ters, live and take walks together, insofar as our noses permit it"
(August 16, 1895). Fliess evidently cauterized Freud's nose in Breslau
a second time, for once home, Freud writes, "My nose is behaving
itself and conveys its thanks" (January 4, 1898).

In Western culture, the nose so commonly substitutes in language for the penis that it is hard to read these letters without hearing a double meaning. In Laurence Sterne's *Tristram Shandy*, for
example, much of the humor depends upon the equation of Uncle
Toby's nose and his penis. When Charmian, one of Cleopatra's waiting women in Shakespeare's *Antony and Cleopatra*, asks Iras, "If
you were but an inch of fortune better than I, where would you
choose it?," Iras replies, "Not in my husband's nose" (1.2.60–62).
When Freud writes about the inclination of his nose "to produce
eruptions like a private Etna" (March 14, 1895), he seems to be describing orgasms of the nose. A sentence like "The condition of the

heart depends upon the condition of the nose" (March 4, 1895) can hardly be read without awakening our shared system of allusions. Since Freud was so alert to multiple meanings, I cannot help but wonder whether he ever heard what I hear. He was so ready to find in his patients displacements upward, did he speculate about whether his symptoms suggested something more problematic than nasal infection or inflammation? I think Freud's symptoms relate at least partially to his desire to be close to Fliess, which he could be if he became Fliess's patient. It is also likely that his unruly, dripping nose reveals the erotic attraction that he must suppress.

Emma Eckstein, a patient whom Freud believed to suffer from hysterical bleeding, also played a part in the drama around Freud's repressed love for Fliess. Many have commented on Freud's overestimation of Fliess and have seen it as the cause of his engaging him to operate on Eckstein's nose and later excusing him for failing to remove surgical packing, a mistake that almost resulted in Eckstein's death. Masson argues that Freud's need to absolve Fliess from blame was so great that it was largely responsible for his relinquishing the seduction theory. Freud's shift from believing that real seductions in childhood played a determining role in hysteria to asserting that patients' fantasies of seduction were the significant determinants and that most of the seductions they described were imagined rather than real was coincident, Masson argues, with Freud's need to exonerate Fliess: "The real operation and its ill effects, and the real seduction, had to cede place to 'bleeding out of longing' and the *wish* to be seduced."[31]

Another mechanism works in the relationship between Freud, Fliess, and Emma Eckstein as well, and it is consistent with the kind of homophobic love Freud felt for Fliess. The operation itself has some of the aura around it that frequently accompanies male bonding that substitutes for more intense love. If, as has been suggested, Freud and Fliess found companionship in undertaking unconventional research and seeing themselves as outsiders among their medical colleagues, the operation links them in a similar way. Though Freud clearly had misgivings, he ventured into the surgery on Eckstein with anticipation as well as anxiety:

> Now only one more week separates us from the operation, or at least from the preparations for it. The time has passed quickly, and I gladly avoid putting myself through a self-examination to ascertain what right I have to expect so much from it. My lack of medical knowledge once again weighs heavily on me. But I keep repeating to myself: so far as I have some insight into the matter, the cure must be achievable by this

route. I would not have dared to invent this plan of treatment on my own, but I confidently join you in it. (January 24, 1895)

Joining in the operation seems to have the feel of adventure, of a dangerous undertaking. Though Freud apparently liked Emma Eckstein, his lack of caution at the outset and his failure to take her side later, at least by acknowledging the grievousness of Fliess's error, recalls another, earlier scene of male bonding in which Freud described how he and his nephew "behaved cruelly" to his younger niece (October 3, 1897). In both instances, he joined with a boy or man for whom he felt affection, admiration, and occasional envy, to the detriment of a girl or woman who mattered less to him and whose interests he forgot under the pressure of the more compelling friendship.

As Freud, in the course of his self-analysis, reflected on the pattern of his relationships that required "an intimate friend and a hated enemy," his erotic attachment to Fliess and his homosexuality began to come more nearly to the surface than they ever had been. Freud writes Fliess, "I still do not know what has been happening in me. Something from the deepest depths of my own neuroses set itself against any advance in the understanding of the neuroses, and you have somehow been involved in it. For my writing paralysis seems to me designed to inhibit our communication. I have no guarantee of this, just feelings of a highly obscure nature. Has nothing of the kind happened to you? For the past few days it has seemed to me that an emergence from this obscurity is in preparation" (July 7, 1897).

Some months later Fliess seemed to imply that Freud had bisexual inclinations. Fliess evidently wanted to associate left-handedness and bisexuality, whereas Freud did not. Freud's letter of January 4, 1898, makes clear that Fliess was upset by Freud's disagreement with him and apparently thought there was something personal in it. Insisting that his disagreement is objective, Freud attempts to explain it, and in so doing, seems to acknowledge his own bisexuality:

> I literally embraced your stress on bisexuality and consider this idea of yours to be the most significant one for my subject since that of "defense." If I had a disinclination on personal grounds, because I am in part neurotic myself, this disinclination would certainly have been directed toward bisexuality, which, after all, we hold responsible for the inclination to repression. It seems to me that I object only to the permeation of bisexuality and bilaterality that you demand . . . I had the impression, furthermore, that you considered me to be partially left-handed; if so, you would tell me, since there is nothing in this bit of self-knowledge that might hurt me. It is your doing if you do not know every intimate detail about me; you have surely known me long enough.

Since Freud thinks that Fliess believes him to be "partially left-handed," he evidently thinks that Fliess believes he is bisexual as well. He suggests that he can confront that possibility.

Later Freud describes an "inner crisis" and says that even though he would like to see Fliess, he is not going to. He continues, "No one can help me in the least with what oppresses me; it is my cross, I must bear it; and God knows that in adapting to it, my back has become noticeably bent" (March 23, 1900). Though Freud's inner crisis may have had to do with his work, his withdrawal from Fliess and his vagueness about what oppressed him suggest that he may have been wrestling with his homosexual feelings.[32]

When Freud stresses how important male friendship is to him, implying, of course, the value of his relationship with Fliess, it evidently provokes an untoward response from Fliess, for Freud writes him:

> As to Breuer, you are certainly quite right about *the* brother, but I do not share your contempt for friendship between men, probably because I am to a high degree party to it. In my life, as you know, woman has never replaced the comrade, the friend. If Breuer's male inclination were not so odd, so timid, so contradictory—like everything else in his mental and emotional makeup—it would provide a nice example of the accomplishments into which the androphilic current in men can be sublimated. (August 7, 1901)

While Freud saw friendships between men as positive in some sense, he also wanted to "sublimate" male love, to channel it into "accomplishments." Since he had chosen in Fliess a man who had contempt for friendship between men, it is clear that Freud did not finally want responsive male love.

When Freud tells Ferenczi that he has "overcome" his homosexuality, "overcome" Fliess, he obviously sees himself as sublimating his love for his friend into something else: "A part of homosexual cathexis has been withdrawn and made use of to enlarge my own ego." But there are signs that Freud simply repressed his feelings and denied the tenacious hold they had on him. Two occasions serve to illustrate how strong his affection for Fliess remained even after they quarreled and parted. It is significant that they occurred in connection with Jung and Ferenczi, both men to whom Freud was strongly drawn.

In the same letter to Ferenczi in which he insists that his "homosexual cathexis has been withdrawn," he also makes clear how strong his feelings for Fliess remain. When Freud and Ferenczi traveled together, Ferenczi was evidently disappointed that Freud was not

more intimate with him and suspected that he kept secrets and
withheld things from him. Freud responded with an explanation and
offered an intimate detail: "That you surmised I had great secrets,
and were very curious about them, was plain to see and also easy
to recognize as infantile. Just as I told you *everything* on scientific
matters I concealed very little of a personal nature. . . . My dreams at
that time were concerned, as I hinted to you, entirely with the Fliess
affair, which in the nature of things would be hard to arouse your
sympathy."[33] Freud's trip with Ferenczi as well as his affection for
him undoubtedly called up memories of Fliess. Although Freud denied his need for a relationship similar to the one he had with Fliess,
his dreams revealed the old longing.

At a meeting in Munich in 1912, when Freud felt the first hint
of Jung's dissension, he fainted. He later writes Ernest Jones, who
was also present at the meeting: "I cannot forget that six and four
years ago I suffered from very similar though not such intense symptoms in the *same* room of the Park Hotel. I saw Munich first when I
visited Fliess during his illness and this town seems to have acquired
a strong connection with my relation to that man. There is some
piece of unruly homosexual feeling at the root of the matter. When
Jung in his last letter again hinted at my 'neurosis,' I could find no
better expedient than proposing that every analyst should attend to
his own neurosis more than to the other's."[34] The first time we hear
of Freud's fainting is the moment when he learns that Fliess has left
surgical packing in Emma Eckstein's nose. It is likely that he felt
both moments as betrayals by men he loved. But his own analysis
of Fliess's continuing importance to him suggests how deeply his
feeling for him ran.

What the letters and Freud's biography reveal are not only his
homosexual feelings for Fliess, but also his continuing homophobia. His fear of homosexuality seduced him, causing him to displace
his feelings into activities or symptoms that expressed his affection
and also evaded it. He had more courage and more self-acceptance
than Fliess: he could finally acknowledge what he felt. But he main-
tained that he was able to "overcome" his homosexual desires while
his dreams and his body betrayed him and refused to be controlled.
Given his cultural milieu, Freud would have had a difficult time
realizing his homosexual longings. Yet running away from them had
terrible consequences for him and sometimes for others.

NOTES

1. Sigmund Freud, *The Complete Letters of Sigmund Freud to Wilhelm Fliess: 1887–1904*, ed. Jeffrey Masson (Cambridge, Mass.: Harvard University Press, 1985), subsequently referred to as *Letters*. All references in the text to Freud's letters to Fliess are to this edition and are indicated by date.

2. For accounts of the dissolution of Freud and Fliess's friendship, see Ernest Jones, *The Life and Work of Sigmund Freud*, 3 vols. (New York: Basic Books, 1953), vol. 1, pp. 311–16; and Max Schur, *Freud: Living and Dying* (New York: International Universities Press, 1972), pp. 199–222.

3. Jones, *Life and Work*, vol. 2, p. 83.

4. In recent years, critics and biographers have been more willing than in the past to see Freud as bisexual, to recognize the strength of his homosexual tendencies and the tenacity of his attachment to Fliess. Patrick Mahony, for example, has argued that Freud's "unresolved and conflictual bisexuality" affected his relationship with Fliess as well as his efforts to deal with bisexuality theoretically ("Friendship and Its Discontents," *Contemporary Psychoanalysis* 15 [1979], 78–89). Though Peter Gay, in *Freud: A Life for Our Time* (New York: Norton, 1988), seems to view Freud's homosexuality as Freud did, i.e., as something that he worked his way "clear of" (pp. 87–88), Gay also acknowledges the persistence of Freud's feelings for Fliess (pp. 274–77).

5. See Jones, *Life and Work*, vol. 1, pp. 21–22.

6. *The Complete Signet Classic Shakespeare* (New York: Harcourt, 1972). Subsequent quotations from Shakespeare are from this edition.

7. Jones, *Life and Work*, vol. 1, p. 292.

8. For a fuller and particularly lucid description of Fliess's theories, see Frank J. Sulloway, *Freud, Biologist of the Mind: Beyond the Psychoanalytic Legend* (1979; reprint ed., New York: Basic Books, 1983), pp. 135–70.

9. Jones, *Life and Work*, vol. 1, pp. 297, 289.

10. Before Freud recognized the addictive qualities of cocaine, he suggested substituting it to cure Fleischl's addiction to morphia, which Fleischl took to stop the pain caused by the "continued growth of neuromas" on his hand (ibid., p. 44). At the end of his life Fleischl suffered not only from his neuromas, but also from his addiction to both painkillers.

11. Freud was a child of his father's third marriage. Jacob Freud had two sons by his first marriage and was already a grandfather by the time of his marriage to Amalie, Sigmund's mother. Therefore, Sigmund was born an uncle to a nephew who was older than he was. For a full account of Freud's parents and siblings, see Marianne Krüll, *Freud and His Father*, trans. Arnold J. Pomerans (New York: W. W. Norton, 1986).

12. Sigmund Freud, *The Standard Edition of the Complete Psychological Works of Sigmund Freud*, ed. and trans. James Strachey et al., 24 vols. (London: Hogarth Press, 1953–74), vol. 6, p. 483.

13. Jones, *Life and Work*, vol. 1, p. 90.
14. Freud writes Fliess that though he had "a delightful dream" about becoming a professor, it could not be published "because its background, its second meaning, shifts back and forth between my nurse (my mother) and my wife and one cannot really publicly subject one's wife to reproaches of this sort [as a reward] for all her labor and toil" (February 9, 1898).
15. Jones, *Life and Work*, vol. 3, p. 219.
16. Since Bonaparte is writing about what Freud told her, the notion that "Martha Freud understood very well that Fliess was able to give her husband something beyond what she could" may have been Freud's hopeful construction of matters.
17. Jones, *Life and Work*, vol. 2, pp. 421–22, 386.
18. Ibid., vol. 1, p. 164; vol. 2, p. 6; vol. 1, p. 153; vol. 2, p. 421.
19. Ibid., vol. 1, p. 153; vol. 2, p. 421. Peter J. Swales has argued at length that Freud and Minna had an affair and that Freud even accompanied Minna to have an abortion when she was pregnant by him. Reviewing the available evidence, Peter Gay finds it inconclusive. My own view is that an affair between them seems plausible. But perhaps the matter will become clearer when the packet of letters between Freud and Minna in the Freud Collection at the Library of Congress becomes available for examination. Swales, "Freud, Minna Bernays, and the Conquest of Rome," *New American Review* (Spring/Summer 1982), 1–23.
20. Jones, *Life and Work*, vol. 1, p. 165.
21. See Jim Swan's fine essay "*Mater* and Nannie: Freud's Two Mothers and the Discovery of the Oedipus Complex," *American Imago* 31 (1974), 1–64. Swan's description of Freud's early experiences with women and his later attitudes toward those experiences may help explain this "split" in Freud's friendships with women.
22. Freud uses such addresses on only two other occasions: "Dear tardily writing friend" (August 17, 1891) and "Excellenza" (August 5, 1897).
23. For an account of the disintegration of Freud and Fliess's friendship, see Jones, *Life and Work*, vol. 1, pp. 253–55.
24. Ernst Kris, introduction to Sigmund Freud, *The Origins of Psycho-Analysis: Letters to Wilhelm Fliess, Drafts and Notes: 1887–1902*, ed. Marie Bonaparte, Anna Freud, and Ernst Kris; trans. Eric Mosbacher and James Strachey (New York: Basic Books, 1954), p. 11.
25. Jones, *Life and Work*, vol. 1, pp. 300–301.
26. See also the letter of August 28, 1895.
27. Whether Freud's illnesses, especially his heart trouble, were physical or psychological has been argued both ways. Jones, for example, tends to view them as psychologically caused; whereas, Schur takes issue with him and looks toward physical sources.
28. See Schur, *Freud: Living and Dying*, pp. 100–104.
29. In *The Freudian Fallacy: Freud and Cocaine* (1983; reprint ed., London:

Paladin Books, 1986), E. M. Thornton has argued that both Freud's and Fliess's difficulties with their noses had to do with their regular use of cocaine (p. 172).

30. See the plate between pp. 112–13 in *Letters*.

31. Jeffrey Moussaieff Masson, *The Assault on Truth: Freud's Suppression of the Seduction Theory* (New York: Farrar, Straus and Giroux, 1984), p. 134.

32. Henri F. Ellenberger has argued that Freud's inner crisis is consistent with "creative illness" (*The Discovery of the Unconscious: The History and Evolution of Dynamic Psychiatry* [New York: Basic Books, 1970], pp. 447–50).

33. Jones, *Life and Work*, vol. 2, pp. 83–84.

34. Ibid., vol. 1, p. 137.

Freud and Dora:
Blindness and Insight

> When I set myself the task of bringing to light what human beings
> keep hidden within them, not by the compelling power of hypnosis,
> but by observing what they say and what they show, I thought the
> task was a harder one than it really is. He that has eyes to see and
> ears to hear may convince himself that no mortal can keep a secret.
> If his lips are silent, he chatters with his finger-tips; betrayal oozes
> out of him at every pore.
>
>   —Freud, "Fragment of an Analysis
>   of a Case of Hysteria" ("Dora")

No one can more insightfully tell us how to read Freud than
Freud himself. Both in the theoretical writings and in the case histories, Freud offers a poetics of narrative enabling us to speculate upon
the meanings at once obscured and preserved in the patient's words.
Works like *The Interpretation of Dreams* and *The Psychopathology
of Everyday Life* become meta-narratives commenting not only upon
the patient's suspect stories, but upon Freud's own accounts, which
do not quite ring true. The case history we refer to as the story of
Dora is just such a suspect account. By now, psychoanalysts, literary
critics, and feminists agree that in his fragmentary analysis Freud
fails Dora, but they continue to differ about the causes and the significance of that failure. They bring forth assorted explanations—
some enraged, others enraging—for the dis-ease that the case history
provokes. As neo-Freudians all, we can only return to Freud himself in yet another attempt to glimpse elusive truths at the heart of
Dora's story.[1]
     In his introductory remarks, Freud himself provides the criteria
by which the "Fragment of an Analysis of a Case of Hysteria" (1905)
can be identified as a symptomatic narrative. He reviews his thera-
peutic technique for the uninitiated: "I begin the treatment, indeed,
by asking the patient to give me the whole story of his life and illness, but even so the information I receive is never enough to let me

see my way about the case."[2] In fact, "the patients' inability to give an ordered history of their life in so far as it coincides with the history of their illness" (*S.E.*, 7:16) becomes a sign of neurosis, even as it points the way to a hypothetical cure, to a story organized around both chronological and causal coherence. With the patient's help, Freud seeks to provide a narrative account of the life that enables the patient to live and to act in time. A story that does not help the patient to act effectively is marked by inadequate causal explanations, by significant gaps, and by confusion about the dates of events. But, of course, the story of Dora is famous for a misdating in which Freud persists long after the publication of the case history in 1905. In both *On the History of the Psycho-Analytic Movement*, published in 1914, and in a 1923 footnote to "Dora," Freud places the analysis in the autumn of 1899, even as, in a telling parenthetical sentence at the end of the account, he correctly dates the final encounter with Dora on April 1, 1902, fifteen months after she has broken off the analysis on a December 31. Though "his lips are silent," Freud "chatters with his fingertips," pointing to the autumn of 1900 as the time of the analysis. Betrayal oozes out of Freud's pen, demanding that anyone with eyes to see perceive the fragment as symptomatic. The confusing account, like "an unnavigable river whose stream is at one moment choked by masses of rock and at another divided and lost among shallows and sandbanks" (*S.E.*, 7:16), compels the editor in his prefatory remarks in the *Standard Edition* to provide a chronology of the significant events in Dora's life. It is the very chronology, with its disturbing causal implications, that Freud's account, punctuated with theoretical asides and with a curious imprecision about dates and events, obscures.[3]

Jeffrey Moussaieff Masson has recently provided a new context in which to reconsider the reasons for Freud's flawed narrative and for his unnerving insistence that Dora's response to Herr K.'s proposition on the shores of the lake near L—— is unjustified, hysterical. In *The Assault on Truth: Freud's Suppression of the Seduction Theory* and in his edition of the letters of Freud to Wilhelm Fliess, Masson returns to seemingly unrelated events in 1895 and 1896 that inform Freud's response to Dora, providing an insight into the sources of his curious distortion of her experience. Masson resurrects the original seduction theory to examine a crucial moment in the history, and the mythology, of the psychoanalytic movement. For, so the story goes, the Promethean insights that followed upon the celebrated letter to Fliess of September 21, 1897, culminating in the formulation of the concept of the oedipus complex, could not have occurred without Freud's repudiation of the original seduction theory, his claim that in childhood his clients had been the victims of an all-too-real seduction by an adult, often a parent.[4]

For Masson, the events precipitating the letter of September 21, 1897, occurred between the spring of 1895 and that of 1896. In February of 1895, Freud handed over to Fliess one of his patients, a woman named Emma Eckstein, who was suffering, in part, from painful menstruation associated, thought Freud, with a history of masturbatory activity. Fliess, with his arcane claim of a connection between the human nose and the genitals, performed an operation on the supposed genital spot in Emma Eckstein's nose, accidentally leaving surgical gauze in the cavity created during the surgical procedure. The inevitable infection, and the hemorrhaging that followed, nearly proved fatal: a Viennese surgeon was called in by Freud in March of 1895 to perform yet another operation, to undo the damage done by Fliess, and to save Emma Eckstein's life.[5] Masson argues that Freud, in his need to excuse himself and Fliess of the responsibility for Emma Eckstein's suffering, determined, as he wrote in a letter dated April 26–28, 1896, that Fliess was "right, that her episodes of bleeding were hysterical, were occasioned by *longing*, and probably occurred at the sexually relevant times" (*C.L.*, 183)—according to Fliess's theory of physiological periodicity. With these words, so Masson argues, Freud sought to explain away Fliess's ineptitude and to implicate Emma Eckstein in an act of pure fantasy, foreshadowing the later claim that hysterics are not victims of adult seduction in childhood, but suffer from suppressed memories of fantasied fulfillments of their own sexual longing for the parent.

But, as Max Schur has explored in *Freud: Living and Dying*, Freud had more on his mind than Emma Eckstein in April 1896. In a letter dated April 16, Freud wrote not only of a "completely surprising explanation of Eckstein's hemorrhages" to be provided in a succeeding letter, but of other worrisome things: "In accordance with your request, I have started to isolate myself in every respect and find it easy to bear. I have one prior commitment, though—a lecture to be given at the psychiatric society on Tuesday" (*C.L.*, 181). Freud was anticipating the delivery of his paper, "The Aetiology of Hysteria," before the Vienna Psychiatric Society on April 21. While he pondered the meaning of Emma Eckstein's hemorrhaging, Freud anticipated the response to the paper in which he was to argue that his female patients had been seduced in childhood, although he would neglect to observe, in public, that the seducer was commonly the father. In the letter dated April 26–28, Freud wrote of Emma Eckstein's bleeding, "occasioned by *longing*," and of the response to the paper he had delivered some five days before: "A lecture on the etiology of hysteria at the psychiatric society was given an icy reception by the asses and a strange evaluation by Krafft-Ebing: 'It sounds like a scientific fairy tale.' And this, after one has demonstrated to them the solution of a more-than-thousand-year-old problem, a *caput Nili*! They can go to hell, euphemistically expressed" (*C.L.*, 184).

In *The Assault on Truth*, Masson seeks to establish a causal relationship between Freud's strained explanation of Emma Eckstein's bleeding and his repudiation of his own seduction theory in September 1897. I want to suggest instead an associative connection through which the Eckstein episode functioned as a complex screen memory, inextricably joined to other moments in Freud's life, but especially to the delivery of "The Aetiology of Hysteria," to the repudiation of the seduction theory, and to events that followed in 1900 and 1901. In his loyalty to Fliess, Freud must have feared that the physicians called in to treat the hemorrhaging Emma Eckstein would see Fliess and Freud as cranks obsessed with wild and unsubstantiated theories. Surely, Krafft-Ebing's response to "The Aetiology of Hysteria" as a scientific fairy tale would stir Freud's doubts both about his own genius and about the professional and general reception of speculations posing a threat to the moral authority of the mother and the father, to the ideological justifications of the bourgeois family. With the passage of time, Freud's commitment to Fliess waned. He could no longer ignore the incompatibility between his own psychological orientation and Fliess's commitment to physiological explanations. He became increasingly skeptical of Fliess's ideas and more sensitive to the stridency of his friend's claims for them. And, with his fuller understanding of parapraxes, Freud could no longer ignore, at some level of his consciousness, the implications of the operation on Emma Eckstein. Fliess's surgical procedure was no accident: obsessed with the genital spots of the nose, Fliess had performed a symbolic clitoridectomy.[6] Freud, who had delivered Emma Eckstein into Fliess's hands, had been involved in an act of terrible violation that sickened him. He compounded the violation in his attempt to explain her suffering away as a fantasy of longing and through his abandonment of the seduction theory: for Freud, the child, and by implication Emma Eckstein, was no longer the victim but, oddly, the culpable party.

The case history of Ida Bauer, the seventeen-year-old girl whom we know as Dora, was written within a context that includes Freud's tortured friendship with Wilhelm Fliess, moving to its inevitable

end, and the repudiation of the seduction theory, a theory that was
not, however, to be laid to rest. The most famous parapraxis in the
case history, Freud's persistent misplacing of the analysis into the
autumn of 1899, was his attempt to return imaginatively to a time
prior to his final meeting with Fliess in the summer of 1900; to a
triumphant moment associated with the appearance of *The Interpretation of Dreams* in November 1899, long before Fliess was to
write, as he did in the summer of 1901, that " 'the reader of thoughts
merely reads his own thoughts into other people.' " Freud's response
to Fliess is revealing: "If that is what you think of me, just throw
my 'Everyday Life' unread into the wastepaper basket. It is full of
references to you—manifest ones, for which you supplied the material, and concealed ones, for which the motivation goes back to
you" (*C.L.*, 447). In misdating the analysis of Dora, Freud alludes to
October 1899, when he eagerly awaited the reception of his great
work, to a moment of fleeting and illusory unity with Fliess, marked
by a birthday gift to Fliess, a copy of the "dream book." Originally
entitled "Dreams and Hysteria," the story of Dora was to stand as a
"continuation of the dream book" (*C.L.*, 433), a final application to
clinical practice of Freud's dream theory. "Dora," published in 1905,
perhaps to seal the estrangement from Fliess, was completed in its
original form by January 24, 1901. Freud worked on the case history
between the writing of *On Dreams* in the autumn of 1900, as the
analysis of Dora was moving to its abrupt end on December 31, and
the completion of *The Psychopathology of Everyday Life* by late February 1901. The three works—*On Dreams*, "Dora," and the *Everyday Life*—constitute a trilogy recording, in Max Schur's words, "the
death of a friendship." In the pages of the three works, the figure of
Wilhelm Fliess appears, asserting its presence in both explicit and
concealed allusions to the man and his ideas.[7]

In the bizarre situation of Dora, Freud confronted a version of
the Emma Eckstein debacle. The liaison between Dora's father and
Frau K. inevitably involved the cuckolded Herr K., Dora's betrayed
mother, and, finally, Dora herself. In the shifting triads of the adulterous relationship, Freud might have glimpsed uncanny repetitions
of the relationships and people figuring in the Eckstein episode of
1895. Just as Freud had once handed Emma Eckstein over to Fliess,
Dora's father had tried to hand her over to K. and, at last, "handed her
over to [Freud] for psychotherapeutic treatment" (*S.E.*, 7:19). Perhaps
Freud sensed parallels between Emma Eckstein and Dora—and between himself and Fliess and the two men in Dora's life. Within the
context suggested by Jeffrey Masson, the father and Herr K. may be

seen as shadowy doubles for Fliess, and for Freud himself, who might have feared he would prove not to be the self-proclaimed Promethean spirit of his letters and published writings.[8] Fliess's operation upon Emma Eckstein and Freud's explanation of the almost fatal hemorrhaging as a form of hysteria are comparable to the self-serving denial by the adults in Dora's life of the liaison between her father and Frau K. and their claim that Dora's story of K.'s sordid proposition was only the girl's fantasy. Freud could have feared an affinity to Dora's father, whose syphilitic condition had led to a detached retina. Like Herr Bauer, Freud was a man suffering from a literal and figurative blindness. As a man "deaf to the most imperative calls of duty," Herr Bauer sees things "in the light which [is] most convenient from the point of view of his own passions" (S.E., 7:38). Such passions are volatile, suggesting the suspect nature of Bauer's motives and those of Herr K., as well as those of Freud and Fliess in the Eckstein affair. In their clumsy attempt to share the women in their lives, the father and Herr K. manifest the homoerotic dimensions in their relationship. In the friendship of Freud and Fliess, the gauze that Fliess left in the cavity produced by his surgery on Emma Eckstein's nose becomes a curious deposit signaling the ways in which he and Freud achieve intimacy through their patient's mediating presence.[9]

What might have been unnerving for Freud was that Dora's plight embodied a possible return of the disavowed seduction theory set forth in 1896 in "The Aetiology of Hysteria." Once Freud had averted his gaze, blinding himself to the meaning of Emma Eckstein's suffering; now he persisted in seeing Dora's response to Herr K. as hysterical. There is nothing more disturbing in the case history of Dora than Freud's insistence upon Dora's love for Herr K. and upon the abnormality of her response to his kiss, when she was fourteen, and to his proposition when she was sixteen. Freud's insistence on Dora's love for K., his obsession with her childhood masturbatory activity, as well as with the sources of her sexual knowledge, divert his attention, and ours, from the events lying behind the two dreams Freud places at the center of his account. In the process, he betrays the very theoretical formulations about dreams and symptoms offered in the case history itself. Freud reminds us that "a regularly formed dream stands, as it were, upon two legs, one of which is in contact with the main and current exciting cause, and the other with some *momentous event in the years of childhood*. The dream sets up a connection between those two factors—the event during childhood and the event of the present day—and it endeavours to re-shape the present on the model of the remote past" (S.E., 7:71, emphasis mine). With this charged figurative language, Freud argues a proposition central to his theory of dreams and symptom formation: events in the present, even a man's fondling of a girl merely fourteen, can cause a dream or a symptom only if such events repeat for the dreamer or the hysteric traumatic moments or fantasies within infancy or childhood.

As long as he explores the immediate events to which one of the legs of Dora's compasslike dreams points, Freud persists in serving what Steven Marcus has called his daimon, his commitment to his version of the truth. Freud flaunts Herr Bauer's expectations and confirms the reality of those facts that the adults in Dora's life conspire to deny. Bauer had handed his daughter over to Freud with the words, "Please try and bring her to reason" (S.E., 7:26): Freud was to compel Dora to acquiesce to the lies of the adults and to their dismissal of her sharp-sighted perception of what was going on around her. Instead, Freud accepted Dora's harsh characterizations of her father. He not only believed her account of the episode by the lake, he helped her to reconstruct the scene in which Herr K. kissed the fourteen-year-old girl and she, Freud speculates, felt the pressure of an erection on her lower body. Freud confirmed not only the existence of the liaison between Dora's father and Frau K., but the fact of the father's venereal disease and his impotence: Dora's story, without symptomatic confusions and omissions, corresponds to "the facts in every respect" (S.E., 7:46). Freud, the man Krafft-Ebing had accused of spinning a scientific fairy tale, the man Fliess was to accuse of reading his own thoughts into other people, sees the facts in ways never anticipated by Dora's father. In his pursuit of the truth, Freud brings to light the very hypocrisy he has been expected to perpetuate.

But Freud betrays Dora, and himself, in his refusal to explore that other realm to which her dreams, her symptomatic acts, and her recollections allude: the realm of the remote past to which, given the anatomical implications of Freud's trope for her dreams, Dora wishes to give birth, as if intuitively reenacting the story of Pandora, her mythic namesake. Such a self-betrayal produces in Freud an odd deafness, not only to Dora's words, but to his own words in "The Aetiology of Hysteria": "The abnormal reaction to sexual impressions which surprises us in hysterical subjects [such as Dora] at the age of puberty is quite generally based on sexual experiences of this sort in childhood, in which case those experiences must be of a similar nature to one another, and must be of an important kind" (S.E., 3: 202). Dora's reactions to Herr K. and her dream of the burning house comment not only upon recent events, however painful; theoretically, they also allude to events in childhood that inform and give meaning to events in the more or less immediate present. Freud's claim that the dream of the burning house occurred for the first time only when Dora was sixteen, in response to Herr K.'s proposition and his appearance at her bedside, obscures less recent sources of the dream that, according to Freud's own theories, must be represented there. The events on the shores of the lake near L—— transport Dora into the suppressed past. Freud must have sensed, uneasily, that they crystallize for her the meaning of earlier events long denied or forgotten.

In discussing the dream of the burning house that has recurred during the analysis, Dora speaks of quarrels between her mother and father. The most recent argument has involved the locking of the doors to the dining room at night, an act that would lock in Dora's brother, whose bedroom is without a separate entrance (*S.E.*, 7:65). An earlier dispute, occurring a year before Herr K.'s proposition to Dora, involved a piece of jewelry: "Mother wanted to be given a particular thing—pearl drops to wear in her ears. But Father does not like that kind of thing, and he brought her a bracelet instead of the drops. She was furious, and told him that as he had spent so much money on a present she did not like he had better just give it to some one else" (*S.E.*, 7:69). The two arguments are part of the long-standing quarrel at the center of the family situation in which Dora finds herself. Each anecdote is itself a figurative dreamscape structured like those narratives Dora offers *as* dreams: they obey the logic of the dream work as they illuminate the domestic secrets by which Dora and her mother are oppressed.

Freud has, at the outset of the analysis, dismissed the insulted and injured mother as a foolish person "without insight into [her own] illness" (*S.E.*, 7:20) and without an understanding of her more sophisticated son and daughter. In fact, her obsessive washing and cleaning, as Freud reluctantly acknowledges, is her symptomatic attempt to purge herself of the physiological and moral infections carried by her syphilitic husband. The mother dwells upon domestic affairs, quarrels peevishly about jewelry, and frets about locking doors: her life has become an unending siege, an attempt to keep locked the rooms, at once literal and figurative, appearing in Dora's dreams and recollections. The household burns with the fever of illness as well as with the fever of ambiguous desires. The embattled mother does her unavailing best to protect her children from the contaminating presence of the father within the context of her fin de siècle bourgeois world.

In her symptomatic acts, the mother both conceals and exposes the circumstances to which Dora's dream of the burning house points, circumstances that include not only Herr K.'s proposal and subsequent events at the lake, but earlier moments in Dora's life. Dora's anecdotal accounts serve to reveal how the father's syphilitic condition had alienated her mother from him. Early in her childhood, Dora had been required to take the place of her inaccessible mother. In his recurring illnesses, the father "would allow no one but [Dora] to discharge the lighter duties of nursing. He had been so proud of the early growth of her intelligence that he had made her his confidante while she was still a child" (S.E., 7:57). This is an intimacy imposed on Dora, not necessarily sought out by her as Freud's words—she "was clearly putting herself in her mother's place" (S.E., 7:56)—might suggest. The father seeks from Dora what he can no longer get from his wife. It is no wonder that with the appearance of Frau K. in her father's life, Dora had "felt and acted more like a jealous wife—in a way which would have been comprehensible in her mother" (S.E., 7:56). Freud aptly surmises that it had been Dora and not "her mother whom Frau K.'s appearance had driven out of more than one position" (S.E., 7:57). He perceives the outrage Dora felt in her identification with the jewels over which her parents had quarreled a year before the events at the lake. She realized the gift was neither for her mother nor for her: she saw herself as a discarded and bartered thing. The gift of love which she had been willing to give her father had been spurned and soon she was to be callously passed on to someone else, to Herr K., as a sop to his injured vanity and sexual needs.[10]

But, in his torturous account, never fully rendered in the proper chronological order, Freud obscures the familial circumstances surrounding and preceding the episode of the proposal. No less than Dora, Freud needs to reorganize the material at hand to illuminate a causal sequence that is, perhaps, latent in past events. Freud fails to do so. In listening to Dora's account, Freud may have felt that her case conformed almost too perfectly to the original seduction theory that he had disavowed in the September 1897 letter to Wilhelm Fliess. There is no conclusive evidence to demonstrate beyond a doubt that Freud sensed that Dora had been the victim of parental seduction during the years she was the father's confidante. Within "Dora" there is, however, circumstantial evidence that Freud fears that a seduction had occurred and that he is engaged in an act of repression to avoid the need to rehabilitate the theory to which Krafft-Ebing and others had responded with scorn.

In "Dora," Freud has reminded us that dreams and hysterical symptoms stand as it were on two legs, one pointing to a recent event, the other to remote childhood experiences. In "The Aetiology of Hysteria," he observes, as I have noted, that "the abnormal reaction to sexual impressions which surprises us in hysterical subjects at the age of puberty is quite generally based on sexual experiences of this sort in childhood, in which case those experiences must be of a similar nature" (*S.E.*, 3:202). Freud's inability to understand why Dora might be legitimately disturbed by her plight suggests that he may have experienced anxiety about those possible earlier events in her life. Dora's history seems to confirm Freud's original speculations as expressed in the seduction theory. Her first neurotic symptoms appeared when she was eight, precisely at the time such symptoms ought to appear according to "The Aetiology of Hysteria." Her father's venereal disease suggests the general moral infection pervading the family circle, harking back to language Freud used in the 1896 paper: "The foundation for a neurosis would accordingly always be laid in childhood by adults, and the children themselves would transfer to one another the disposition to fall ill of hysteria later. . . . Might not this appearance of a family neurosis naturally lead to the false supposition that a hereditary disposition is present where there is only a *pseudo-heredity* and where in fact what has taken place is a handing-on, an infection in childhood?" (*S.E.*, 3: 208–9). The rhetorical question provides another context in which to understand the actions of Dora's mother, and Freud's potential awareness of the contagion she seeks to stem. Evidence accumulates to suggest that the abandoned seduction theory may have threatened to reassert itself, to compel an unwilling Freud "to recognize that, after all, the later scene only owes its power of determining symptoms [in the present] to its agreement with [an] earlier one" (*S.E.*, 3: 216) in the patient's childhood.

The episode by the lake, followed by Herr K.'s appearance at Dora's bedside, agrees with an earlier episode reconstructed by Freud. In the dream of the burning house, Dora's father takes the place of the menacing Herr K.: "If there were a past situation similar to [the] present one, and differing from it only in being concerned with one instead of with the other of two persons mentioned in the wish, that situation would become the main one in the dream. But there *had* been such a situation. Her father had once stood beside her bed, just as Herr K. had the day before [after the proposal], and had woken her up, with a kiss perhaps, as Herr K. may have meant to do" (*S.E.*, 7:86). Herr K.'s clumsy effort at seduction recalls an earlier scene whose nature, at this point in the analysis, remains shadowy, elusive. In dreaming of the father rather than of K., Dora not only appeals to the father who had awakened her to prevent her from wetting the bed; she indicts the father who had "brought [her] into danger" (S.E., 7:90) not only as a girl of sixteen, but presumably as a child. The dream of the burning house, informed by the theoretically requisite conflict of long standing, reveals Dora's childhood love for her father, her desire to give him that which her mother understandably withholds. It also captures her childhood terror and her desire to be saved from the man whose victim she may have become. Freud bullies Dora about her childhood love for her father and exults in bringing to the light of day the masturbatory activities no other physician has been keen enough to see, even as he reveals in a footnote the darker implications of that love, the cruel irony of her desire that her father preserve her virginity. The bed-wetting becomes a screen memory for the vice of masturbation, and for something else. In the footnote that explains the fixation of the child's "rudimentary feeling of love" for a parent, Freud observes, "The decisive factor in this connection is no doubt the early appearance of true genital sensations, either spontaneously or as a result of seduction or masturbation" (S.E., 7:57, n. 1).

In the face of Freud's apparent blindness to the many meanings of her story, Dora plays with her reticule; she relates the anecdote of the cousin who wills the mother's death so that she may marry Daddy; or, like Cordelia, she is silent.[11] Caught up in this web of symptomatic communications, Freud resorts to footnotes and to other gestures to reveal the implications of Dora's story. Like all compromise formations, the footnotes in the case history are structured like dreams. In On Dreams, the little essay to which he refers in the same letter that announces the appearance of "a new patient, an eighteen-year-old girl" (C.L., 427), Freud reminds us that the language of the unconscious possesses no "no," no "either-or": "Dream-interpretation has laid down the following rule: in analysing a dream, if an uncertainty can be resolved into an 'either-or,' we must replace it for purposes of interpretation by an 'and,' and take each of the apparent alternatives as an independent starting-point for a series of associations" (S.E., 5:649–50). Freud's footnote, with its ambiguous "or," points to a causal connection between seduction and masturbation: Dora's bed-wetting has replaced the practice of masturbation; the masturbatory activity has succeeded the earlier appearance of what Freud calls, unnervingly, "true" genital sensations. The passage from On Dreams suggests that in the footnote Freud is unconsciously equating masturbation and seduction, pointing indirectly to an event, not a fantasy, that he cannot fully acknowledge.[12]

With his reconstruction of Dora's masturbatory acts, Freud implicitly returns to the case of Emma Eckstein and to Wilhelm Fliess's operation to correct the nasal abnormality associated, by Fliess, with that childhood vice. The analysis of Emma Eckstein may have been one of the thirteen cases to which Freud referred in two papers completed before the delivery of "The Aetiology of Hysteria" to the Vienna Psychiatric Society in April 1896. In them Freud anticipated the fully developed seduction theory of the later paper, observing in "Further Remarks on the Neuro-psychoses of Defence" that childhood masturbation is not itself the cause of hysterical symptoms at puberty: "Although it is found so very often side by side with hysteria, this is due to the circumstance that masturbation itself is a much more frequent consequence of abuse or seduction than is supposed" (S.E., 3:165). One can imagine the disavowed words of "The Aetiology of Hysteria" asserting themselves at some level of Freud's consciousness as he reconstructed Dora's past: "Sexual experiences in childhood consisting in stimulation of the genitals, coitus-like acts, and so on, must therefore be recognized, in the last analysis, as being the traumas which lead to a hysterical reaction to events at puberty and to the development of hysterical symptoms" (S.E., 3: 206–7).[13]

In his apparent attempt to deny the relevance of his original seduction theory to the case at hand, Freud ignores the other implications of Dora's habit of masturbation and misconstrues her symptomatic communications to him. Dora's addendum to the dream of the burning house, that she remembers awakening on each occasion of the dream to the smell of cigar smoke, is surely no more an expression of her "longing" for a kiss than Emma Eckstein's bleeding announced her suppressed desire. It can be seen, rather, as a sign that Freud chooses to misread. Dora has identified Freud with her father and Herr K., and with all the self-mystified physicians who conspire against her by seeing things only in the light most suitable to their desires. Dora plays with her reticule—"opening it, putting a finger into it, shutting it again, and so on" (S.E., 7:76)—pointing, as it were, to Freud's violation of her person and to that premature stimulation of her genitals in childhood that lies behind her masturbatory activity. Freud responds by proclaiming, "The circumstantial evidence of her having masturbated in childhood seems to me complete and without a flaw" (S.E., 7:78), only to refer, in the next breath, to Wilhelm Fliess and the suspect hypothesis about the genital spot in the nose. Freud comments on the gastric pains experienced by a cousin with whom Dora had identified: "It is well known that gastric pains occur especially often in those who masturbate. According to a personal communication made to me by Wilhelm Fliess, it is precisely gastralgias of this character which can be interrupted by an application of cocaine to the 'gastric spot' discovered by him in the nose, and which can be cured by the cauterization of the same spot" (S.E., 7:78). With this reference to Fliess, Freud returns to the Emma Eckstein episode. He by implication identifies Dora with Emma Eckstein and himself with Fliess. Freud has participated in the violation of a patient in the past and may fear that, in his refusal to provide the explanation of Dora's situation offered by his own seduction theory, he is engaged in yet another violation at this very moment. Appropriately, the allusion to Fliess occurs only two paragraphs after Freud has observed: "He that has eyes to see and ears to hear may convince himself that no mortal can keep a secret. If his lips are silent, he chatters with his finger-tips; betrayal oozes out of him at every pore" (S.E., 7:77–78).

The dream of the burning house, with the associations it evokes, can be seen as Dora's plea to the father, and to Freud, that she not be violated again in the present as she had been, we may now suspect, in her childhood. Playing with her reticule, Dora points to that earlier violation and reveals the gap in her consciousness about those events, not yet spoken of, and the gap that threatens the analysis itself. In the words of "The Aetiology of Hysteria," a case history is "exactly like putting together a child's picture-puzzle: after many attempts, we become absolutely certain in the end which piece belongs in the empty gap; for only that one piece fills out the picture and at the same time allows its irregular edges to be fitted into the edges of the other pieces in such a manner as to leave no free space and to entail no overlapping" (S.E., 3:205). In her second dream, in which she finds herself walking in a strange town, Dora provides a sequel to the first dream. She unconsciously offers to Freud the piece needed to fill out the picture, to fill the gap in her history and in her self. She presents Freud with another opportunity to be true to her history and to himself before she admits defeat and wills the death of the father and the end of the analysis.

Again the exciting cause of the dream, a seemingly trivial event of the previous evening, establishes the context in which the dream becomes intelligible: "They had had company, and afterwards her father had asked her to fetch him the brandy: he could not get to sleep unless he had taken some brandy. She had asked her mother for the key of the sideboard; but the latter had been deep in conversation, and had not answered her" (*S.E.*, 7:97). Dora returns to the ongoing domestic crisis, to the skeletons in the family closet. Freud's comments reveal his uneasy awareness of the situation. He observes that Dora "understood very clearly what it was that her father needed when he could not get to sleep without a drink of brandy" (*S.E.*, 7: 98), only to add in the now inevitable footnote, "There can be no doubt that sexual satisfaction is the best soporific, just as sleeplessness is almost always the consequence of lack of satisfaction. Her father could not sleep because he was debarred from sexual intercourse with the woman he loved" (*S.E.*, 7:98, n. 1).

But, as Freud and Dora know, the father is a "man without means." He is impotent and the sexual satisfaction he seeks involves deviations from conventional practices: Dora "knew very well, she said, that there was more than one way of obtaining sexual gratification. (The source of this piece of knowledge, however, was once more untraceable)" (*S.E.*, 7:47). Freud's parenthetical observation is yet another evasion, a refusal to consider that perhaps Dora had been initiated into such knowledge neither by Frau K. nor by Paolo Mantegazza's *The Physiology of Love*, but by her father. Bauer's marriage had foundered long ago through his own acts. He had needed his soporific, in one form or other, before the appearance of Frau K. in his life. Seen within the context of "The Aetiology of Hysteria," the anecdote of the sideboard may be seen to allude to those nights before the liaison with Frau K., when the father materialized at Dora's bedside to awaken her, "with a kiss perhaps," as a possible prelude to something else.[14]

The implications of Dora's plight become ever more grotesque, for Freud and for us. The father's impotence and Dora's picturing to herself "a scene of sexual gratification *per os* between the two people whose love-affair occupied her mind so incessantly" (*S.E.*, 7:48) can be linked to a passage in "The Aetiology of Hysteria": "The idea of these infantile sexual scenes is very repellent to the feelings of a sexually normal individual; they include all the abuses known to debauched and impotent persons, among whom the buccal cavity and the rectum are misused for sexual purposes. . . . People who have no hesitation in satisfying their sexual desires upon children cannot be expected to jib at finer shades in the methods of obtaining that satisfaction; and the sexual impotence which is inherent in children inevitably forces them into the same substitutive actions" (*S.E.*, 3: 214–15). Such insights, with their relevance to the girl before him, might have acted upon Freud like the return of the repressed. He

refuses to revive the original seduction theory to throw light upon
Dora's thumb-sucking, her symptomatic cough, or her masturbatory
activities. He weaves a mystery to obscure, for himself and for us,
a more probable source of Dora's sexual knowledge, a relationship
characterized in "The Aetiology of Hysteria" as one involving an
ill-matched pair in "a love relationship . . . with its mental side developed—which has often lasted for years" (S.E., 3:208). Dora's pre-
cocity, in which the father had taken such pleasure, can be partly
explained with these observations: she has been cast into the role of
surrogate wife and lover in her childhood, thrust into that premature
adulthood that has been the mark of her personality.[15]

So it is that Freud dwells upon the present and only selectively
upon certain aspects of Dora's past, significantly "leaving gaps un-
filled, and riddles unanswered" (S.E., 7:16). He forgets the year in
which Dora and her mother, then suffering from a venereal infection
handed on to her by the husband, visit a spa in Franzensbad. He interprets her cough as proclaiming aloud, "I am my father's daughter. I
have a catarrh, just as he has. He has made me ill, just as he has made
Mother ill" (S.E., 7:82): he is almost forced to ask Dora whether she,
too, was suffering from a venereal infection at the time of the visit
to the spa. But he curiously neglects to do so. "By inadvertence"
—his own words—Freud leaves "a gap in the analysis" of the first
dream. He fails to inquire into the source of the words the father
speaks: *I refuse to let myself and my two children be burnt for the
sake of your jewel-case* (S.E., 7:64). The speech, as Freud must have
suspected, appropriates words said by the mother and the father in
the course of their unending recriminations and self-justifications.
Transformed, they appear in the dream as Dora's condemnation both
of the mother and the father for their shared complicity in her fate
as victim and wifely surrogate. The mother's understandable need to
protect herself from the father has placed her children in jeopardy:
he turns to them for the satisfaction of his desires. The mother's
attempts to protect the remnants of her own integrity through her
symptomatic gestures fail to shield her daughter, perhaps even her
son, from the contaminating influence of the father. In the dream,
the father ironically speaks for Dora. She and her brother have been
sacrificed to the father's unchecked desires because the mother cares
more for her figurative jewel case than for her children. The mother
abandons them by retreating into ineffectual symptomatic behavior.
But the dream as a whole reveals the persistence of Dora's ambivalence: she remains tempted to yield to the father's will, summoning
him to her bedside, even as she cries out to be saved from his desires,
both in the present and presumably in the past.

Apparently, in response to the disturbing implications of Dora's plight, Freud suppressed "The Aetiology of Hysteria" while relentlessly eroticizing the analysis. Just as he has exploited the presence of the jewelry in the first dream, detecting a veiled trope for vaginal discharges and drops of semen, he dwells upon the thick woods in the second dream, in the midst of which Dora encounters a strange man, as the "symbolic geography of sex!" (S.E., 7:99). Freud sees the dream in which Dora moves through a strange town, in and out of various buildings, into and out of the vaguely threatening woods as, in part, a figurative reenactment of a defloration. But this is not only, if at all, a fantasy expressing Dora's homosexual longing for Frau K. In accord with the theories Freud discusses in the case history, recollections "derived from the impressions of later years do not possess sufficient force to enable them to establish themselves as symptoms" (S.E., 7:103), or as dreams. The second dream appears to allude more explicitly than the first to the past, to those acts following upon the moment when the father, that debauched and impotent man, has awakened Dora, with a kiss perhaps. In his evasion of certain possibilities, Freud will remind Dora of Herr K. and her father, for like the father, Freud persists in seeing things "in [a] light . . . most convenient from the point of view of his own passions" (S.E., 7:38) and of those theories to which he remains passionately committed. Freud presses his constructions, unconsciously seeking not to seduce Dora, but to drive her into flight.[16]

On the last day of the analysis, Dora appears to announce, "Do you know that I am here for the last time to-day? . . . I made up my mind to put up with it till the New Year. But I shall wait no longer than that to be cured" (S.E., 7:105). Dora then offers what may be the solution to the puzzle, the missing piece to fill the gap to which Freud has himself referred. Only now does she mention the governess at the K.s', revealing the full significance of the slap with which she had responded to Herr K.'s proposition. Freud claims that Dora slapped K. because he had spoken to her the same words he used to seduce a mere governess. K.'s words, "You know I get nothing out of my wife" (S.E., 7:98), move Freud to observe, in an aside relegated to a footnote, "It is not a matter of indifference, perhaps, that Dora may have heard her father make the same complaint about his wife, just as I myself did from his own lips. She was perfectly well aware of its meaning" (S.E., 7:106, n. 1).

But Freud will not pursue the implications of Dora's story of the governess or of those words her father has used upon more than one occasion. His case history does not consider the possibility that just as Herr K. had once seduced the family governess, Dora's father had perhaps victimized his own daughter during the time that she attended him in his illness and had justified his acts with Dora with the same words spoken by K. The anecdote of the governess may be the final disconcerting confirmation that the fantasy of defloration in the second dream is no fantasy at all, but an allusion to "a man seeking to force an entrance into the female genitals" (S.E., 7:100), and, in his frustration, turning to "all the abuses known to debauched and impotent persons" (S.E., 3:214).[17] The anecdote elliptically explains why Dora cannot forgive her father for acts she cannot remember, why she enigmatically proclaims that her father has made her ill. Freud can only respond, as he did in the case of Emma Eckstein, by turning Dora's latest revelation against her: for him, the story of the governess reveals Dora's longing for Herr K. He lamely speculates that Herr and Frau K. might actually divorce, freeing Dora to marry him: "The scheme would by no means have been so impracticable. Your father's relations with Frau K.—and it was probably only for this reason that you lent them your support for so long—made it certain that her consent to a divorce could be obtained; and you can get anything you like out of your father" (S.E., 7:108). Freud's words are stunningly irrelevant, a falsification of the history he has so far set forth: they fly in the face of reason. But they are a way in which he can deny the relevance of his own seduction theory to the case before him. Dora responds as she must: "She seemed to be moved; she said good-bye to me very warmly, with the heartiest wishes for the New Year, and—came no more" (S.E., 7:109). Dora breaks off the analysis on December 31, 1900. She has despaired of Freud's supposed Promethean capacity to cast light into the darkest corners of her life.

Nevertheless, fifteen months later on April 1, 1902, Dora reappears in Freud's consulting room. Freud has not completely failed her. She has confronted the father, Frau K., and Herr K. with those facts they can no longer deny, thwarting their attempt to subvert her sure understanding of the world. She has returned to Freud to celebrate victory over the conspiracy of silence in the hope that he will renew the analysis and complete it. He has enabled her to confront the present; the past remains to be explored. Freud rebuffs Dora with the disclaimer that he does "not know what kind of help she want[s] from [him]" (S.E., 7:122). But, of course, he must sense what Dora wants from him. The recurring allusions to Fliess in the case history, connected as he is to Emma Eckstein and to the suppression of the seduction theory, suggest that Freud may fear where the analysis might lead: "Deaf to the most imperative calls of duty," he prefers not to resurrect the theory and abandons Dora to her fate. Perhaps he is checked by memories of Krafft-Ebing's mocking words, "It sounds like a scientific fairy tale"; perhaps by his association of Dora with Emma Eckstein and his memory of how he has failed her. Freud belies the heroic pose he strikes within the case history itself: "No one who, like me, conjures up the most evil of those half-tamed demons that inhabit the human breast, and seeks to wrestle with them, can expect to come through the struggle unscathed" (S.E., 7:109). He betrays his own Promethean aspirations. With his pen as his fennel stalk, the embattled Prometheus confronts the paradox of his situation: he has defied the Krafft-Ebings of the world to illuminate the murky affairs of two troubled families. Yet, in seeing Dora's dreams and symptoms only as signs of hysterical longings rather than as evidence of events in her childhood with far darker implications, Freud has failed Dora and himself. The would-be Prometheus is cruelly punished for his audacity—by an eighteen-year-old girl who, in playing with her reticule, chatters with her fingertips about the ills and horrors denied first by a world blind and deaf to the truth, and now by himself. Dora's flight inflicts the humiliation he deserves.[18]

In his account of the analysis, Freud retaliates against the historical Ida Bauer by choosing for her the pseudonym Dora. As Janet Malcolm observes in *Psychoanalysis: The Impossible Profession*, Freud's own account of the choice of the pseudonym in *The Psychopathology of Everyday Life* remains suspect. The story of his sister's nursemaid who must relinquish her own name and assume that of Dora, is, like any screen memory, only partially true. In the *Everyday Life*, so Malcolm suggests, "Freud stopped associating too soon: . . . he would eventually have arrived at the name whose potent allusiveness and compelling symbolism were the cause of its insistent, all-effacing primacy in Freud's mind. Who could Dora be but Pandora?"[19] The Pandora of myth appears to punish Prometheus and all men. Freud transforms Pandora into Dora, alluding to his sister, Rosa; to Emma Eckstein, part of the premonitory triad of 1895 and 1896; to Ida Bauer, with her "pitilessly sharp" perception of those about her; and to all victimized women who seek their revenge upon a patriarchal order and those figures in authority who defend it.[20]

Like her father, Freud sacrifices Dora in his need to see things in the light which suits him best. But in the trilogy upon which he is at work throughout the autumn and winter of 1900–1901, Freud remains true to his Promethean aspirations in spite of himself. In the trilogy, he sets forth the telltale signs of an inadequate account. He offers a hermeneutic system that permits others to reinterpret his own fragment of an analysis. In the references, both explicit and implicit, to Wilhelm Fliess, Emma Eckstein, and "The Aetiology of Hysteria," he compels us to ponder the very bases of psychoanalytic orthodoxy with its emphasis on fantasy and an intrasubjective model of the mind. Freud's unconscious refusal to return to the abandoned seduction theory points to an earlier and, I think, truer intersubjective basis for psychoanalytic speculation.[21] More significantly, in anticipation of *Moses and Monotheism*, Freud enables us to demythologize Freud himself, to glimpse the man behind the legend and the officially sanctioned history of the psychoanalytic movement. In the story of Dora, we see, however darkly, the historical circumstances out of which psychoanalytic theory emerged. We are compelled to doubt the claims of Anna Freud, Ernst Kris, and others that the formulation of the oedipus complex is impossible without the rejection of the reality of infantile seductions. There are neither logical nor empirical reasons for claiming an incompatibility between the seduction theory of the 1896 paper on "The Aetiology of Hysteria" and the theory of the oedipus complex formulated in the autumn of 1897. In fact, the apparent contradiction arises from ideological concerns, from profound personal and cultural fears accompanying the possibility that "the *father*, not excluding [Freud's] own, [has] to be accused of being perverse" (*C.L.*, 264). In the face of such a possibility, it is not altogether surprising that Freud may have chosen not to see with the clarity to which he aspired, even as he bequeathed to us the account that betrays his blindness and a method of glimpsing, however darkly, its shadowy origins.

NOTES

1. See Erik H. Erikson, *Insight and Responsibility: Lectures on the Ethical Implications of Psychoanalytic Insight* (New York: W. W. Norton, 1964), pp. 159–215; Philip Rieff, *Fellow Teachers* (New York: Harper and Row, 1973), pp. 85–87; Mary Daly, *Gyn/Ecology: The Metaethics of Radical Feminism* (Boston: Beacon Press, 1978); Hyman Muslin and Merton Gill, "Transference in the Dora Case," *Journal of the American Psychoanalytic Association* 26 (1978), 311–28; Cynthia Chase, "Oedipal Textuality: Reading Freud's Reading of *Oedipus*," *Diacritics* 9 (Spring 1979), 54–68; Suzanne Gearhart, "The Scene of Psychoanalysis: The Unanswered Questions of Dora," *Diacritics* 9 (Spring 1979), 114–26; Mark Kanzer and Jules Glenn, eds., *Freud and His Patients* (New York: Jason Aronson, 1980); Maria Ramas, "Freud's Dora, Dora's Hysteria: The Negation of a Woman's Rebellion," *Feminist Studies* 6 (1980), 472–510, reprinted in *In Dora's Case: Freud—Hysteria—Feminism*, ed. Charles

Bernheimer and Claire Kahane (New York: Columbia University Press, 1985); Jane Gallop, *The Daughter's Seduction: Feminism and Psychoanalysis* (Ithaca, N.Y.: Cornell University Press, 1982), pp. 132–50; Juliet Mitchell, Introduction-1 to *Feminine Sexuality: Jacques Lacan and the école freudienne*, ed. Juliet Mitchell and Jacqueline Rose (New York: W. W. Norton, 1982), pp. 1–26; Jacqueline Rose, Introduction-2 to *Feminine Sexuality*, pp. 27–57; Jacques Lacan, "Intervention on Transference," in *Feminine Sexuality*, trans. Jacqueline Rose, pp. 61–73; Sharon Willis, "A Symptomatic Narrative," *Diacritics* 13 (Spring 1983), 46–60. "A Symptomatic Narrative" is one of the essays appearing in the special issue of *Diacritics* entitled *A Fine Romance: Freud and Dora*, ed. Neil Hertz. I am particularly indebted to the indispensable bibliography accompanying the issue.

2. Sigmund Freud, "Fragment of an Analysis of a Case of Hysteria," in vol. 7 of *The Standard Edition of the Complete Psychological Works of Sigmund Freud*, ed. and trans. James Strachey et al., 24 vols. (London: Hogarth Press, 1953–74), p. 16. All further references to Freud's psychological works are from the *Standard Edition* and will be indicated by the use of the abbreviation *S.E.*, volume number, and page number in parentheses.

3. Any further discussion of Freud and the "Fragment of an Analysis of a Case of Hysteria" inevitably owes a debt to Steven Marcus's *Representations: Essays on Literature and Society* (New York: Random House, 1975), pp. 247–310.

4. See Jeffrey Moussaieff Masson, *The Assault on Truth: Freud's Suppression of the Seduction Theory* (New York: Farrar, Straus and Giroux, 1984); and Max Schur, *Freud: Living and Dying* (New York: International Universities Press, 1972) for extensive accounts both of the Freud-Fliess relationship and the episode involving Emma Eckstein. See also Jeffrey M. Masson, "Freud and the Seduction Theory," *Atlantic Monthly*, Feb. 1984, pp. 33–60; and Janet Malcolm, *In the Freud Archives* (New York: Alfred A. Knopf, 1984). The main repository of the psychoanalytic myth is *The Origins of Psycho-Analysis: Letters to Wilhelm Fliess, Drafts and Notes: 1887–1902*, ed. Marie Bonaparte, Anna Freud, and Ernst Kris (New York: Basic Books, 1954). The editorial deletions in the letters are significant. Masson's new edition of the letters, *The Complete Letters of Sigmund Freud to Wilhelm Fliess: 1887–1904*, trans. and ed. Jeffrey Moussaieff Masson (Cambridge, Mass.: Belknap Press, 1985), is designed to restore the unedited letters to us and to make possible a reinterpretation of events crucial to the origins of Freud's ideas. In quoting Freud's letters to Fliess, I will refer to the *Complete Letters*, using the abbreviation *C.L.* and page number in parentheses.

5. I am drawing here upon Schur, *Freud: Living and Dying*, pp. 63–92; Masson, *Assault on Truth*, pp. 55–106; and Malcolm, *In the Freud Archives*.

6. For a discussion of the nose and the sense of smell, with its significance for Freud and Fliess, see Catherine Clément, "The Guilty One," in *The Newly Born Woman*, by Catherine Clément and Hélène Cixous, trans. Betsy Wing, Theory and History of Literature, vol. 24 (Minneapolis: University of Minnesota Press, 1986), pp. 37–39. For discussions of masturbation and the use of clitoridectomy as a surgical procedure, see George Frederick Drinka, *The Birth of Neurosis: Myth, Malady, and the Victorians* (New York: Simon and Schuster, 1984); Peter Gay, *Education of the Senses*, vol. 1 of *The Bourgeois Experience: Victoria to Freud* (New York: Oxford University Press, 1984); Elaine Showalter, *The Female Malady: Women, Madness, and English Culture, 1830–1980* (New York: Pantheon Books, 1985); and Jeffrey Moussaieff Masson, ed., *A Dark Science: Women, Sexuality, and Psychiatry in the Nineteenth Century* (New York: Farrar, Straus and Giroux, 1986).

7. See Felix Deutsch, "A Footnote to Freud's 'Fragment of an Analysis of a Case of Hysteria,'" *Psychoanalytic Quarterly* 26 (1957), 159–67; and Arnold A. Rogow, "A Further Footnote to Freud's 'Fragment of an Analysis of a Case of Hysteria,'" *Journal of the American Psychoanalytic Association* 26 (1978), 331–56, for discussions of the identity and history of Ida Bauer, Dora, and for comments on the circumstances of the analysis. See especially Rogow, p. 337: "Freud's misdating of Dora's analysis, in other words, like his omitting of Fliess's name from his later discussions of bisexuality, may have owed something, perhaps even a good deal, to the deterioration of their relationship after 1900." For the dating of the works written in 1900–1901, see the editor's introductions to individual works in the *Standard Edition*, the *Complete Letters*, and Schur, *Freud: Living and Dying*. Many of the important essays on "Dora," including Deutsch's "A Footnote to Freud's 'Fragment of an Analysis of a Case of Hysteria,'" appear in *In Dora's Case*, ed. Bernheimer and Kahane. *In Dora's Case* provides useful introductions by the editors, biographical information about Ida Bauer, and a bibliography to supplement the earlier bibliography in *A Fine Romance: Freud and Dora*.

8. See Masson, *Assault on Truth*, pp. 55–106. On pp. 66–67, Masson writes, "It was 'abnormal' of Freud to hand Emma Eckstein over to Fliess and it was 'abnormal' of Fliess to operate at all and then to bungle the operation." I assume Masson quite consciously uses the phrase, "hand over," thinking of Freud's own use of the phrasing in "Dora." The story of Dora becomes a form of romantic narrative with the structure and motifs of uncanny tales. See Freud, "The 'Uncanny,'" *S.E.*, 17:217–56; Tzvetan Todorov, *The Fantastic: A Structural Approach to a Literary Genre*, trans. Richard Howard (Ithaca, N.Y.: Cornell University Press, 1975); Neil Hertz, "Dora's Secrets, Freud's Techniques," *Diacritics* 13 (Spring 1983), 65–76.

9. Joyce Zonana of the University of Oklahoma alerted me to the full implications of Wilhelm Fliess's "slip."

10. For a similar discussion of "Dora," see Showalter, *The Female Malady*, pp. 158–61.

11. See Freud, "The Theme of the Three Caskets," *S.E.*, 12:289–301. In her silence, Dora is like the Cordelia who refuses to answer Lear's question with what he wants to hear. Freud discusses Cordelia in "The Theme of the Three Caskets" only after dealing with Portia and *The Merchant of Venice*. Cordelia and Portia are associated with the three caskets among which Portia's suitors must choose. Pandora is associated, of course, with a vase or "box." The three stand for the mystery posed by women to the men who silence them and for those ambiguous gifts women deliver into the world in patriarchal mythology. For a discussion of the problem of silenced women see Hélène Cixous, "Castration or Decapitation?" trans. Annette Kuhn, *Signs: Journal of Women in Culture and Society* 7 (1981), 41–55.

12. For a discussion, influenced by Jacques Lacan, of the seduction theory and the role of "fantasy" in the creation of sexuality and the self, see Jean Laplanche and J.-B. Pontalis, "Fantasy and the Origins of Sexuality," as translated in *International Journal of Psychoanalysis* 49 (1968), 1–18. Although I shall argue that Freud suspects that an actual seduction has occurred, one could argue that Dora is moved by a repressed fantasy of seduction that is not an expression of a longing to be seduced by the father, but the psychic trope around which her sexuality and her self become organized: the suppressed fantasy captures Dora's sense of her violation by the men in her life.

13. In *Assault on Truth*, pp. 87–94, Masson suggests that Emma Eckstein's case was one source of the speculations in "The Aetiology of Hysteria."

14. For a different reading of the fantasy of fellatio, see Madelon Sprengnether, "Enforcing Oedipus: Freud and Dora," in Bernheimer and Kahane, eds., *In Dora's Case*, pp. 254–75.

15. See Edith Wharton's fragment about an incestuous relationship between daughter and father, "Beatrice Palmato," printed in R. W. B. Lewis's *Edith Wharton: A Biography* (New York: Harper and Row, 1975), pp. 544–48. Robert Con Davis of the University of Oklahoma drew my attention to the fragment, with its relevance for "Dora."

16. See Mark Kanzer, "Dora's Imagery: The Flight from a Burning House," in Kanzer and Glenn, eds., *Freud and His Patients*, for a discussion of the ways in which Freud eroticizes the therapy and uses a sexual trope to describe Dora's first dream. See, particularly, p. 79: "Was it really an unknown resemblance between Herr K. and himself which made Dora feel rebuffed and take her revenge [on Freud] by leaving him? Could there have been a wish to have her leave him which militated against his recognizing until too late that it would have been possible to do so?" Where Kanzer poses an apparently rhetorical question, I have acted upon the implications of the question to argue that Freud wills Dora's breaking off of the analysis.

17. See Isidor Bernstein, "Integrative Summary: On the Reviewings of the

Dora Case," in Kanzer and Glenn, eds., *Freud and His Patients*, p. 90: "I should also like to suggest the possibility of a prepuberty or early puberty trauma—an exhibitionistic display by an important male figure." Bernstein does not pursue the full implications of his words. I am aware that both Maria Ramas and Sharon Willis would object to my reading here—yet another male interpretation in which Dora's sexuality is explained in terms of male sexuality. See the problem of reading explored by Jonathan Culler in *On Deconstruction: Theory and Criticism after Structuralism* (Ithaca, N.Y.: Cornell University Press, 1982), pp. 43–64.

18. For a book-length discussion of "Dora," see Phillip McCaffrey, *Freud and Dora: The Artful Dream* (New Brunswick, N.J.: Rutgers University Press, 1984). McCaffrey dwells upon Dora's second dream and Freud's failure of his client; he explores the father's betrayal, without dealing with the possibility of seduction.

19. Janet Malcolm, *Psychoanalysis: The Impossible Profession* (New York: Alfred A. Knopf, 1981), p. 96. Also see Dora and Erwin Panofsky, *Pandora's Box: The Changing Aspects of a Mythical Symbol*, Bollingen Series, no. 52 (New York: Pantheon Books, 1956).

20. For other discussions of Freud's choice of the name Dora, see Steven Marcus, in *Representations*, who connects Freud's Dora with Dickens's Dora, David Copperfield's child-wife in *David Copperfield*; Hannah S. Decker, "The Choice of a Name: 'Dora' and Freud's Relationship with Breuer," *Journal of the American Psychoanalytic Association* 30 (1982), 113–36; and Madelon Sprengnether, "Enforcing Oedipus: Freud and Dora," in Bernheimer and Kahane, eds., *In Dora's Case*.

21. See Samuel Slipp, "Interpersonal Factors in Hysteria: Freud's Seduction Theory and the Case of Dora," *Journal of the American Academy of Psychoanalysis* 5 (1977), 359–76, for a different reading, but one emphasizing intersubjective realities rather than intrasubjective fantasies. And see Alice Miller, *Thou Shalt Not Be Aware: Society's Betrayal of the Child*, trans. Hildegarde and Hunter Hannum (New York: Farrar, Straus and Giroux, 1984) for a lengthy revision of Freud's basic assumptions.

PART THREE

Seduction of the Reader

Seduction and the Voice of the Text: *Heart of Darkness* and *The Good Soldier*

In *Reading for the Plot*, Peter Brooks explores the relation between teller and listener by retelling what he calls Maupassant's "dirty joke," the story "Une Ruse," in which a doctor tells his female patient, a recent bride in the flush of erotic exhaustion, a tendentious story about his assistance to another wife in an extramarital "situation" and offers to assist her also should she need it. Noting that listening to the tale itself implicates the woman as listener and that the teller knows this, Brooks describes this act of narration as aggressive, "a forcing of attention, a violation of the listener." But even more, as he points out through the motives of the doctor, the act of narration is seductive: "Seduction appears as a predominant motive . . . be it specifically erotic and oriented toward the capture of the other, or more nearly narcissistic, even exhibitionistic, asking for admiration and attention."[1] Brooks constitutes the relation of narrator to listener as analogous to that of text to reader, and both as classic instances of psychoanalytic transference. Yet as in the transference situation, although the narrator-text appears to be dominant, seducing a reluctant and passive listener-reader, the speaker is also dependent upon the listener's engagement with the narrative. Ultimately, as Brooks insists, the narrative relation between teller and listener, like transference, involves dynamic exchange; the narrator depends on the listener as an interlocutor who makes speech possible; the meaning of the narrative is the product of the listening as well as the telling.

Of course, Brooks is not the only literary critic to rely on the psychoanalytic process as a model for discussing narrative effects. From its inception, psychoanalysis has staged a relation between talker and listener that has stimulated a good deal of theorizing about texts and readers. But I would like to meditate on one issue that Brooks raises, the particular relation of seduction to the act of storytelling and listening. Starting with Freud's *Studies on Hysteria*, seduction has constituted the originary text of psychoanalysis —hysterics told stories of seduction—and is enacted in the very dynamic of talking and listening. Unlike the relation between text and reader, however, psychoanalysis, the talking cure, demands the *embodied* presence of two subjects. Indeed, the talking cure constitutes an acoustic relation between a teller and a listener, who are connected by the voice which vanishes, leaving only the trace of its effect.

Most present to the senses and yet evanescent, both there and not there, the voice is uncanny in its effects. As articulated sound, the voice makes most flagrant what Julia Kristeva calls the semiotic register of discourse: tone, rhythm, music—the body speaking, which is the privileged register of the mother.[2] Yet the voice speaks language, symbolic discourse which theoretically signifies maternal absence. The speaking voice stands somewhere between the body and the symbolic system; like a transitional object, it binds the speaker to the listener at the same time that it signals separation. A sensitive reflector of emotion, it reveals to the listening ear, through a tone and timbre that is not always under the speaker's control, the state of the speaker's interiority, while it also invades the open ear of the listener, who is thus put into a passive position that he or she cannot control. Perhaps most significant, the speaking voice marks the gender of the speaker, marks a difference in the speaking body of which the listener is always aware.

What is the relation between this embodied voice and the speaking text? To what extent does the written text have a bodily voice, a gendered voice, what Roland Barthes calls the "grain" of the voice?[3] What is the place and function of the voice in the written text? I will suggest that the voice of the text is the presence of the body in writing, or that which gives the illusion of presence in the midst of absence, an illusion which is a primary pleasure of the text. While some texts attempt to exorcise the voice, to present writing that wears the mask of impersonality, others pointedly pretend to be oral storytelling rather than acts of writing in order to seduce the reader into a transferential relation, into hearing with the inner ear the written words as spoken by an imagined embodied other. Modernist fictions in particular, moreover, substitute voice for plot, seducing the reader through a projection of the voice of the other rather than through the suspenseful turns of plot. It is such a seduction of the reader posited as listener that characterizes much of the writing of Henry James, Joseph Conrad, and Ford Madox Ford.

In her comprehensive reading of *The Turn of the Screw*, Shoshana Felman describes the way in which the prologue frames the inner story of the governess through a chain of narrative voices: the reader hears the story from a narrator who has heard the story from his friend Douglas, who reads the manuscript of his former governess to a circle of listeners seated around a fire. James thus draws the reader and the narrator into the story, as members of that circle, "enclosing [in the story] what is usually outside it: its own readers." But as Felman notes, the frame at the same time does the very opposite, pulling the inside outside: for "in passing through the echoing chain of the multiple, narrative voices, . . . the interior of the story . . . becomes somehow exterior to itself, reported . . . by a voice inherently alien to it, a voice whose intrusion compromises the tale's secret intimacy and whose otherness violates the story's presence to itself."[4] That is, the narrator in telling someone else's story is essentially alienated from it; story and narrator thus split, the "meaning" of the story cannot be directly interrogated or assured. The frame thus acts to blur the difference between inside and outside and the narrating voice becomes our link to a truth to which we have no access.

A similar dynamic informs Conrad's *Heart of Darkness*, as well as *The Good Soldier* by Ford Madox Ford, Conrad's onetime friend and colleague. Indeed, like James, Conrad and Ford each make use of framed narratives to incorporate the listener into the discourse of the speaker, who tells someone else's story. Each locates the reader as listener within a circle of oral storytelling, and as in the psychoanalytic dialogue, each posits the ear of the listener as necessary to the speaker's articulation and understanding. Perhaps most strikingly, each evokes a seductive scene of hearing that echoes the ur-scenes of psychoanalysis in a discourse whose power is primarily auditory. Just as in *The Turn of the Screw* the narrator hears in Douglas's reading "a rendering to the ear of the beauty of his author's hand," so in the works of Conrad and Ford the seductive power of auditory discourse is itself a principal theme as well as technique in their work. What is this power? From where does it derive?

Psychoanalysis and the Voice: The Etiology

In his early theorizing, Freud pointed to an aural source of hysterical fantasy, of voices heard in preoedipal infancy, articulations whose meaning was deferred.

> The point that escaped me in the solution of hysteria lies in the dis-
> covery of a new source from which a new element of unconscious pro-
> duction arises. What I have in mind are hysterical phantasies, which
> regularly, as it seems to me, *go back to things heard* by children at an
> early age and only understood later. The age at which they take in in-
> formation of this kind is very remarkable—from the age of six to seven
> months onwards.[5]

These "things," heard before the child understands language, leave
a memory trace which is activated at a later moment, when voiced
sound "means," by a repetition which strikes a chord over the in-
terval. (That repetition is also a reconstruction, since memory is
mediated by fantasy and the desire of the subject.) But the resonance
between past and present can be experienced as a dissonance, pro-
voking that repression whose issue is neurotic symptoms.

Freud had named the initial scene of repression the primal scene,
a structural moment in psychic development when the child first
sees and interprets sexual relations between parental figures. Although as Juliet Mitchell points out, Freud's work subsequently emphasized the primacy of vision in the etiology of neurosis, in this
early formulation Freud first suggests that auditory phenomena must
be equally if not more important to the construction of primal fantasies—a suggestion he repeats throughout his works.[6] If the child
can close its eyes and blot out the visible universe, it cannot close
its ears; it remains vulnerable through this orifice to the outside as
sound which penetrates its being and remains as a trace. The experience of the voice precedes Winnicott's transitional object as a bond
to a world whose boundaries are totally indeterminate. It is the voice
that is the first other to invade the child's boundaries, that speaks
as the first internal object, in a dynamic which eventually becomes
that inner anterior voice called conscience, named God.

Indeed, one can argue that the structure of the unconscious itself is acoustic, a thesis implied by Freud's figure of the dream as
rebus, defined as "a riddle composed of words or syllables depicted by
symbols or pictures that suggest the *sound* of the words or syllables
they represent" (italics mine);[7] the dream work translates the more
primary verbal sounds into visual images to disguise unconscious
thoughts, while understanding the dream reverses the process, returning visual images into their phonetic sources. In their discussion
of Freud's interpretation of the noise heard by a woman patient as the
fantasied sounds of the primal scene, "an indispensible part of the
fantasy of listening," Laplanche and Pontalis also privilege the aural
register of discourse. Hearing, they note, "breaks the continuity of

an undifferentiated perceptual field and at the same time is a sign
(the noise waited for and heard in the night) which puts the subject
in the position of having to answer to something"; and hearing is
related to the family sounds and sayings, a "spoken or secret discourse going on prior to the subject's arrival, within which he must
find his way. Insofar as it can serve retroactively to summon up the
discourse, . . . noise . . . can acquire this value."[8]

Not surprisingly then, the scene of hearing, and especially overhearing, appears regularly to complicate narrative plots, a repetition
of a primal scene in which sound is privileged rather than sight. In
Heart of Darkness, Marlow overhears a conversation about Kurtz
which excites his interest in the man who becomes his obsession. In
The Good Soldier, the deaths of Edward's mistresses, Maisie's heart
attack and Florence's suicide, as well as Edward's own suicide, are
consequences of intimate conversations each has overheard. Moreover, as Laplanche and Pontalis indicate, the scene of overhearing
need not involve language, but can be constituted by any meaningful
noise. Recall the vivid passage in *Sons and Lovers*, in which the children lie awake in bed late at night hearing the wind howl through
the old ash tree. These sounds become intermingled with the sounds
of their father and mother arguing:

> Often Paul would wake up, after he had been asleep a long time, aware
> of thuds downstairs. Instantly, he was wide awake. Then he heard the
> booming shouts of his father, come home nearly drunk, then the sharp
> replies of his mother, then the bang, bang, of his father's fist on the
> table, and the nasty snarling shout as the man's voice got higher. And
> then the whole was drowned in a piercing medley of shrieks and cries
> from the great wind-swept ash-tree. The children lay silent in suspense,
> waiting for a lull in the wind to hear what their father was doing. He
> might hit their mother again. There was a feeling of horror, a kind of
> bristling in the darkness, and a sense of blood. . . . The wind came
> through the tree fiercer and fiercer. All the cords of the great harp hum-
> med, whistled and shrieked. And then came the horror of the sudden
> silence, silence everywhere. . . . What was it? Was it a silence of blood?
> What had he done?[9]

The syntax and rhythm of Lawrence's text rise to a climax, a cre-
scendo of aural images that conflate violence, sexuality, and then,
silence with the classic question, "What had he done?" Lawrence's
representation vividly evokes a prototypical primal fantasy of paternal brutality and maternal suffering, constructed around those uncanny sounds in the night. When those sounds specifically involve
language, the primal scene becomes a primal text; the voice takes

on its human dimension as both sound and sense, and registers the symbolic, the Lacanian signifier of the cultural system of signs and symbols in which we live.

The voice (the emission) and the ear (the receiver) have long been culturally coded by gender: men have traditionally wielded the power of articulation, the gift of tongues, while women typically have served as the perfect ear. Indeed, as Shakespeare suggests in his representation of King Hamlet's literal poisoning and of Othello's metaphoric corruption through Iago's insinuations, when male figures are represented as listening, or receiving through the ear, it signifies their vulnerability and emasculation. Julia Kristeva speaks to this difference and its effect in her meditation on the idealized body of the Virgin Mary: "Of the virginal body we are entitled only to the ear, the tears, and the breasts. That the female sexual organ has been transformed into an innocent shell which serves only to receive sound may ultimately contribute to an eroticization of hearing and the voice, not to say of understanding."[10] The ear of the Virgin, into which the Holy Ghost whispers and through which she conceives, is the most blatant fiction of the woman as receptive ear which runs through Western cultural forms.[11]

But the talking cure undermines the image of woman as ear listening to male speech. Psychoanalysis marks a transfer of the voice; it is the patient—and the classic hysterical patient of Freud's was a woman—who speaks, who tells stories, while the analyst listens, although he listens with a difference. The talking cure evokes the classic image of seduction, the lips whispering into an ear,[12] yet it also raises the question of who is seducing whom.

On Seduction and Hysteria

Hysterics told stories when they talked, and Freud listened to tales of seductions, the narration of which was to rid the hysteric of her symptoms, the sign of repression. Yet the liberated tongue of the hysteric and the listening ear of the analyst did not constitute a neutral intercourse. Although Freud defensively insisted on keeping his aural/oral technique dry,[13] he realized that often the fantasies were themselves a production of the talking cure, of the embodied relation between doctor and patient: as he subsequently wrote, "I was at last obliged to recognize that these scenes of seduction had never taken place, and that they were only phantasies which my patients had made up or *which I myself had perhaps forced on them*" (italics mine).[14] That is, Freud's own vocal interventions could constitute the fantasy of seduction and contribute to the silencing of the hysteric; the voice of the father could capture hers, if she listened. But hers could also seduce him, if she talked.

The father's voice has long signified dominance for the vulnerable heroines of the English novel. From Clarissa Harlowe, who feared her father's thunderous voice, to the even more virginal Nancy Rufford in Ford's *The Good Soldier*, whose father's voice causes her to shriek in the night, a series of middle-class daughters fear and tremble at the father's voice, experienced as an avatar of the voice of God, a God who traditionally can be heard but not seen. But the voice of the analyst is not only the voice of paternal authority; it is also the soft voice of suggestion, of comfort; ideally it can speak the mother tongue as well. Insofar as this voice seductively calls the body into language, it recalls the voice of the preoedipal mother who through her bodily ministrations is, as Freud had written, the first seducer of the infant.

Since the mother is not only the first love object, associated with the body, but also first experienced as part of the infant's body before separation and individuation, a scene of seduction seems to recreate this amorphous interchange between mother and child. Seduction plays on a desire for submission, a desire to yield, to merge the separate self into the body of the seducer. Desire in this form, as an eroticized submission as object rather than subject of desire, as receiver rather than speaker, is the desire that Freud ultimately located in the death drive, in a primary masochism in which the subject seeks pleasure in a return to nonbeing, to nondifferentiation, to silence.[15] Seduction thus typically leads one to cross the boundary from speech to silence; it climaxes in a "petit mort," an orgasmic dying out of language.

How appropriate, even uncanny then, was the fact that in Freud's major case history of hysteria, the Dora case, Dora's primary symptom was aphonia, a hysterical loss of voice. While Freud attributed Dora's aphonia to the absence of Herr K., the suitor he imagined would suit her, it was just as conceivably a consequence of her being left alone to talk with—and listen to—Frau K., the woman Freud eventually concluded was her most important love-object. Significantly, in the Dora case Freud imagined the intimacy between Dora and Frau K. as a series of conversations on sexual matters, conversations which mimicked the very nature of the talking cure in which he was engaged. Although in this analogy Freud occupied the transference position of Frau K., his narrative insists on his link with Herr K., the virile male in the heterosexual romance plot. It is no accident that Freud's failure in the Dora case turned on the transference, for it revealed Freud's inability to acknowledge the transference implications of Dora's relation to Frau K., which would have placed him in the position of the sexual mother, or to admit his identification with Dora, with the vulnerable hysterical daughter, though his text shows him caught up in his fantasy of her desire.

That feminine identification takes us back to the scene of hearing; for it structurally repeats Freud's position as ingenue to the patriarchal establishment of Viennese medicine of his time, which, as Neil Hertz has pointed out, is inscribed into the history of psychoanalysis as a classic scene of overhearing: Freud overhears the elders of his profession narrating a sexual joke, which turns on sexual frustration as the source of female hysteria. In this scene, as Hertz remarks, Freud plays ingenue overhearing the joke and thus occupies the feminine position in his own theory of obscene joke telling:

> Freud's distinctly marginal relation to this scene of professional knowingness, almost out of earshot, listening to two men talking—in French, of course—about suggestive matters, *secrets d'alcove*, locates him close to the position of the woman in his analysis of obscene jokes, just as his being paralyzed with amazement aligns him with the (mostly female) victims of hysterical paralysis. In his innocence, in his capacity to receive impressions, he is feminized.[16]

Culture defines the position of the listener, the receiver of impressions, as feminizing whether or not the listener is a woman. The anxiety associated with that position as well as the pleasure of being seduced by the erotics of the voice informs both the structure and thematics of *Heart of Darkness* and *The Good Soldier*.

Seduction and Narration

In Conrad's *Heart of Darkness*, the object of the narrative quest is Kurtz, who is valued for "his ability to talk, his words," whom Marlow remembers as "a voice, a voice."[17] Conrad's fiction, which is about the primitive impulses that can erupt in the most idealistic of men when external restraints are removed, enacts in its very structure of talking and listening, as well as in its diction, the primal oral/aural desire that is its subject.

"*Heart of Darkness* is a tale told *viva voce* by a ship's captain on the deck of a cruising yawl," Ford Madox Ford writes, stressing Conrad's aural technique.[18] Indeed, *Heart of Darkness* places us as readers-listeners to an anonymous narrator, locates us with him on

board a becalmed ship, compelled to listen, as darkness falls, to the
tale of Marlow, an untypical seaman who sees differently. Unlike
other seamen, Marlow believes "the meaning of an episode was not
inside like a kernel but outside, enveloping the tale which brought
it out only as a glow brings out a haze in the likeness of one of
these misty halos that sometimes are made visible by the spectral
illumination of moonshine."[19]

In a mystifying discourse which blurs distinctions while playing
on sensuous sound, especially long vowels and lulling *l*'s, Conrad seductively describes meaning as located in the outside, but not seen;
what he describes in fact is the resonance of language, the play of
meanings which Roland Barthes similarly calls an "immense halo"
of implications, a play which is heard rather than seen. Although
elsewhere in his famous dictum on writing Conrad insists that the
purpose of his fiction is to "make you see," his diction makes you
hear. Thus, at the end of *Heart of Darkness*, when Marlow, sitting
in the darkness, appeals to the eyes of his listeners to confirm the
truth of his story, speaking the familiar metaphor of truth as vision,
"you see," ironically they cannot see him; they can only hear him
in the obscurity. *Heart of Darkness* substitutes voice for vision as a
conduit toward truth, truth in the spoken word.

Marlow is seduced by the voice of Kurtz even before he meets
him:

> I had travelled all this way for the sole purpose of talking with Mr.
> Kurtz. Talking with . . . I . . . became aware that this was exactly what
> I had been looking forward to—a talk with Kurtz. I made the strange
> discovery that I had never imagined him as doing, you know, but as dis-
> coursing. . . . The man presented himself as a voice. . . . The point was
> in his being a gifted creature, and that of all his gifts the one that stood
> out preeminently, *that carried with it a sense of real presence,* was his
> ability to talk, his words—the gift of expression." (p. 48; italics mine)

Talking and listening: this is the shape of Marlow's desire, both aural
and oral. Yet although Kurtz's gift of expression is said to be a figure
of presence, the voice of Kurtz is beyond language: Conrad cannot
communicate it; he can merely allude to it. In *Heart of Darkness*
what we have instead of Kurtz's voice is Marlow's; it is Marlow who
as darkness settles becomes a voice to a circle of listeners, Marlow
who whispers into their ears. But finally even Marlow's voice lapses
into silence, and only an anonymous narrator is left to retell the tale.
Indeed, the story must be told and retold, we discover, not only as
a warning that the lapse into silence and darkness is dangerous, but

as a means of sustaining through the voice and the word the human bond which Kurtz had violated.

However, the only word that continues to echo through the heart of darkness, behind the eloquence of Marlow's tale, is "the horror, the horror," the repetition of a word on the edge of the unspeakable, as Peter Brooks notes in his suggestive reading, a primal cry which effectively stops discourse.[20] Yet Brooks omits from his ostensibly psychoanalytic reading any link between this "primal cry" in the heart of darkness and the infantile prelinguistic relation to the maternal body which it suggests. For the particular nature of Kurtz's horror to which the text alludes is his regression to a primal voraciousness, the satisfaction of an unspeakable oral desire before language: "I had a vision of him on the stretcher, opening his mouth voraciously, as if to devour all the earth with all its mankind." Yet this "as if" is no metaphor, as the row of human skulls adorning Kurtz's jungle house implies.

Conrad's fascination with cannibalism and its relation to pre-oedipal fantasies has been explored by Bernard C. Meyer in his psychobiography. As Meyer writes, "In [Conrad's] fiction the love of a man for a woman is so fused with fantasies of nursing as to confer upon all masculine aggression the significance of unrestrained biting."[21] Marlow discovers the horror of unrestrained orality and its concomitant narcissism, but he justifies Kurtz. "No fear can stand up to hunger, no patience can wear it out, disgust simply does not exist where hunger is." It is not Kurtz who is blamed for his primitive savagery, but the object of his desire, which has seduced him. Kurtz, we are told, falls prey to "the heavy mute spell of the wilderness—that seemed to draw him to its pitiless breast by the awakening of forgotten and brutal instincts, by the memory of gratified and monstrous passions" (p. 67). The wilderness, figured as a maternal breast which is pitiless and mute, and associated with the "savage and superb" woman who gestures in formidable silence, "awakens" cannibalistic desire, evokes a "memory" of infantile passions acted out by the adult Kurtz, who "lacked restraint in the gratification of his various lusts" (p. 58).

The antithesis of this mute wilderness is embodied in that quasi-allegorical shadow, the Intended. Yet as Marlow listens to her speak of Kurtz's great gift of speech, "the sound of her low voice seemed to have the accompaniment of all the other sounds, full of mystery, desolation, and sorrow, I had ever heard—the ripple of the river, the soughing of the trees swayed by the wind, the murmurs of the crowds, the faint ring of incomprehensible words cried from afar, the whisper of a voice speaking from beyond the threshold of an eternal darkness" (p. 77). In language pronouncedly assonant and alliterative, Marlow describes both her seductive plea to hear Kurtz's last words, a truth which he will not utter, and her voice—the low and sensuous voice of the speaking woman which evokes for him those sounds from another place, the chora from the immense wilderness whose primal lure Marlow must resist.

To foreclose his seduction by the wilderness, here evoked by the woman's voice, Marlow lies: "The last word he pronounced was—your name" (p. 161). Yet Marlow's lie—his substitution of the name of the Intended, the figure of ideality, for "the horror" also gives textual voice to Conrad's "truth," his anxious equation of the woman's name—itself absent in its particularity from the story—with the horror. Insofar as the word "horror" is voiced, it can be heard as one of those Freudian switchwords, a word which homonymically functions in a parallel unconscious discourse.[22] The "horror" echoes its homonym "whore," its embedded, embodied repressed term, suggesting that what is revealed through the voice is a fear of and rage at woman, whose innocence masks her sexual being, and who provokes that oral desire which elsewhere in his fiction Conrad repeatedly represents in the biting, voracious, dangerous mouths of mute women. Finally, even though it is Kurtz, recalled as a voice, who becomes the voracious figure with the dangerous mouth, like Marlow's blaming of Kurtz's descent (or ascent, for "he had kicked the very earth to pieces") on the desires evoked by the mute wilderness, the subtext adheres to the masculinist tradition and blames the female figure for the fall of man. It is woman, represented by the double figures of the Intended and the Wild Woman, and associated with the idealized/sexual mother, she who can never satisfy the raging desires of the infant, who is blamed for arousing them.

In Conrad's fiction, the extremity of this oral desire which the text confronts is displaced as the desire to speak to a listener who will totally understand. The drive to talk, the passion that drives narrative, is this desire for communication with the other in a fullness that eradicates difference. But that eradication is also dangerously aggressive, simultaneously destroying what is desired—the otherness of a validating listener, the otherness of a text. Paradoxically, this desire for full communication leads to silence. As Peter Brooks astutely remarks, what Conrad's fictions insist is that the quest of life is full utterance to the perfect ear;[23] at the same time they insist that neither full utterance nor the perfect ear is possible. "Are not our lives too short for that full utterance which through all our stammerings is of course our only and abiding intention?" Conrad writes in *Lord Jim*.[24] We can also formulate this intention as a desire to be one with a primal figure, a preoedipal desire for the mother who can transform our childlike stammerings—the primal cry—into a communion that does not destroy its desired object.

Seduction and the Narrator: *The Good Soldier*

In Ford Madox Ford's *The Good Soldier*, the narrator Dowell muses that the essence of love is to be one with the object of passion: "The real fierceness of desire, the real heat of a passion long continued and withering up the soul of a man is the craving for identity with the woman he loves."[25] Dowell's desire, perhaps Ford's too, is analogous to Conrad's desire for full utterance. But while Conrad represents the speaking voice as constituting a necessary intercourse, Ford makes clear the dangers of that desire to be the other through talking and listening. Talking in *The Good Soldier* becomes the medium of an erotic interchange which can destroy the listener.

The Good Soldier is at least a thrice retold tale. Most evidently, *The Good Soldier* is a retelling by Dowell, who knows this saddest story before he begins. He has heard it twice before, from "the lips" of two of its principals: Edward, the good soldier whose adulterous affairs generate the narrative movement, and Leonora, his wronged but commanding wife, who herself emerges as the victorious soldier in this domestic warfare. The repetition of this image of transmission—lips whispering into an ear—emphasizes the seductive intimacy with which Dowell will now engage the listener-reader.

But in the preface Ford tells us his novel is also a retelling, although significantly, he had the story from the male voice only, from Ashburnham, the good soldier. Moreover, Ford confirms his transmission of the tale through a series of anecdotes which exploit the image of intimate listening to male voices. First, Ford records that his friend, John Rodker, said in his clear, slow drawl, "Ah yes. It is . . . the finest French novel in the English language" (p. xx). The allusion to the clear slow drawl of his friend's voice confirms in its sensual notation the remark that *The Good Soldier* is more French than English, French also because it is a narrative of adultery analogous to the story of courtly love within the novel—the story of the troubador Peire Vidal that Dowell tells—and similarly is set in Provence, original site of romance narrative. Like the novel, the story of

Peire Vidal, which Dowell calls the story of culture, represents mo-
nogamy and fidelity as sentimental rather than, as in the Protestant
English novel, at the heart of its value system. In this logic, it follows
that Ford then tells the anecdote about the adjutant who looks sick
because, having just gotten engaged to be married, he is now reading
The Good Soldier, which tells and foretells of betrayal and infidelity.

Finally, Ford tells us that while he was on military parade, pet-
rified with nervousness, "one of the elderly red hatbands walked
close behind my back and said distinctly in my ear: "Did you say
The *Good* Soldier??" (p. xxi). This seductive whispering into his ear,
which questions the meaning of the "good" soldier, articulates the
subversion of precisely those ethical certainties of English society
—honor, virtue, strength, honesty—which the good soldier represents. Moreover, it does so through the trope of the voice and the
ear, foregrounding their insidious place in this "French" version of
the English novel.

Dowell stages his relation to the reader as a tête-à-tête, and even
a talking cure,[26] imagining the listener as a silent interlocutor, who
can perhaps make sense of his sad story. "So I shall just imagine
myself for a fortnight or so at one side of the fireplace of a country
cottage, with a sympathetic soul opposite me. And I shall go on talking, in a low voice while the sea sounds in the distance and over head
the great black flood of wind polishes the bright stars" (p. 12). This
is seductive talk, reminiscent of Conrad's diction, lulling the listener with maternal overtones. But if this image of intimacy suggests
trust—and the mouth is the first locus of trust—the story Dowell
tells the reader-listener is about ultimate betrayal: about intimacy
as inevitable pain, even torture. What Dowell does is replay with
his imagined interlocutor the two scenes of his disillusion, his listening to Edward and to Leonora. "I trusted in Edward and Leonora
and in Nancy Rufford . . . as I had trusted in my mother's love.
And that evening Edward spoke to me" (p. 202). From both Edward
and Leonora, he learns the nature of the intricate oedipal triangle
in which they are all involved and of his essential betrayal; in both
cases he as listener has been forced "to get it full in the face" (p. 105).

Indeed, the image of listening with which Dowell begins—the
lips speaking into an ear—is increasingly replaced by this more
violent image, being hit "full in the face," a violence with which
the listener-reader is in turn threatened by Dowell's narrative. Even
Dowell's repeated "I don't know," the psychoanalytic signifier of repression which punctuates his discourse, repeatedly transmits to the

reader the experience of fragmented knowledge until both narrator and reader are mutually implicated in a hysterical attempt to make the story cohere, while apprehensive about what it will say.

The novel repeatedly stresses the need for an interlocutor so that unconscious knowledge and desire can be heard. For example, Leonora, "like a person who is listening to the sounds in a sea shell held to her ear" (p. 97), hears in Dowell's naive remark that Edward is "a good husband" and "good guardian to your ward" her own unconscious knowledge of Edward's illegitimate desire for Nancy, in great part because the repetition of the word "good" in the first phrase "good husband," a phrase which Leonora knows to be false, casts doubts on the structural repetition, "good guardian"—and of course on "the good soldier." Dowell's words thus ironically bring to the surface Leonora's repressed knowledge. Similarly, when after Florence's death, Leonora says to Dowell, "You might marry her" (p. 103), he had no thought of it before; "It made things plainer, suddenly" (p. 104).

This articulation of the subject's unrecognized desire is most consequential in the case of Edward, in the scene of his sudden recognition of his desire for Nancy: "It was as if his passion for her hadn't existed; as if the very words he spoke, without knowing that he spoke them, created the passion as they went along. Before he spoke, there was nothing; afterwards, it was the integral fact of his life. Well, I must get back to my story" (p. 116). In the double irony that inhabits Dowell's last remark, in the "recollection" that is his story, as he remembers voices of those presumed to know, the story itself as he speaks it creates for the narrator "the integral fact of his life." Paradoxically, this fact of his life, his story, is represented as the story of others. Indeed, by the end of the novel, it is everyone's: "the story of culture," the archetypal narrative of adultery with which Western romance narrative begins.

It is Florence the talker, who compels them all into the orgy of talking, Florence who seduces Edward through her stories, most pointedly when she explains the significance of the document, the Protest, while physically touching Edward on the wrist. As Carol Jacobs argues, this document, the Articles of Marburg, records an argument over the phrase "This is my body," over whether it is to be taken figuratively or literally.[27] The phrase is extraordinarily resonant to this novel, for it is precisely this question which echoes through the novel in its many ramifications—from Florence's touch which asserts her body and speaks through it, to the question of marriage as a sacrament, of whose body is possessed, whose circulated, of language itself as embodied presence, transmitting forbidden knowledge through the voice.

Significantly, the novel distinguishes between male talk and female talk while indicating that both exploit the body under discussion. In the world of male anecdotes and joke telling, as in the male enjoyment of "gross" sexual narratives to which Dowell alludes, it is the body of a woman that is being circulated; the counterpart of this male talk is the conversation among women, in which, as Dowell makes clear, the body that circulates is the man's. As in Freud's case of Dora, Dowell represents this female talk not only as threatening to male identity, but as a physical torture to the man who listens: "It was as if Leonora and Nancy banded themselves together to do execution, . . . upon the body of a man who was at their disposal. . . . Night after night he would hear them talking; talking . . . seeking oblivion in drink, he would lie there and hear the voices going on and on" (p. 239). What begins as an erotic relation between talking and listening in the novel increasingly becomes a sadomasochistic orgy. Even though Leonora "had been drilled to keep her mouth shut" (p. 177), when she gives in to her desire for communication, "What had happened was just hell. Leonora had spoken to Nancy; Nancy had spoken to Edward. Edward had spoken to Leonora—and they had talked and talked" (p. 201).

This implicit violence to the listener is made most manifest in the repeated scenes of overhearing which structure the novel. Maisie Maiden overhears Edward and Florence talking about her, and her realization that she is no longer the central figure for Edward causes her death. Florence overhears Edward speak his love for Nancy; she "heard the words from behind the tree" (p. 117), and commits suicide. In retelling the scene of Florence's overhearing, Dowell's language reveals his own sadistic pleasure in imagining that "Florence must have got it in the face, good and strong" (p. 110).

For Nancy, the scene of overhearing is linked to her father's "booming" voice (p. 128). In an allusion to the horror of *Heart of Darkness*, Dowell and Nancy overhear her father talking of the Congo and of the proper treatment of natives: "Oh, hang humanity," he says, and the effect of overhearing these words on the daughter is terror. But it is the sound of his voice—"that peculiar note of his voice, used when he was overbearing or dogmatic, [that] could unman her" (p. 129). While this "unmanning" speaks to Dowell's own feminized position in listening, it also figures the daughter's disintegration when penetrated by the violent voice of the oedipal father.

In the climactic scene of overhearing, however, Nancy's terror is transmuted by Edward, whose voice seduces even when it carries the paternal prohibition. As Nancy and Leonora are talking,

> The half-opened door opened noiselessly to the full. Edward was there
> . . . "I forbid you to talk about these things. . . . I am the master of this
> house." . . . And at the sound of his voice, heavy, male, coming from a
> deep chest, in the night, with the blackness behind him, Nancy felt as
> if her spirit bowed before him, . . . that she desired never again to talk
> of these things. (pp. 229–30)

Nancy's submission to the seduction of Edward's voice, figured as a desire for silence, is reiterated as Edward telephones to arrange for her mother's care:

> She sat there in a blissful dream. She seemed to see her lover, sitting
> as he always sat, in a round-backed chair, in the dark hall—sitting low,
> with the receiver at his ear, talking in a gentle, slow voice, that he re-
> served for the telephone—and saving the world and her, in the black
> darkness. She moved her hand over the bareness of the base of her throat,
> to have the warmth of flesh upon it and upon her bosom. (p. 231)

Edward's telephone voice, the voice of the savior carried over the cord, is the other side of the feared paternal voice; an unthreatening seductive voice associated with caretaking, with the bodily relation between mother and child suggested in Nancy's touching of herself "to have the warmth of flesh . . . upon her bosom."

Ford's text reveals speech as the very carrier of desire, a caress or an assault. As a caress, it soothes us into the illusion of intimacy, as when Leonora takes Edward's whispering to her as a sign of his returning affection: "He whispered little jokes about the odd figures they saw up at the Casino. It was not much to make a little joke —but the whispering of it was a precious intimacy" (p. 189). Paradise itself is figured by a whisper: "Is there any terrestrial paradise where, amidst the whispering of the olive-leaves, people can be with whom they like and have what they like?" In such passages Ford, like Conrad, represents the speaking voice seducing through a linguistic felicity based on sound.[28] But while this semiotic maternal discourse promises gratification, it delivers instead frustration, the explosion of trust "full in the face."

In sum, Ford's fiction, like Conrad's, accords the speaking voice a fantasmatic power, a power, moreover, that is represented most sa- distically when women speak, as in the repeated image of Edward being flayed by the talking women. In representing women talking as an assault which can destroy the listener, Ford/Dowell reveals a hysterical fear of the voice as the destructive phallus of the fantasmatic mother which reduces men to stammerers, to a silence that has traditionally figured the feminine relation to discourse. Perhaps this is why Ford tells us he has had the story from Ashburnham, and not from Leonora. To have listened to the woman talking, to have heard the story from Leonora, Ford implies, would have silenced him.

NOTES

1. Peter Brooks, *Reading for the Plot: Design and Intention in Narrative* (New York: Vintage, 1985), pp. 217, 236; all quotations are from this edition.
2. See Julia Kristeva, *Revolution in Poetic Language*, trans. Margaret Waller (New York: Columbia University Press, 1984) for Kristeva's elaboration of this place of the mother in discourse.
3. Roland Barthes, *Image, Music, Text*, trans. Stephen Heath (London: Fontana, 1977), pp. 179–89.
4. Shoshana Felman, "Turning the Screw of Interpretation," *Yale French Studies* 55/56 (1977), 123.
5. Sigmund Freud, *The Standard Edition of the Complete Psychological Works of Sigmund Freud*, ed. and trans. James Strachey et al., 24 vols. (London: Hogarth Press, 1953–74), vol. 1, pp. 244–45. (My italics.)
6. For Mitchell's remarks on the primacy of vision, see *Women: The Longest Revolution* (New York: Pantheon, 1984), p. 298.
7. See Gallop's discussion, in *The Daughter's Seduction: Feminism and Psychoanalysis* (Ithaca: Cornell University Press, 1982), p. 57; Also see Paul Kugler's Jungian discussion of language as sound-image in "The Phonetic Imagination," *Spring* (1979), 118–29.
8. Jean Laplanche and J.-B. Pontalis, "Fantasy and the Origins of Sexuality," *International Journal of Psychoanalysis* 49 (1968), 10–11.
9. D. H. Lawrence, *Sons and Lovers* (New York: Penguin, 1980), p. 60.
10. Julia Kristeva, "Stabat Mater," in *The Female Body in Western Culture*, ed. Susan Rubin Suleiman (Cambridge: Harvard University Press, 1986), p. 108.
11. See Ernest Jones's classic article on the insemination of the Virgin through the ear in *Essays in Applied Psycho-Analysis* (New York: International Universities Press, 1964), vol. 2, pp. 266–357. For other representations of the ear as receptive organ of insemination, see also *The Ear of the Other*, a collection of discussions with Jacques Derrida, English edition, ed. Christie V. McDonald, trans. Peggy Kamuf (New York: Schocken Books, 1985); Thomas G. Pavel, "In Praise of the Ear (Gloss's Glosses)," in Suleiman, ed., *The Female Body in Western Culture*.
12. The opening frames of the feminist film *Sigmund Freud's Dora: A Case of Mistaken Identity* (1979) by Anthony McCall, Claire Pajaczkowska,

Andrew Tyndall, and Jane Weinstock focus in extreme close-up on the lips of a woman, in profile, speaking.

13. Freud's text repeatedly uses metaphors of dry and wet to signify neutral versus sexual issues; for example, in justifying his talk about the sexual body to his patients, Freud insists that his technical language is "dry." Commentators on this issue include Neil Hertz and Jane Gallop in "Dora's Secrets, Freud's Techniques" and "Keys to Dora" respectively, in *In Dora's Case*, ed. Charles Bernheimer and Claire Kahane (New York: Columbia University Press, 1985).

14. Freud *On the History of the Psycho-Analytic Movement, S.E.*, 14:34 (1914).

15. See *Beyond the Pleasure Principle (1920), S.E.* 18:7–64, for Freud's discussion of primary masochism.

16. Hertz, in Bernheimer and Kahane, eds., *In Dora's Case*, p. 239.

17. Joseph Conrad, *Heart of Darkness*, Norton Critical Edition, ed. Robert Kimbrough (New York: W. W. Norton, 1971), pp. 48, 69, respectively. All page number references are to this edition.

18. Ford Madox Ford, "Heart of Darkness," *Portraits from Life* (1936, 1937) pp. 59–60; reprinted by permission from Houghton Mifflin in *Heart of Darkness*, Norton Critical Edition, p. 127. Ford mistakes the narrator, who is not the captain. Ford also reveals the importance of sound to Conrad's technique, and his own, when he writes of the ending of the tale, "The last paragraph of a story should have the effect of what musicians call a coda—a passage meditative in tone, suited for letting the reader or hearer gently down from the tense drama of the story, in which all his senses have been shut up, into the ordinary workaday world again" (Norton Critical Edition, p. 135).

19. In Conrad's manuscript version, the phrase "not inside like a kernel, but outside" is followed by "in the unseen." *Heart of Darkness*, p. 5.

20. Brooks, *Reading for the Plot*, p. 250.

21. Bernard C. Meyer, *Joseph Conrad: A Psychoanalytic Biography* (Princeton: Princeton University Press, 1967), p. 182.

22. As an anonymous reviewer pointed out to me, Shakespeare also played with the relation between this particular phoneme in Desdemona's "I cannot say 'whore.' It does abhor me now I speak the word." *Othello*, 4.2.161–62.

23. Brooks, *Reading for the Plot*, p. 253.

24. Brooks uses this as the epigraph to *Reading for the Plot*.

25. Ford Madox Ford, *The Good Soldier* (New York: Vintage, 1955), p. 115. All subsequent page references appear in the text and are to this edition.

26. My gratitude to Deborah Kloepfer, who pointed out the analogy between the narrative of *The Good Soldier* and the psychoanalytic dialogue in an unpublished paper.

27. Carol Jacobs, "*The* (Too) *Good Soldier*: 'A Real Story,'" *Glyph* 3 (Spring 1978), 32–51.

28. See Shoshana Felman's remarks in *The Literary Speech Act: Don Juan with J. L. Austin, or Seduction in Two Languages,* trans. Catherine Porter (Ithaca: Cornell University Press, 1983): "To seduce is to produce felicitous language" (p. 28).

Anne Sexton and the Seduction of the Audience

In the most famous seduction poem in English, Andrew Marvell reminds his coy mistress that "The grave's a fine and private place / But none, I think, do there embrace."[1] The final turn of his syllogism then begins:

Now, therefore, while the youthful hue
Sits on thy skin like morning dew,
And while thy willing soul transpires
At every pore with instant fires—

We are all familiar with the strategy: thy willing soul transpires at every pore with instant fires—or crudely paraphrased, you're blushing, baby, I know you really want it, don't be shy. Earlier in the poem Marvell has engaged in some clever bullying, mocking the conventions of courtship and of courtly love poetry he pretends to respect. At its close he anticipates a lovemaking that will transgress social and literary rules in its combination of indelicate violence and startling intimacy. "Like amorous birds of prey," the lovers must "Rather at once our Time devour / Than languish in his slow-chapt power." It is either eat or be eaten, in the world of the flesh. This metaphor is followed by one yet more insistently carnal, and at the same time more genuinely loving than the rhetoric of flattery the poet has rejected:

Let us roll all our strength, and all
Our sweetness up into one ball,
And tear our pleasures with rough strife
Through the iron gates of life.
Thus, if we cannot make our sun
Stand still, yet we will make him run.

If we take Marvell's poem as an epitome of seduction, the activity of seduction is quite a subtle matter. It differs on the one hand from the act of rape, where X subdues Y by force, and on the other from the proposal, where X promises Y an exchange of goods and services: come live with me and be my love and I'll give you this and that. In both rape and the proposal, X and Y remain distinct beings with separate sets of wishes. In the seduction this separation is less certain, less absolute. As Marvell suggests, seduction depends on X convincing Y that she already secretly desires the same amorous play that X desires, and that she has the potential to amalgamate with Y into a single being, a "we" that will replace "I" and "you" as it does at the poem's close. Note that Marvell does not make the gender distinction we would expect, my strength and your sweetness, but invokes "all our strength and all our sweetness," implying that both man and woman possess both strength and sweetness.

"To His Coy Mistress" is a poem about poetry, and not only about a poetics of the contraconventional, composed under pressure of lust and of mortality; it is a poem about the poet-reader relation. For if all works of literature construct their proper readers, a work which addresses a "you" within itself does so doubly. In the transaction taking place between "To His Coy Mistress" and each of its readers, the reader as well as the mistress plays the part of "you," and the poet is seducing the reader by suggesting that the reader's resistance disguises a deeper desire to be seduced. The poet promises the reader that when certain foolish literary formalities are dropped, the reader can become—excitingly, violently, strongly, and sweetly, transcending gender distinction and the distinction between self and other—one with the poet.

Anne Sexton's poem "For John, Who Begs Me Not to Inquire Further" (1960), composed as the apologia for what we might call an erotic poetics at the very outset of Sexton's career, resembles "To His Coy Mistress" (c. 1650) in a number of ways. First, the title constitutes a witty piece of bullying mockery, as we learn from Diane Middlebrook's reconstruction of Sexton's early apprentice relationship with John Holmes.[2] Holmes, Sexton's teacher, fellow poet, and supposed friend, wrote her an admonitory letter after seeing the manuscript which was to become *To Bedlam and Part Way Back*, advising her not to publish the poems she had written about her mental breakdowns and hospital experiences:

> I am uneasy . . . that what looks like a brilliant beginning might turn out to be so self-centered and so narrowed a diary that it would be clinical only. Something about asserting the hospital and psychiatric experiences seems to me very selfish—all a forcing others to listen to you, and nothing given the listeners, nothing that teaches them or helps them. . . . It bothers me that you use poetry this way. It's all a release

for you, but what is it for anybody else except a spectacle of someone experiencing release?

Holmes accuses Sexton, in other words, of what might be called an analog of attempted rape. His assumption is that her experiences are not only painful but intrinsically without interest, and that others cannot identify with her or them.

Sexton's reply begins by accepting the premise of difference between "I" and "you" but, like Marvell, gives that difference a twist of the tail. She has quoted as her epigraph to *To Bedlam and Part Way Back* a letter from Goethe to Schopenhauer: "The true philosopher must be like Sophocles' Oedipus, who, seeking enlightenment concerning his terrible fate, pursues his indefatigible inquiry, even when he divines that appalling horror awaits him in the answer. But most of us carry in our heart the Jocasta who begs Oedipus for God's sake not to inquire further." The title "For John, Who Begs Me Not to Inquire Further," then, accomplishes a neat role reversal. Anne Sexton assumes the mantle of the tragic hero-philosopher (male, of course, and celebrated by a long line of high-culture men), while John Holmes is relegated to the position of timid female. As Marvell mocks the coy mistress, Sexton mocks the resistant mentor.

Second, as Marvell seems to agree that conventional courtship would be desirable if we had world and time enough, Sexton seems to agree that her poetry is "not beautiful." Echoing Holmes's own language, she calls her mind a "narrow diary" and herself "selfish." She appears to accept his values: "I tapped my own head; it was glass, an inverted bowl. / It is a small thing / to rage in your own bowl." We may take these concessions to the adversary as sincere or insincere; they are probably in some sense both; either way, they establish a kind of authority of empathy. The poet knows what the adversary thinks and likes, and this gives the poet a bit of moral edge, or at any rate wedge.

A third and crucial similarity is that Sexton tells Holmes he is not really different from her: "At first it was private. / Then it was more than myself; / it was you, or your house / or your kitchen." As Diane Middlebrook has observed, "Sexton insists to Holmes that his rejection of her poetry is in part a defense against the power of her art, which tells not a private but a collective truth, and, to his horror, includes and reveals him." For Holmes's first wife was a suicide, and he himself was a recovered alcoholic. The poet then continues:

And if you turn away
because there is no lesson here

> I will hold my awkward bowl,
> with all its cracked stars shining
> like a complicated lie,
> and fasten a new skin around it
> as if I were dressing an orange
> or a strange sun.

As Marvell reminds his coy mistress of human mortality, so Sexton in this beautiful passage offers her resisting reader the truth of human vulnerability. The awkward bowl of her creativity, mysteriously precious, will be wounded by his disdain. Still, she will continue to care for it, continue to write, even if her truths are taken to be a lie. There is fear of rejection and contempt here, but also a pursuit of the point that rejection of one another derives precisely from the dread of contemplating our shared, frightening lives, and that denial can only exacerbate suffering:

> This is something I would never find
> in a lovelier place, my dear,
> although your fear is anyone's fear,
> like an invisible veil between us all . . .
> and sometimes, in private,
> my kitchen, your kitchen,
> my face, your face.

The tone is at once pleading and condescending, with its masterstroke rhyming of "dear" and "fear." The idea of the personal as transpersonal expands, as she urges Holmes to recognize that his fear of accepting a shared human condition is itself a shared fear; that it is perhaps responsible for making that human condition as sad as it is; and that resistance is a kind of spiritual virginity. The "invisible veil" returns us to the image of Holmes as woman, as Jocasta, while it suggests that all of us may be in the position of protecting ourselves like fearful women. But as Jocasta already intuitively knows the secret she hopes to deny, so Holmes is not really a virgin. He has suffered like Sexton, even if he wishes to deny it, and she has already penetrated his veil by naming his disapproval "fear." They are, as the undifferentiated parallelism of kitchens and faces urges, alike.

As a poem of seduction and an apologia for a poetics of seduction, "For John" addresses—indeed creates by addressing—a reader who is at once in the poem and outside it, who is both John and anyone, and who both resists the poet's claim and secretly wants to accept it. That "I" and "you" are different and also the same, is the claim; and the attempt is to seduce the reader into empathizing both with

Holmes's position and with Sexton's, into finding both the Oedipus and the Jocasta within the self, and, ultimately, into recognizing that our normal sense of self as rigidly bounded ego committed to protecting its boundaries is a fiction that damages more than it sustains us. As a critique of conventional aesthetics, "For John" does not so much dismiss conservative expectations that poetry must be impersonally "beautiful" as it introduces the liberal possibility that poetry may legitimately be personal and intimate and that a poet's introspection may yield a "certain sense of order . . . worth learning" to others as well as herself. Note, however, that while Sexton offers the notion that such poetry is cognitively significant, something one can "know," a "lesson," the poem's most original and provocative metaphoric sequence is generated by the expectation of rejection. If the cracked stars of the poet's glass head shine "like a complicated lie," which is to say that poetry is a truth that seems to be a lie, the poet will veil it with new skin "as if dressing an orange / or a strange sun," which is to say that she will write irrationally, surreally, healingly, ornamentally, childishly, playfully, protectively. The absurdity of trying to put the peel back on an orange, the impossibility of "dressing" a sun strange or otherwise, the simultaneous analogy and disjunction between sun and orange, combined with the vividness of the image (one can "see" it), make this figure a startlingly appropriate one for the paradoxically simultaneous truth and falsity of poems, the simultaneous connection and failure of connection inherent in the invention of metaphor. Notice, too, the richness of the figure's polysemy. One dresses wounds, one dresses dolls, one dresses meat. These are metaphors that recur in Sexton's poems, and they are metaphors for the activity of metaphor-making. Thus the critic-reader's assumed antagonism becomes incorporated into the act of the poem, which states it, accepts it, rejects it, and transforms it to poetic energy. It is at this point that the site of the poem shifts from the author's single personal self to a relationship between two personal selves, which then stands as a trope for all relationship and, potentially, for all poetry.

To penetrate the invisible veil between us all was Anne Sexton's literary calling, much as the justification of God's ways to men was Milton's, the articulation of the true voice of feeling was Keats's, or the recovery of the tale of the tribe was Pound's. The poetic program Sexton announced in her first volume of poems continued to be hers throughout her career. She had committed herself to an erotic view of art and life and remained committed to it. Having grown up in a family and society which resisted reading her and each other, among "people who seldom touched— / though touch is all,"[3] she places the issue of human intimacy at the center of her writing, both thematically and as the source of poetic language itself. In a letter to a psychiatrist friend Sexton wrote:

> It is hard to define. When I was first sick I was thrilled . . . to get into the Nut House. At first, of course, I was just scared and crying and very quiet (who me!) but then I found this girl (very crazy of course) (like me I guess) who talked language. What a relief! I mean, well . . . someone! And then later, a while later, and quite a while, I found out that [Dr.] Martin talked language. . . . By the way, Kayo [Sexton's husband] has never understood one word of language.[4]

When she began taking classes in poetry, and meeting poets, Sexton discovered another group who spoke "language." "I found I belonged to the poets, that I was *real* there." As Diane Middlebrook observes, what Sexton means by "language" is something compressed, elliptical, metaphoric. "Schizophrenics use language this way, and so do poets: 'figurative language' is the term Sexton might have used here, except she meant to indicate that the crucible of formation was urgent need."[5] Clearly, too, "language" in Sexton's account is what people speak when they are free of the censor's invisible veil of ordinary intercourse; "language" is intimacy, authenticity, love in a loveless world; it is what the inner self uses to communicate with other inner selves. What a relief! But inevitably temporary, inevitably to be sought and resought. Longing always "for something to touch / that touches back" ("The Touch," *C.P.*, p. 173), a kiss is for her "Zing! a resurrection" ("The Kiss," *C.P.*, p. 174); a lover caressing a breast is "the key to everything" ("The Breast, *C.P.*, p. 175); at the consummation of any lovemaking, "Logos appears milking a star"; and with a variation on the figure of the hymeneal veil of separation, the man and woman "with their double hunger / have tried to reach through / the curtain of God" ("When Man Enters Woman" *C.P.*, p. 428) much as Sexton has tried to pierce the veil of the anxious male authority. All her books contain recurrent images of undressing, nudity, skin, the parts and parcels of the body. Her work repeatedly implies that self is constituted by other(s) or that self and other overlap: "Mother, father I'm made of" is for her one key constellation; another is what she confesses to her daughter, "I made you to find me" ("The Double Image," *C.P.*, p. 42). She remembers becoming "a *we* . . . a kind company" in infancy, inventing her imaginary supportive twin Christopher (based on Christopher Smart, another mad-

man who spoke "language") for the times "when the big balloons
did not bend over us" ("O Ye Tongues: Fourth Psalm," *C.P.*, p. 402).
Lovers "gnaw at the barrier because we are two" and swim "up and
up / the river, the identical river called Mine" ("Eighteen Days without You," *C.P.*, p. 214). Friends "reach into my veins" ("The Witch's
Life," *C.P.*, p. 423). In *The Awful Rowing toward God*, Sexton advises
us to take off our lives like trousers, shoes, underwear, take off our
flesh, "In other words / take off the wall / that separates you from
God" ("The Wall," *C.P.*, p. 446).

That opening the self to intimacy means leaving oneself open
to pain and guilt continues to be a deep assumption in Sexton's late
work as in her early. As in "For John," the desire for erotic connection is usually seen as doomed, while at the same time that doom
is converted into pyrotechnically vivid poetic language. The same
poem that advises stripping ourselves for God also describes us as
earthworms underground, who, were Christ to come in the form of
a plow, "would be blinded by the sudden light / and writhe in our
distress. / As I write these lines," she adds, "I too writhe." To surrender a lover is to annihilate the self: "As for me, I am a watercolor. /
I wash off" ("For My Lover, Returning to His Wife," *C.P.*, p. 190).
In the posthumously published "Food," the dependency on love is
described as profoundly infantile, a need that continuously reproduces the infant's need for the breast: "I want mother's milk, / that
good sour soup," a need that can never be satisfied. Rejection takes
the form of impersonal discourses antithetical to the "language" of
intimacy:

> I am a baby all wrapped up in its red howl
> and you pour salt into my mouth. . . .
> I am hungry and you give me
> a dictionary to decipher. . . .
> Tell me! Tell me! Why is it?
> I need food
> and you walk away reading the paper.
>   (*C.P.*, p. 489)

From the beginning, Sexton saw readers and audiences as potential intimates, and consequently potential sources of pain, much as
she sees the other beings who populate her poems. Indeed the condition of her poetry is the presence of an audience, whom she needs
to need her; Sexton's vocation as a poet was determined to an extraordinary degree by an assumption of and dependence on readerly
empathy. "My doctor encouraged me to write more. 'Don't kill your-

self,' he said. 'Your poems might mean something to someone else someday,' " she says of her first poems.[6] Recalling the course she took with Robert Lowell, she describes letting her poems "come up, as for a butcher, as for a lover" (*No Evil Star*, p. 6). Describing the agonies she endured as a performer reading her poetry to thrill-seeking audiences in the essay "The Freak Show," she also makes clear how significant performance was to her: "Don't kid yourself. You write for an audience. I think of myself as writing for . . . that one perfect reader who understands and loves" (*No Evil Star*, p. 33). She touchingly relates occasions when audience members shouted encouragement, declares that readings traumatize her for a month, and quotes in full an adulatory letter from a fan. Her letters, too, are full of references to her "fans," references which are at once self-dramatizing, self-congratulatory and self-pitying.

We may easily find Sexton's addiction to love, her insistence on need, infantile and repellent. She clearly finds it repellent herself, thereby somewhat outflanking us. What must mitigate our judgment is the recognition that we too are such addicts, were truth told. Imagine the veil lifted, "language" spoken. Hence, for Sexton, the centrality of a strategy of seduction.

The single most crucial device whereby Sexton pursues a seductive poetics is her use of "you," a pronoun which she employs, I would not be surprised to learn, more than any other poet in English. Over and over the poems address a "you" who may be mother, father, daughter, husband, lover, friend, psychoanalyst or God, and who is always also the reader. More powerfully than any other poet in English (only D. H. Lawrence comes close), she renders the complexity of intimate relationships—the way they involve the desire to merge with the other and the desire to resist merger; the way the other can be seen both as antagonist and as lover-beloved; the way joy, sympathy, affection, admiration, resentment, fear, anger, and guilt may (must?) coexist at any moment in a relationship of sufficient nearness and dearness. When we include the inevitable actuality of the readerly "you" within the dynamic of these poems, their potential meaning increases severalfold, for the reader may at any moment be identifying / resisting identification with both the "I" and the "you" of the poet's text. Further, those Sexton poems which deal most self-referentially with language gestures of various kinds are often precisely addresses to "you," in effect inviting "you" to reconsider the meaning of language, of poetry.

For example, the early elegy "The Division of Parts" oscillates as do all Sexton's mother-poems between entanglement and disen-

tanglement of the mother's and the daughter's two identities, and
between motherly and daughterly dominance. The mother is half
identified as a martyred Christ whose daughter is "one third thief"
of her inheritance; "division" signifies both the dividing of the dead
from the living and the apportionment of the dead among the living
—whether or not they want her "parts." The poet describes her discomfort with the mother's burdensome legacy of money, coat, jewels, furs, the mother's Christ and the mother *as* Christ. Simultaneously this is a text about textuality, "your will" (a legal, moral, and
religious text, especially if we hear the echo of "thy will be done")
versus the poet's work: "I . . . poke at this dry page like a rough /
goat." Visited in a dream by her dead mother, Sexton writes, "I cursed
you, *Dame! keep out of my slumber. / My good dame, you are dead.*"
At the poem's climax, however, she wants both to "curse / you with
my rhyming words" and to "bring you flapping back, old love . . .
god-in-her-moon . . . my lady of my first words." The poet speaks, as
we all do, a mother tongue; to recognize this is to recognize that the
mother-daughter bond is the source of the poetic language whereby
the poet both exorcises the mother, rupturing the connection, and
guarantees her perpetual presence.

Like her mother-poems, Sexton's daughter-poems revolve around
issues of identification and separation, and around the inevitable
superseding of mother by daughter. Just as "I did not know / that
my life, in the end, / would run over my mother's like a truck," so
to the growing daughter, "I'm there, an old tree in the background."
In "Mother and Daughter" (*C.P.*, pp. 305–7), Sexton celebrates the
advent of her daughter's puberty:

> Linda, you are leaving
> your old body now.
> You've picked my pocket clean
> and you've racked up all my
> poker chips and left me empty.

I have presided over more than one classroom of women arguing
over whether this is a poem of love or hate, pleasure or jealousy, satisfaction or dread. I have tried to suggest that it is all these things, and
that it is also a poem about language, juxtaposing an aging mother's
discourse of words with a ripening daughter's discourse of proud
bodily gesture. "Question you about this" is the poem's refrain:

> Question you about this
> and you hold up pearls . . .
> Question you about this—

> you with your big clock going,
> its hands wider than jackstraws—
> and you'll sew up a continent . . .
> Question you about this
> and you will see my death
> drooling at these grey lips
> while you, my burglar, will eat
> fruit and pass the time of day.

The daughter's response is frightening, gratifying, tragic, comic. It is both a failure of response, as the daughter cannot or will not answer the mother in words, and precisely the response the mother desires, as it indicates that the daughter has successfully entered her own life; therefore the mothering has succeeded. One must perhaps be a mother to recognize in these lines the maternal wry pride in the daughter's free vitality; but that the daughter is a new Eve whose casual fruit-eating is being endorsed as safe to herself if fatal to her mother, and that the mother would not have it otherwise, should be apparent to any reader.

Another ambiguous alternative to the "language" of intimate communication in Sexton is laughter, specifically the laughter of the fathers. The first poem of "The Death of the Fathers," called "Oysters" (C.P., pp. 322–23) again has puberty as its subject:

> Oysters we ate,
> sweet blue babies,
> twelve eyes looked up at me,
> running with lemon and Tabasco.
> I was afraid to eat this father-food
> and Father laughed
> and drank down his martini,
> clear as tears.

She eats the oysters, successfully completing an initiation that she also calls a death, as she joins her father's laughter: "Then I laughed and then we laughed / for I was fifteen / and eating oysters / and the child was defeated / the woman won." But won what, we are made to wonder. The child has been seduced (or is it raped?) into woman-hood, in a scene that seems to balance intimidation and enticement. One becomes a woman by eating "father-food" which suggests both the father's genitals and the unborn children she may now bear, but which also suggests that she will now be *like* her father, able to do frightening adult things. To enter womanhood, sexuality, is to enter a condition in which sophistication and humiliation, power and grief ("his martini, clear as tears") will be inextricably combined. The powerful and sinister paternal laughter of this poem resembles that of "Death, with his ho-ho baritone." It reappears in "Santa," "Grandfather, Your Wound," and above all, "The Rowing Endeth," where the Father God's laughter rolls out of His mouth and into the speaker's after the notorious crooked game of poker. The scene of daughterly compliance with paternal force is at once physical and spiritual. In the tremendously glamorous shadow of the Father, one must die to be saved; one ceases to speak in words. Whether or not the paternal laughter can be said to constitute a superior "language" of intimacy remains a question. Sexton's propitiatory tone at the close of "The Rowing Endeth" suggests that it is and is not. For her, however, it is unquestionably seductive.

Let me indicate two issues which I believe the foregoing discussion of Sexton opens up. The first is the relation of Sexton's work to gender issues, the second, its relation to the issue of the boundary between life and art.

Readers of feminist theory will of course recognize the context in which this discussion of Sexton's poetics belongs. Students of female psychology such as Jean Miller, Nancy Chodorow, and Carol Gilligan define female personality in terms of its fluid ego boundaries, its permanent tendency to oscillate between mother and father as erotic objects, its often self-destructive capacity for empathy, its relatedness. The consensus is particularly striking because it is shared by Freudians and non-Freudians, by those who see women's fluid ego boundaries as a weakness, by those who see them as a strength.[7] Literary critics including Sanda Gilbert and Susan Gubar, Nancy Miller, Judith Kegan Gardiner, Mary Jacobus, Rachel DuPlessis and others concerned with avant-garde writing propose that the woman writer's culturally marginal status gives her what DuPlessis calls a "both/and vision" opposed to the "either/or" of the dominant culture. The French feminist philosopher Luce Irigaray tells us that the female sex is never "one" but is always fluid, multiple, plural:

> "She" is indefinitely other in herself. This is doubtless why she is said to be whimsical, incomprehensible, agitated, capricious. . . . It is useless, then, to trap women in the exact definition of what they mean, to make them repeat (themselves) so that it will be clear; they are already elsewhere in that discursive machinery where you expected to surprise them. . . . Their desire is often interpreted, and feared, as a sort of insatiable hunger, a voracity that will swallow you whole. Whereas it really involves a different economy more than anything else, one that upsets the linearity of a project, undermines the goal-object of a desire, diffuses

the polarization toward a single pleasure, disconcerts fidelity to a single discourse.[8]

Female difference, according to certain currents in feminist thought in our time, is female fluidity, diffusion, affiliation, multiplicity. Accordingly, to write in ways that violate our normal notions of a unitary self and of simply definable self-other relationships, then, is to write like a woman. Readers of contemporary women's poetry will recognize that others besides Sexton attempt to engage the reader in participatory acts that rupture both literary rules and the rule that we must not try to penetrate "the invisible veil between us all." Writers as various as Sylvia Plath, Diane Wakoski, Adrienne Rich, Ntozake Shange, June Jordan, Audre Lorde, and Judy Grahn—to name a few—employ strategies designed to put the reader in a problematic position, to make it impossible for us to read objectively whether or not we identify with the author or approve of her strategies. "I imagine," writes Marge Piercy, "that I speak for a constituency, living and dead, and that I give utterence to energy, experience, insight, words flowing from many lives." Ntozake Shange, in a poem called "inquiry," declares, "poetry is unavoidable connection." Denise Levertov in her essay "Origins of a Poem" describes "the communion between the maker and the needer within the poet; between the maker and the needers outside him." Adrienne Rich describes the motivation of poetry as "the drive to connect. The dream of a common language."[9] Much of the critical hostility to feminist poetry stems precisely from the discomfort of the critic confronted by work which is not only ideologically threatening but which insists on emotion and emotional intimacy. Forced to relinquish the role of reader-looking-at-artifact, forced to respond personally to the poetic fiction of a direct address expressing need, hope, pain, joy, anger, and despair, calling on our love and sympathy, or attacking us for our indifference and neglect, we may be delighted, we may be repelled. Either way, we have been, to some undetermined degree, seduced. Insofar as we believe that love is woman's topic, and that the need to transform phallocentric literature woman's larger project, the seductiveness of women's writing is almost an inevitable consequence.

Yet does it make sense to look at literature in this rigidly gendered fashion? I began this essay by noticing the way Andrew Marvell invokes, at the climax of his poem, not man's strength and woman's sweetness, but all our strength, all our sweetness. I should add that this gesture moves me deeply; I am very grateful for it. I went on to suggest that Anne Sexton at the outset of her career perceived that self and other may, when they penetrate the invisible veil of fear between them, discover likeness as well as difference. Now I must wonder what I am liable to find when I penetrate the veil of other poets I love, men as well as women.

In her powerful study of Anne Sexton's poetry, Diana George argues both that Sexton's work constitutes a "psychic biography of a gender" and that it tells not merely a gendered but a human story, "not the story only of personal pathology but of a people, a culture, perhaps all cultures, all individuals."[10] This is contradictory only if we are unwilling to suppose that a generic "she" may represent humanity, may probe the universal human condition, in precisely the way the generic "he" has always done. It has been the assumption of our culture that the male subject may always potentially represent mankind, while the female subject—even if she does arrive at a status change from object to subject—is always a special case. Yet the past, as they say, is a prologue. It is by no means destiny, and the marginalization of women's vision in today's literary milieu, which is full of powerful and successful women writers, can no longer be taken for granted. What if we were to *expect* the woman writer to compose in "the first-person universal?" Would we not then *expect* the male writer to write like a woman?

The woman reader, the woman critic, should, I think, be especially alert to the possibility that "female" literary techniques, values, forms, exemplify human universals. For are not writers marginal just as women have been marginal? May not the search of women writers for continuity and community exemplify a larger, though veiled, quest implicit in all literature? Thus it is proper to hypothesize that if we reexamine the long tradition of poetry by men with the light offered us by a poet like Sexton, we may well find more "female" eroticism, more fluidity, more dissolving of self-other boundaries than we had supposed. Certainly with the help of Sexton and other writers like her we may learn to recognize that the quality of relationship between poet and reader is never neutral. A poem is never simply an artifact, is always a transaction, a personal transaction. We do not have a critical vocabulary to describe the many types and kinds of responses poets may demand of their readers, or the many types and kinds of responses readers may bring their poets. But by asking ourselves what happens to us when we read, we might begin to develop one.

A second issue raised by Sexton's seductiveness has to do with the moral resonance of her art and its relation to the real lives of women. There is a sense in which all art affirms what it represents, a sense in which all viewers consent to what is viewed. A few years ago in a session of the Modern Language Association devoted to "Anne Sexton: The Daughter's Seduction," several members of the audience were distressed at my neutral-to-positive use of the term "seduction." We had just heard a paper by Diane Middlebrook on Sexton's play about incest, *Mercy Street*, and a paper by Diana George on the theme of incest in Sexton's poetry and life. We had in our audience women who were or who knew incest victims, and who were appalled at the absence of protest in my, in our, discussion of "seduction." That absence of protest, it must be said, is a defining characteristic of Sexton. Both in *Mercy Street*, where the daughter's adolescent body is the locus of the father's and the great-aunt's selfish desires, and in the lyrics which hint at incestuous desire and/or exploitation by Anne Sexton's father and grandfather, Sexton withholds the anger we wish her to feel, just as she withholds it when she writes of/to her mother, daughter, lover, God. The story Sexton tells about love says, in part, that normative femaleness means falling in love with the father, being seduced by him, being complicit in that seduction, and proceeding to resurrect his deified image in other men. This is a plain enough pattern in Sexton. But it is complicated by the poet's awareness of male failure. The father in all his incarnations is, as Diana George points out, "a god not sufficiently omnipotent, a man not sufficiently humane, a male principle not sufficiently able to accommodate feminine powers and desires. But this ultimate failure is never judged harshly. . . . In the world of Sexton's poetry the men born into their myths are often as helpless and hapless as the women born into theirs."[11] If love, in Sexton, is inextricable from pain, it is also inextricable from compassion. To love is to experience an other as a self in a way that undermines anger, protest, judgment. When Sexton claims to write "with mercy for the greedy," she means by "the greedy" not merely herself but everyone. And it is to this vision that her art is ultimately designed to seduce us.

How is the feminist reader, or any woman who is committed to changing her own life and society, to respond to an art which seems so complicit with female victimization? I believe there is no plain and simple answer to this question. Therefore I would like to suggest a set of possible responses. First, it may well be that for some readers the values of Sexton's erotic poetics will be thoroughly repellent; they will view her neediness and greediness, her insistent vulnerability and excessive generosity with horror; they will not find these qualities in themselves, and they will not be led by her into doing so. Other readers may recognize the Sexton in themselves and want to expel or alter her. Yet others may believe that Sexton's "weird abundance" of erotic openness is or might be normative and benign, and that it is society that needs transforming. It is a conviction of one branch of feminism, at least, that if everyone spoke the "language" of intimacy we would be, as it were, out of the woods. When Adrienne Rich speaks of "the dream of a common language," she speaks for a wide readership which already shares that dream. I do not think Sexton encourages simple imitation—there was never a Sexton cult comparable to the Plath cult—and I think this is because she does not herself glamorize madness, suicide, pain. She represents; she does not endorse, just as she does not condemn. However we respond to her poetry and life, it will be useful to remember that she looked "for uncomplicated hymns / but love has none" ("A Little Uncomplicated Hymn," C.P., p. 152).

NOTES

1. Andrew Marvell, "To His Coy Mistress," Selected Poetry and Prose, ed. Denis Davison (London: George G. Harrap, 1952), pp. 83–84.
2. See Diane Wood Middlebrook, " 'I Tapped My Own Head': The Apprenticeship of Anne Sexton," in Coming to Light: American Women Poets in the Twentieth Century, ed. Diane Wood Middlebrook and Marilyn Yalom (Ann Arbor: University of Michigan Press, 1985), pp. 195–203, to which the following discussion is indebted.
3. Anne Sexton, "Rowing," in The Complete Poems (Boston: Houghton Mifflin, 1981) (hereafter cited in the text as C.P.), p. 417.
4. Anne Sexton, Anne Sexton, A Self-Portrait in Letters (Boston: Houghton Mifflin, 1977) (hereafter cited in the text as Letters), p. 244.
5. Middlebrook, "I Tapped My Own Head," p. 198.
6. Anne Sexton, No Evil Star: Selected Essays, Interviews, and Prose, ed. Steven Colburn (Ann Arbor: University of Michigan Press, 1985), p. 85.
7. Jean Miller, Toward a New Psychology of Women (Boston: Beacon Press, 1976); Nancy Chodorow, The Reproduction of Motherhood (Berkeley: University of California Press, 1979); and Carol Gilligan, In a Different Voice (Cambridge, Mass.: Harvard University Press, 1982) are key texts which share a similar view of women's affiliative characteristics while not agreeing on the value of those characteristics.
8. Luce Irigaray, This Sex Which Is Not One, trans. Catherine Porter with Carolyn Burke (Ithaca: Cornell University Press, 1985), pp. 28–32. See also Judith Kegan Gardiner, "On Female Identity and Writing by Women," Critical Inquiry 8, no. 2 (Winter 1981); Elizabeth Abel, "(E)merging Identities: The Dynamics of Female Friendship in Con-

temporary Fiction by Women," *Signs* 6, no. 3 (Spring 1981); Mary Jacobus, "The Difference of View," in *Women Writing and Writing about Women*, ed. Mary Jacobus (London: Croom Helm, 1979); Rachel Blau DuPlessis, "For the Etruscans," in *New Feminist Criticism*, ed. Elaine Showalter (New York: Pantheon, 1985).

9. Marge Piercy, Preface to *Circles on the Water* (New York: Knopf, 1982), p. xi; Ntozake Shange, *Nappy Edges* (New York: St. Martin's, 1978), p. 57; Denise Levertov, *The Poet in the World* (New York: New Directions, 1973), p. 65; Adrienne Rich, *The Dream of a Common Language* (New York: W. W. Norton, 1978), p. 7. See also Alicia Ostriker, *Stealing the Language: The Emergence of Women's Poetry in America* (Boston: Beacon Press, 1986), pp. 205–9.

10. Diana Hume George, *Oedipus Anne: The Poetry of Anne Sexton* (Urbana: University of Illinois Press, 1987), pp. 24, 181.

11. George, *Oedipus Anne*, p. 25.

Seduced by Witches: Nathaniel Hawthorne's *The Scarlet Letter* in the Context of New England Witchcraft Fictions

> No play is deeper than its witches.
> —Herbert Blau, on Arthur
> Miller's *The Crucible*

In 1692, over a period of three months which has become famous as the New England witch craze, Salem, a little town in Massachusetts, which also happens to be the birthplace of Nathaniel Hawthorne, witnessed twenty-one executions on account of witchcraft. Another 150 accused, including a four-year-old girl, were held in chains for months. Women were not the only ones to die at the gallows. Among the twenty-one victims—seventeen of whom were female—were also two men and two dogs. This happened at a time when the witch craze in Europe was already nearing an end and even in New England the legal proceedings of the witch trials had begun to be challenged.

A century later, this period of the witch-hunts resulted in a flood of adaptations in American nineteenth-century literature whose trail of influence reaches well into the present. I will present a contextual reading of Nathaniel Hawthorne's *The Scarlet Letter*, choosing this historical frame and its fictional adaptations as the horizon of interest. I would like to show that though *The Scarlet Letter* does not, like some of Hawthorne's other texts, directly focus on Salem witchcraft, it can still be seen as deeply influenced by the theme. The central motivation of my reading, however, reaches beyond this frame of literary history in the narrow sense and aims at psychohistorical cultural criticism. Hawthorne's text appears as a cultural critique that does not so much concentrate on a historical period, but on the effects of a cultural internalization of certain patterns of interpretation, in this specific case the witchcraft pattern.[1] This pattern had been formed during the Middle Ages and used as the basis of direct social action until about the end of the seventeenth century, that is, about the time of the Salem trials. At that time, however, the pattern was already about to dissolve gradually, and in the eighteenth century it disappeared from the surface of social semantics.[2] But at the same time, the witchcraft pattern had been internalized and lived on in displaced forms as a part of the political unconscious. To put it more concretely, I am concerned here not with the literary depiction of historical witches, but with an internalized pattern of witchcraft which was effective on a much larger scale in the cultural representation of women in general. The witch appears, in this perspective, as other in the cultural production of female subjectivity. *The Scarlet Letter* offers an outstanding paradigm with which to study this cultural pattern because this romance not only undercuts the literary stereotypes of presenting historical witches, but also reveals the fundamental ambiguities of the witchcraft pattern through its highly overdetermined symbolism.

My analysis proceeds in three steps. First, I outline some aspects of the cultural use of the witchcraft pattern as a mode of interpretation and action. Here I focus on male phantasms of seduction or, more precisely, on fantasies of women seduced by the devil. The witchcraft trials, staged as public spectacles, allowed these fantasies to be acted out collectively. In this context "the gaze"—the public gaze of the Puritan community in its cultural function as well as the fantasmatic cathexis of the witch-gaze or the evil eye—is crucial. In a second step, I point out how conventional literary witchcraft narratives are based on a specific witch stereotype that they then perpetuate by reenacting those very phantasms of seduction in various forms of displacement. Usually these narratives create a romance around a witch not unlike a Freudian "family romance" that allows the phantasms to be acted out in the reading process.[3] Third, I read *The Scarlet Letter* as a narrative that, instead of fictionalizing historical witches, reveals the witch stereotype as a cultural pattern of interpretation used by the New England Puritans against deviant women in general.

Since its cultural formation in the Middle Ages, one of the basic functions of the witchcraft pattern had been to symbolize and interpret the relationship of historical subjects to society and external nature—as, for example, the relationship of a gradually professionalized male system of medicine to women who provided traditional medical care as midwives and healers. But, at the same time, the witchcraft pattern was also an expression of a cultural relationship to inner nature, that is, to specific psychological dispositions or states. Thus it could absorb, for example, the male fear of seductive women on the one hand, and of strong, independent women on the other. In both cases, the pattern was used in the cultural attempt to overcome or subdue nature—be it as wilderness, as native Indian, or as untamed and earthbound women. Moreover, the witchcraft pattern functioned on the basis of a double code, according to which all *visible* signs of the phenomenal world gain their deeper meaning as manifestations of an *invisible* world ruled either by divine or diabolic powers.

An epistemological framework in which the essential meaning of the world is concealed behind its visible representations requires a special code that allows one to read the manifestations of the invisible world. Otherwise, social semantics would cease to function as a reliable system of orientation. In Puritan New England the logic of the "Covenant" provided such a code that allowed one to interpret signs of grace.[4] This code remained, however, highly problematic and unstable. For there was the suspicion that the devil or his allies, the witches, aimed, in their perfidiousness, at outwitting precisely this system of interpretation provided by the covenant. Devils and witches were supposed to do what God did not do: use signs to deceive, and also to seduce. Their cunning was believed to rob the Puritan search for redemption of its reliability, confronting it with a semantics of deceit and a rhetoric of seduction. Therefore the invisible diabolic world was supposed to have its own code with its own visible and readable symbolic objects and signs of witchcraft. Be it the flight on the broomstick or the suspended gait, tearlessness or the evil eye, the repertoire of witch attributes and signs of the witch code were precisely delineated. They were, in other words, perceived as visible signs of the invisible world, and accordingly they could be used to bring this world under control by persecuting the carriers of the signs. Thus, the signs of the witch code were not merely seen as the stereotypes transmitted by deranged imagination, but also as symbolic vehicles used to control the invisible world through the coding of visible objects. Thus a negative fixation on the gaze evolved, and in Puritan New England this fixation was reinforced even more by the Calvinistic search for signs of redemption. The public sphere was organized according to an overall cultural attempt to expose the invisible to the gaze. In addition to the precise coding of visible manifestations of witchcraft, the community also established ritualistic forms of publicly exposed punishment in which bodies were inscribed with visible symbols of offences against the divine order. The gaze as medium of interpretation became a guarantor, albeit an ambivalent one, of a reality that was actually invisible.

Accordingly, the witchcraft trials and executions were staged as institutionalized visual spectacles in which the community actively participated. In Puritan New England, the function of these spectacles was even enhanced by the fact that they were the only allowed form of festive gathering. Those members of the community who believed themselves to be bewitched by the accused performed their symptoms of affliction under the community's gaze. Their ecstatic convulsions, betraying an erotic semantics of the body carried to the brink of insanity, visually demonstrated the art of witchcraft through encoded gestures of demonic possession. The bewitched imitated and outdid the gestures displayed by the alleged witches. If the latter, for example, crossed their fingers while pleading innocent, the victims would throw themselves immediately to the floor with splayed arms and spastic movements. The body became the medium of an interaction, enacting a spectacle of seduction where the gestures devalued the spoken word, that is, the affirmations of innocence. The culturally institutionalized body-language became a visual (dis-)play which split off from and devalued spoken language. Whatever the alleged witches would say, the community would interpret through a reading of their bodies.

These trials gave the accused virtually no chance not to assume the role of a witch. The puritanical cleric George Burroughs claimed during his own trial, for example, that in fact one had to be a witch to prove that one wasn't one. He referred to the split in social semantics and the paradox inherent in the historical "reality" of witches. The most striking example was that one had to admit to being a witch in order not to hang as one. In this paradoxical language game, any plea of innocence was construed as an indication of firm adherence to the devil's covenant. As a sign of repentance, however, official admission could prevent a death sentence. In both cases the reality of witchcraft was a given. The "witch" herself had, in fact, been forced to cooperate actively in establishing a social consensus.

The witchcraft pattern served therefore, in the historical context of the Salem trials, among other things, to publicly reaffirm the reality of witchcraft, which had long since become precarious. On a more subtle level, however, the public trials staged an erotic spectacle of seduction and punishment, acted out collectively on the basis of a tacit knowledge about the highly ambivalent status of the witch in the context of the Puritan ethics. On this basis, then, a concrete social practice could develop which lent a tangible symbolic framework to the battle between the internal and external attacks on Puritan beliefs.

In the flourishing literary discovery of witchcraft as a favorite Gothic and romantic theme in nineteenth-century New England literature, this historical drama of the Salem witchcraft period revealed itself as an exotic heritage whose ambivalence could be reenacted under new historical and epistemological premises. One of the crucial aesthetic challenges lay in the fact that the secular perception of what has to be perceived as historical reality had changed in the meantime. In retrospect, only the belief in witchcraft and the witch craze were considered real. In contrast, the invisible world and all its manifestations were seen, according to the new cultural code, as imaginary projections of the historical protagonists. The retrospective view added its own interpretation to the concurrent one and thus doubled the already double-edged semantics of witchcraft.

There is an abundant corpus of fictional literature which deals explicitly or implicitly with New England witchcraft. The roughly forty works which are direct literary renditions of the Salem events exceed the even more narrow scope of Gothic literature. The most important ones range from Lydia Maria Child's *The Rebels: or Boston before the Revolution* (1825); John Neal's *Rachel Dyer* (1828); Whittier's *Legends of New England* (1831); Mary Lyford, *The Salem Belle: A Tale of Love and Witchcraft in 1692* (1842); John W. De Forest's *Witching Times* (1857); Longfellow's *New England Tragedies* (1868); Caroline Derby's *Salem* (1874); Pauline B. Mackie, *Ye lyttle Salem Maide: Story of Witchcraft* (1898); Amelia E. Barr, *The Black Shilling* (1903); Marvin Dana, *A Puritan Witch* (1903); L. F. Madison, *Maid of Salem Towne* (1906); Henry Peterson, *Dulcible: A Tale of Old Salem* (1907); Esther Forbes, *Mirror of Witches* (1928); up to Arthur Miller's *The Crucible* (1952).[5] It seems to me that they all fail to solve aesthetically the crucial problem of the period, namely that, retrospectively, the status of what was considered to be reality or imagination had changed. But this failure is in itself highly significant, because it reveals the persistence of the seductive power of the witch as much as the desire for "displaced" witch-hunts. Although the historical interest in the witch craze is central to these texts, their precarious proximity to melodrama and to the Gothic novel allows one to surmise that they are, in fact, whetting quite a different reading appetite, which thrives less on the historical interest than on the witch as a feared but seductive object of desire. The historical witch had already been persecuted on the basis of a witch stereotype; in order to deal with this phenomenon aesthetically, the stereotype had to be undermined. Otherwise it would be reenacted under a fictional guise.

It is no coincidence that the literary interest in witchcraft arose in America almost simultaneously with the demand for a "genuine American" literature. Aesthetically, this demand remained, however, oriented toward the English model. Walter Scott had already discovered the thematic reservoir with which to realize this demand: the historical past, on the one hand, and the miraculous, on the other. Significantly this discovery was made along the path of the Gothic novel. The New England witchcraft episode seemed to meet this double interest in the historical and the miraculous ideally, endowing America with its own piece of a belated Middle Ages that could simultaneously satisfy the hunger for history and the desire for the supernatural. Witchcraft literature is, in fact, nostalgic about this past inasmuch as it reenacts the witch stereotype and its inherent pattern of seduction and punishment on the basis of a romantic, or even more narrowly Gothic, imagination of femininity.

Nonetheless, this promising historical material resists in a peculiar way aesthetic treatment in the narrower sense. Even the literary fictionalizations of witchcraft as a historical theme draw on the Gothic imagination as their basic source of aesthetic effect. The Gothic novel's romantic interest in the occult, however, poses a problem when it interferes with the presentation of witchcraft as a historical event, since the heritage of the Enlightenment obliges one to present the witches as innocent victims, thus setting a dynamic force in motion that is aimed at the demystification of the occult. Aesthetically, historical witchcraft fictions are torn between two genres and desires: the Gothic novel and historical fiction. Instead of being one or the other, they are, in most cases, a literary compromise with a built-in disappointment. Their dilemma is that they cannot afford witches historically or ethically, and yet are aesthetically dependent on them.

The aesthetic compromise of literary witchcraft narratives is usually based upon the age-old ambivalence toward the witch as a symbolic representation of the female—an ambivalence that can be traced throughout the historical transformations of the witchcraft pattern in the split cultural language game. After the supernatural lost its claim to reality status in the wake of the Enlightenment, one could assume that social and cultural activities would no longer be based on the witchcraft pattern. This was true, however, only insofar as this pattern vanished from the surface of public discourse.

Far from losing its symbolic value, the witchcraft pattern now became interiorized and would henceforth form part of the political
unconscious. This process of cultural interiorization of the witchcraft pattern can be seen as a specific form of what the psychohisto-
rian Norbert Elias describes on a larger scale as the gradual cultural
transformation of outer into inner restrictions.[6]

When, about 130 years after its dismissal as a pattern of sociocultural organization and interpretation, the witchcraft pattern re-
emerged in the guise of fiction, this internalization had already been
achieved. Hence the fictional witchcraft literature had to take the
changed cultural status of the witch into account. The aesthetic experience had to allow, in other words, a deliberate and artful return of
the repressed political unconscious. Moreover, the former repression
had to be worked through aesthetically, in order to avoid a simple reenactment of the old pattern. The belief in witches was now in need
of interpretation as an ideological construct. Writers and historians
alike focused on socioeconomic and psychological motives which,
at the time of the witch craze, had been withheld from public consciousness. As indicated above, the emergence of a specialized male
medical system was one of the socioeconomic factors relevant here,
whereas the psychological factors were all connected with deeply
rooted fears of women. Retrospectively, however, one can also see
how these very motives already formed the basis of a tacit knowledge
enacted in the tacit language games of the witch trials. Both historical and fictional witchcraft narratives thus drew their resources
from attempts to reconstruct or act upon the presumed political unconscious of earlier times. These narratives perceived behind the
witchcraft pattern a linguistic structure of double meaning, and a
divided sociocultural language game. They assumed, in other words,
that a cultural motivation for the persecution of witches lay behind
the official cultural code of the time. Accordingly, the historical or
aesthetic function of these narratives lies in recuperating for the
realm of public discourse and communication parts of what was repressed in the past. How they attempt this recuperation varies of
course greatly from text to text. While the historical witchcraft narratives have to "rationalize the irrational," the fictional texts in a
romantic countermotion to the Enlightenment discover in this very
irrationality potential for aesthetic and psychological effects.

The aesthetic use of the irrational or the miraculous produces,
however, problems of a particular nature for the witchcraft fictions.
Along with and partly as a reaction to the cultural desymbolization
and interiorization of the witchcraft pattern in the wake of the En-

lightenment, phantasms of the witch survived in cultural cliches and stereotypes which absorbed the repressed irrational desires and fears connected with the witchcraft pattern.[7] Fictional witchcraft narratives tend to draw their effect from reviving or acting out such phantasms. Thus, although the culturally tacit and split language game that allowed for the witch craze is the object of these fictional narratives, the split in the language game remains intact in the aesthetic recuperations. This can be illustrated by retracing a basic scheme in these texts.

Most striking is the reevaluation of values which stems partly from Enlightenment and partly from romantic values. Women who during the actual witch-hunts were supposed to have been seduced by or to have sold themselves to the devil, now became, from a retrospective point of view, victims of an age blinded by the witch craze. They now develop uncensored the erotic charm of their seductive play, formerly considered to be a sign of their sinful nature. These women center a plot whose historical roots are communicated through their fictionalized relationship with specific historical characters.

To take a classic example, in John Neal's *Rachel Dyer*, Rachel is a strong, mysterious, and attractive woman, who nevertheless carries a stigma considered one of the capital signs of an alliance with the devil: a deformed body. Her sister, Elizabeth, on the other hand, is portrayed as a beautiful, fragile child-woman. Both women love the male hero of the novel, the Reverend George Burroughs, historically one of the two men put to death during the Salem trials. Burroughs symbolizes, in Neal's novel, the other of colonial history. Son of an English Quaker woman and a native Indian, he represents heretic belief and native Indian devil-worship in one person. As the Byronic hero of a witchcraft romance, he also acts as an enlightened skeptic in his public defense of the two Dyer sisters. He finally dies at the gallows, together with Rachel, while Elizabeth is saved. A dense network of historical allusions forms part of an intertextual web of family relationships between the historical figures used as characters in the New England witchcraft fictions. Rachel and Elizabeth Dyer, for example, are daughters of the legendary Mary Dyer who, before her execution, uttered the curse on the Salem judges and their descendants to which Nathaniel Hawthorne refers in his introduction to *The Scarlet Letter*. Moreover, on her way to the gallows, Mary Dyer was accompanied by Ann Hutchinson, the heretic who founded the Antinomian sect. Ann Hutchinson, in turn, plays a crucial role in *The Scarlet Letter*. Thus, the two Dyer sisters, and later

Hester Prynne, are linked to the first sectarian movement which offered women an alternative to the misogyny and sexual repression of Puritan orthodoxy, and which could therefore recruit large circles of women.

In general, the stereotypes underlying the relationships between the protagonists in the New England witchcraft fictions activate, beneath the surface of the fictionalized historical event, phantasms of the witch. The network of those relationships that are in all the texts dominated by familial organization reveal fantasies of a wish-family that are strikingly similar to those in the Freudian family romance. The witch is the center of desire in these fictional elective families, or, more precisely, it is always one of two witch types: the beautiful wild witch (who will become the model for Hester Prynne) or the child-woman witch (a classic model is Doll Bilby in Esther Forbes's *A Mirror for Witches*, about whom the narrator says that she "with more than feminine perversity preferred a Demon to a Mortal Lover," and who destroys all the men who fall prey to the magic of her seduction). Significantly, both stereotypes underlying the witchcraft pattern are complementary male stereotypes of female seducers. A third type of witch—the most common historical victim—may, in the fictional texts, occupy only the position of a peripheral figure: the old or deformed witch possessing magic powers, who comes to represent, in fact, the inverse of seduction.

In addition to these pure types, we find, of course, female characters who are condensations of different types, as, for example, Rachel Dyer, who is a condensation of the strong, mysterious witch and the deformed witch. In contrast to the third type of the old or deformed witch, the seductive types of women, stigmatized as witches and desired by the male protagonists, are at the same time classified as antagonists to the so-called normal woman. The latter had now, in turn, to assume the negative feminine attributes that had been formative for the witch stereotype. Note the very significant displacement in these fictional texts: they reevaluate the historical witches by romanticizing the two seductive types, while at the same time displacing the pattern of the third and nonseductive witch-type onto the normal woman. Be it as the frigid or infertile wife, prototype of antiseduction, or as the jealous mother, the normal woman is unwittingly stylized as the affective driving force behind the witch craze. Thus she is used not only to reproduce the old pattern of male fear of women, but also to serve as a scapegoat who can absorb the displaced guilt stemming from the witch craze.

We can find this schema even in Arthur Miller's *The Crucible*, which was not conceived as a romantic adaptation of the historical material, but as an historical projection of the McCarthy era. Miller's drama relies much more on the documented witchcraft trials than do the earlier adaptations. Witchcraft itself is presented under a rationalizing perspective: the "bewitched" young girls suffer from adolescent hysteria; behind the accusations lie dramas of jealousy and revenge as well as political or economical interests. All the more interesting is the fact that the classic witch family romance remains intact. The play's hero is the historical John Proctor, whose identity is threatened by two women: by his wife Elizabeth, who is, of course, portrayed as frigid, and by her opponent, Abigail Williams, a nymph who seduces Proctor and blackmails his wife as a witch. Thus the classic phantasms underlying the witchcraft pattern are preserved: the nymph represents the seductive child-woman witch; the hysterical woman is a descendant of the possessed woman; and the frigid wife represents a contrasting social paradigm of antiseduction, itself a threat to masculinity. While Miller's play is supposed to show that there are no witches, but only witch hysteria, it also shows, if read against the grain, how the phantasms that underlie the witchcraft pattern have survived as phantasms of male fear and desire.

It is precisely this witch family romance that, in the fictional witchcraft narratives, functions as a literary compromise, making the old witch phantasms aesthetically palatable. Even if the romanticized (or, as in Miller, "hystericized") witches function, in one way, as a demystification of the historical witches, their aesthetic effect is drawn from the phantasm of the desirable but also threatening witch who, because of her seductive powers, retains an aura of the supernatural, even in a disenchanted world. Since, moreover, the distribution of negative and positive witch phantasms is preserved by stigmatizing the normal woman and by thus maintaining the two polar evaluations of female types, these texts do not overcome the witchcraft pattern; they only achieve an inversion of the manifest and the latent cultural codification of the witch. If in the historical context the cultural cathexis of the witchcraft pattern was governed for the most part by the fear of the witch, the literary texts now invert this cathexis by focusing on the complementary fantasies and desires that had been concealed in the historical context. Nevertheless, the old fear lurks beneath the surface, since even after the pattern of desire and seduction has surfaced, the men who are the objects of seduction perish along with their objects of desire. To make matters worse, the driving force seen behind the destruction of the male protagonists is now the old witch disguised as an ordinary woman.

The aesthetic and psychohistorical weakness of this type of fictional witchcraft narrative, the witch-family romance, rests on the fact that it reevaluates the witchcraft pattern, yet leaves its underlying phantasms intact. Fixed cultural cliches thus find literary transposition.

This is the specific context in which I read Nathaniel Hawthorne. Even if his texts do not belong to the direct renditions of the Salem events, seduction in New England Puritanism is one of his prominent themes; and he often treats his subject by using an aura of witchcraft, or by reflecting on the internalization of a witchcraft pattern. As I am less concerned here with the fictional representation of historical material than with the literary reproduction of a witchcraft pattern, it turns out that those of Hawthorne's texts in which witchcraft as such is displaced from the center of the plot are the most interesting. *The Scarlet Letter* seems to me paradigmatic not only in exposing the witchcraft pattern in a displaced context, but also in displaying devices that undercut its aesthetic reproduction. In "The Custom-House," his introduction to *The Scarlet Letter*, Hawthorne presents himself as the descendant of two notorious persecutors of witches and heretics, William and John Hathorne. The latter is said to have been the harshest judge of the Salem trials. Nathaniel Hawthorne declares himself to be superstitious enough to see his fictional dealings with witchcraft as an answer to the curse which the famous heretic Mary Dyer leveled against the Hathorne family. It is to the credit of Hawthorne that he did not give us yet another spectacular dramatization of the witch craze, but a fictional analysis of the witchcraft pattern in a broader framework not limited to the empirical witch. In *The Scarlet Letter*, historical witchcraft is only the background for the witch stereotype. It is this stereotype that becomes the actual subject of the novel.

Hester Prynne, the protagonist, is indicted not as a witch, but as an adulteress. The prominent drama of seduction has been displaced from a supernatural to a secular stage. Even so, the basic traits of the stereotype remain obvious. At the onset of the novel, Hester is established as an outcast woman. The scene is the Puritan performance of public punishment. Exposed to the gaze of the collected community, Hester stands at the pillory bearing both emblems of her disgrace: sewn to her dress the scarlet letter *A* for adulteress, and in her arms her illegitimate daughter, Pearl. Since Hester does not name the father, the Reverend Arthur Dimmesdale, the parishioners suspect a diabolic paternity. Hester's exposure to the humiliation of the public gaze coincides with the arrival of her husband, who had been presumed dead after his disappearance, and who, through secret gestures, now commits Hester to silence about his identity. The network of family and love relationships is thus concealed from the public but revealed to the reader—a device that creates a kind of complicity with Hester, who is the only one to know all the threads of the network. Following this scene, the reader becomes witness to a drama of revenge which could—as far as the plot itself is concerned—easily occur in a Gothic novel. In silent revenge, Hester's husband, a doctor with the allegorical name of Chillingworth, himself suspected of witchcraft because of his affiliations with native Indians and their use of herbal plants, moves into Dimmesdale's house under the pretense of investigating the reverend's "heart problems."[8] Dimmesdale will perish under Chillingworth's penetrating gaze because he has concealed his guilt from the community. In contrast, Hester lives with Pearl at the edge of town and learns to overcome the role which the stigmatic *A* has imposed on her by changing its symbolic cathexis not only for herself but also for the community.

Like the conventional witchcraft narratives of the time, Hawthorne's novel is based on the scheme of a complicated family romance. Not only are the entanglements of family and love relationships similar to those in a witchcraft narrative, but there are also secular representations of the three types of witches which together form the witchcraft pattern. Apart from Hester, who corresponds to the image of the beautiful, wild witch, her daughter Pearl is stylized as the child-woman witch. The third type of the old and ugly witch is represented by Ann Hibbins, a peripheral character modeled after one of the historical witches who was hanged for witchcraft in Salem in the year 1656. However, while the conventional witch-family romance uses the witch to seduce the reader into acting out the passions that she represents, Hawthorne reveals these passions to be the result of the repressed desire which has historically underlain the witchcraft pattern. The text points to a social semantics in which the stereotype of the witch transmits cultural norms of femininity via the repression of sensuality and desire. In so doing, *The Scarlet Letter* foregrounds the dominance of the gaze in the historical formation of the witchcraft pattern.

The gaze, in fact, becomes the organizing principle for the whole text: as puritanical gaze, it steers the dynamics of the narration; as the gaze of the narrator, it inserts a normative perspective to guide the reader's response. Thematically, the gaze becomes a medium of social formation, be it through the dynamics of seductive or of punitive exposure to the gaze, or even—as in Hester's interaction with the community—through a dialectic of seduction and punishment.

Finally, as aesthetic device, the gaze is used as metaphoric visual-
ization, as an exposure of images to the gaze of the reader. All the
central symbols in the book are visual images derived from the puritanical gaze-mediated code. The text presents the gaze of the scopo-
philic community, fixed on the marked woman and her child, as a
social ritual staged in order to establish the power of social consensus via visual interactions. The letter *A*, which Hester has to bear
her entire life, is a visible codification of her body. Under the Puritan
gaze it becomes the vehicle of a new identity; and Hester is deindi-
vidualized into a representation of sin until she learns to deallegorize
and resemanticize the symbol *A*.

Hester's internalization of the social gaze becomes identity-
forming for her daughter. Pearl does not see herself mirrored in the
eyes of her mother but in the golden reflection of the scarlet *A*:

> The very first thing which she had noticed, in her life, was—what?—not
> the mother's smile, responding to it, as other babies do, by that faint,
> embryo smile of the little mouth. . . . But that first object of which Pearl
> seemed to become aware was—shall we say it?—the scarlet letter on
> Hester's bosom! One day, as her mother stooped over the cradle, the
> infant's eyes had been caught by the glimmering of the gold embroidery
> about the letter. (Pp. 110f.)

As Pearl's mirror stage[9] of psychological development is determined by the scarlet letter, she will have internalized its fantasmatic
cultural significance, the witchcraft pattern, long before she grows
up to understand its codified meaning. Hester reinforces this pattern
through her interactions with her daughter. In keeping with current
superstitions of the time, Hester does not see herself mirrored in the
eyes of her daughter. Instead she sees Dimmesdale's image, which as
in a dream, is very tellingly condensed with the image of the devil:

> Once, this freakish, elfish cast came into the child's eyes, while Hester
> was looking at her own image in them . . . suddenly . . . she fancied
> that she beheld, not her own miniature portrait, but another face in the
> small black mirror of Pearl's eye. It was a face, fiend-like, full of smiling
> malice, yet bearing the semblance of features that she had known full
> well, though seldom with a smile, and never with a malice, in them.
> It was as if an evil spirit possessed the child, and had just then peeped
> forth in mockery. Many a time afterwards had Hester been tortured,
> though less vividly, by the same illusion. (P. 120)

This reflection not only reveals that Hester herself has unconsciously linked her own stigma to the witchcraft pattern, but also
shows that she transfers it to her own daughter. Pearl develops as an

elfin, witchlike girl, persecuted by the suspicious gaze of the community as much as of her mother, who fears in the daughter the
stigma she herself bears. With these problems, the text introduces
a dimension which leads out of the historical polarization of supernatural reality and sensual manifestation: this new dimension is the
sociopsychological genesis of an identity formed by the witch stereotype. This process is mediated by the gaze; and this gaze condenses
the psychological function of the mirroring process between mother
and daughter with the social function of the gaze in the Puritan
cultural code. Pearl's gaze has carried the stigma of "a born outcast" (p. 117) since her early infancy. "It was a look so intelligent,
yet inexplicable, so perverse, sometimes so malicious, but generally
accompanied by a wild flow of spirits, that Hester could not help
questioning, at such moments, whether Pearl was a human child"
(p. 116).

When Pearl screams as a reaction to being persecuted by the
other children, the narrator, who in another context openly talks
about "Pearl's witchcraft" (p. 118), describes her "shrill, incoherent
exclamations that made her mother tremble, because they had so
much the sound of a witch's anathemas in some unknown tongue"
(pp. 117f.). So it is Pearl, more than Hester, who has to embody the
fantasmatic cathexis of the scarlet A—to a point that even the towns-
people consider her as "a demon offspring" (p. 122). Pearl clearly
assumes and spitefully plays the role of a witch-child whenever she
communicates about her missing father or about the scarlet A which,
for her, also symbolizes the absent father. The text leaves no doubt,
however, that this role is assumed in a collusion between mother
and daughter. The mother makes the child into a mirror reflection of
her own fears, a literal embodiment of the witch stigma: "It was the
scarlet letter in another form; the scarlet letter endowed with life!
The mother herself—as if the red ignominy were so deeply scorched
into her brain, that all her conceptions assumed its form—had care-
fully wrought out the similitude; lavishing many hours of morbid
ingenuity, to create an analogy between the object of her affection,
and the emblem of her guilt and torture" (p. 125).

Thus, the crucial irony in Pearl's stigmatization lies in the fact
that Hester is the active agent who unconsciously transfers to her
daughter what she herself tries consciously to control. For in her
relationship to herself Hester uses the social stigma against itself
by inverting its ambivalent social cathexis. Decisive for Hester's lib-
eration from the witch stereotype is the ambivalent function of the
letter A and Hester's use of its double symbolic potential, and hence

its reversibility.[10] While the exteriority and physical visibility of the linguistic sign affixed to the body is supposed to codify this body for the gaze, it also enables Hester to find a partial redemption by inverting its codified cultural meaning. As soon as Hester learns to understand the letter as carrier of the Puritan code rather than as emblem of disgrace she can distance herself from this code and finally even develop her own free heterodox philosophy.

This process, experienced as a new realization of her forcefully derealized personality,[11] also reflects back on her social existence. What saves Hester as a person is the *A* as letter, because she can reverse its codified meaning. She does this by using all its ambivalence. From the outset she not only bears it as an emblem of shame but also wears it proudly as an item of seduction. She achieves this through her artful embroidery, which reworks the letter into a brilliant jewel. This in itself is a spiteful violation of the Puritan sumptuary laws that restricted any rich and decorative display:

> On the breast of her gown, in fine red cloth, surrounded with an elaborate embroidery and fantastic flourishes of gold thread, appeared the letter A. It was so artistically done, and with so much fertility and gorgeous luxuriance of fancy, that it had all the effect of a last and fitting decoration to the apparel which she wore; and which was of a splendor in accordance with the taste of the age, but greatly beyond what was allowed by the sumptuary regulations of the colony. (P. 80)

By embroidering her stigma as a seductive jewel "which drew all eyes" (p. 81), she plays with the duplicity within the Puritan law, thus influencing the imaginary cathexis of the letter by the community, while at the same time removing herself beyond its reach. The scarlet letter thus "had the effect of a spell, taking her out of the ordinary relations with humanity, and enclosing her in a sphere by herself" (p. 81). She uses the silence imposed on her by law in the same way: she sustains it with such exotic grace that it envelops her in an aura of mystical saintliness. The emptiness of both, sign and silence, seduces the community into filling it with projections of their own fears and desires. Thus Hester uses both the ambivalence of the letter's symbolic potential and the emptiness of her proud silence to assimilate the witch to her cultural counterpart: the image of the saint. She supports this assimilation by performing the original social activities of the historical witch as healer, midwife, or advisor to suffering women. The mutual exclusiveness and irreconcilability of opposites may be sublated in the letter *A*. Witch or saint, adulteress or angel—even the community is drawn into the current of its own phantasms and puzzles over the true meaning of the letter. As the title suggests, a story is mediated through a letter, and the ambiguity of this letter illuminates the ambivalence of the Puritan code. Since the *A* can carry meanings that are socially accepted as well as others that are rejected, one could even say that the letter reflects the split Puritan language game. Thus it allows the witchcraft pattern to appear in its ambivalent double-edgedness.

Already in Hawthorne's autobiographical satire, "The Custom House," which introduces the romance, the red embroidered *A*, unearthed from a file cabinet, assumes a dual function. On the one hand, as a historical relic, it insures authenticity; on the other hand, it functions as a "magic object," making its finder feel as though it were burned into his skin. The visionary experience of the narrator thus evokes the continued efficacy of the magic object and hence of the old stereotypes some two hundred years after it had been in use.

This dual function of the letter as a historical relic and a magical object is rooted in the narrator's notion of history. Influenced by the aesthetic of the Transcendentalists, Hawthorne's historical consciousness is decidedly subjective; he cherishes the romantic notion of liberating the real from the distortions of the factual. The narrator's voice incorporates this notion of aesthetics. His personal insertions not only mediate diachronically between the different perspectives of the seventeenth and nineteenth centuries, but also create synchronic references which remain implicit in the plot.

This strategy of synchronic mediation is further elaborated in the many references throughout the text to the heretic Ann Hutchinson, whose story mirrors Hester's fate on a more political level.[12] Female heretics like Ann Hutchinson can be seen as the philosophical sisters of witches, judged and persecuted on the basis of the very same stereotypes. Like Hester Prynne, Ann Hutchinson was in the Boston jail, where a rosebush is said to have "sprung up under the footsteps of the sainted Ann Hutchinson, as she entered the prison-door" (p. 76). Like Hester she had a decisive influence on a leading cleric, John Cotton, who publicly disavowed her—as Dimmesdale disavows Hester. Significantly, in order to describe Ann Hutchinson's heretical writings, the witchcraft specialist Cotton Mather used the metaphor of an illegitimate child of orthodox belief begotten by the devil. These heretical writings, in turn, mirror Hester's secret philosophy in the historical context of protest movements against orthodox Puritanism. Unlike Ann Hutchinson, Hester does not openly protest; the narrator attributes this silence to the existence of Pearl. "Yet, had little Pearl never come to her from the spiritual world, it might have been far otherwise. Then, she might have come down to us in history, hand in hand with Ann Hutchinson, as the foundress of a religious sect. She might, in one of her phases, have been a prophetess. She might, and not improbably would, have suffered death from the stern tribunals of the period, for attempting to undermine the foundations of the Puritan establishment" (p. 183).

As these foundations are sternly patriarchal and misogynist, Hester's secret heresy is, at its core, a feminist heresy, which the narrator describes by inserting his own antifeminist bias:

> The whole system of society is to be torn down, and built up anew. Then, the very nature of the opposite sex, or its long hereditary habit, which has become like nature, is to be essentially modified, before woman can be allowed to assume what seems a fair and suitable position. Finally, all other difficulties being obviated, woman cannot take advantage of these preliminary reforms, until she herself shall have undergone a still mightier change; in which, perhaps, the ethereal essence, wherein she has her truest life, will be found to have evaporated. (P. 184)

What is for Hester a necessary condition to make "existence worth accepting" for women is for the narrator an evaporation of woman's "ethereal essence." A true woman, then, is in this view neither witch nor heretic. Hester's secret affinities to both of these roles are rejected as deviations. Again it is Pearl who seems to prevent Hester from choosing the other alternative for dealing with her social stigma: the active assumption of the witch role. Ironically the historical witch Ann Hibbins, Governor Bellingham's sister, brings this alternative into play while addressing Hester after her encounter with the governor:

> "Wilt thou go with us to-night? There will be a merry company in the forest; and I wellnigh promised the Black man that comely Hester Prynne should make one."
>
> "Make my excuse to him, so please you!" answered Hester, with a triumphant smile. "I must tarry at home, and keep watch over my little Pearl. Had they taken her from me, I would willingly have gone with thee into the forest, and signed my name in the Black Man's book too, and that with mine own blood!" (P. 139)

The fact that Hester is mirrored by two historical women who evoke, in their function as mythological figures, two rejected possibilities of dealing with social stigma, adds to the already overdetermined function of the letter A. Ann Hibbins embodies the stereotype of the aged witch who tries to use Hester's stigma, the scarlet letter

A, as an item to seduce Hester to join the covenant with the devil. Ann Hutchinson, on the other hand, persecuted as a heretic and venerated as a saint, embodies the witch stereotype as much as its social counterpart, the stereotype of the angel. Adulteress or angel, witch or saint, Ann Hibbins or Ann Hutchinson—all of these cultural stereotypes stem from the secularization of mythologies and are cited in the text to mirror Hester, albeit only in order to lend her psychological depth in contrast to the historical cliche.

Along with the historical witch stereotype, the text also undermines conventional forms of literary revitalization. The characters as well as the plot are not only staged as reflections of historical figures and events; they function as well as intertextual quotations of characters from the Gothic novel. Behind the individual makeup of the characters, there is always an ironical quotation of the genre. Be it Hester as the dark, wild beauty, Dimmesdale as the hero who is seduced by her, or even Chillingworth as the classic villain, they all echo their Gothic counterparts. Ann Hibbins imbues this device with traces of a carnivalesque parody of history. The historical witch is transfigured into an ironic quotation of the literary stereotype of the old witch. By using the conventional cliches of the code of witchcraft, she tries to seduce Hester to participate in the Witches' Sabbath or to inscribe her name in the Black Book. Thus the woman who, in the historical context, was executed as a witch, is ironically used, in *The Scarlet Letter*, as a character who provides comic relief for the tragic development of the plot. The narrator's irony leaves it up to the reader to decide the undecidable, namely whether to read Hester's encounters with Ann Hibbins as a quotation of historical reality, as a parable, or as a historical allegory. Decisive for the strategies guiding aesthetic response is the fact that it is precisely the historical witch who appears as the ironic quotation of the witch stereotype.

The literary revitalization of the witchcraft pattern in *The Scarlet Letter* has to be evaluated in light of all these mirroring effects. While the conventional witchcraft narratives only reverse the ambivalent cathexis of the witch stereotype, *The Scarlet Letter* uses the same ambivalence as a field of tension. While Hester emancipates herself from the stigma which the community has imposed on her, she at the same time reveals that the cultural witchcraft pattern is restricted neither to historical witches nor to the romanticized witches in literary witchcraft narratives. Precisely because she is never explicitly accused of being a witch, it becomes all the more clear how the pattern has been culturally internalized, surviving as part of the political unconscious in the social stigmatization of certain types of women whose bodies and behavior might nourish male phantasms of the witch.

The different modes of treating the witch stereotype in *The Scarlet Letter* with respect to the different female characters—Hester, Pearl, Ann Hutchinson, and Ann Hibbins—produce a common effect: the witch has lost her ontological status and is, instead, seen as a cultural symbol. At this point the reality status of the witch regains a new and fundamental ambiguity. The question whether the allusions to witchcraft in Hawthorne's text are staged as fictional reality or as the parabolic evocation of a past witchcraft craze ultimately misses the point. The text focuses instead on the more important dimension of the flexibility and hence the continuous psychosocial efficacy of the witchcraft pattern which reaches far beyond the historical context in which the existence of witches was to be "empirically" tested. In his fictitious romance, Hawthorne exposes the roots of the historical ambivalence of the witch stereotype which eventually led to its reevaluation, to the disappearance of the witchcraft pattern from the public social practice and discourse, but at the same time also to its continuing fantasmatic effects.

There is one further device with which Hawthorne takes into account the changing ways in which the witchcraft pattern is effective: it is the polarization between Hester and the narrator.[13] Even though the latter clearly exposes the cruelty and destructiveness of the Puritan moral law, and even though his allusions to witchcraft are mediated by ironic distance, he nevertheless constantly chastises Hester's development, and especially her own emancipation from the witchcraft pattern as a deviation from her womanhood.

> There seemed to be no longer any thing in Hester's face for Love to dwell upon; nothing in Hester's form, though majestic and statue-like, that Passion would ever dream of clasping in its embrace; nothing in Hester's bosom, to make it ever again the pillow of Affection. Some attribute had departed from her, the permanence of which had been essential to keep her a woman. Such is frequently the fate, and such the stern development, of the feminine character and person, when the woman has encountered, and lived through, an experience of peculiar severity. (P. 182)

There is a significant ambivalence in the narrator's romantic imagination of women which leads him to describe Hester's emancipation as a loss of femininity. "She who has once been woman, and ceased to be so" (p. 182) is supposed to have lost her womanhood because "her life had turned, in a great measure, from passion and feeling, to thought" (p. 182). The seventeenth-century Puritans persecuted women for passion as well as for thought. (Reading, for example, was brought up in several of the Salem trials as an indication that a woman stood under the influence of the devil.) The nineteenth-century Puritan narrator frowns upon woman's thought while romanticizing her passion. And yet, even with respect to the latter, he retains some ambivalence. When Hester manages to win over the community "with a woman's strength" (p. 180), the narrator comments: "society was inclined to show its former victim a more benign countenance than she cared to be favored with, or, perchance, than she deserved" (p. 180f.).

The reason why she does not deserve, in the narrator's eyes, the benevolent gaze of the community is Hester's secretly developed anti-Puritan intellect, which, as he rightly thinks, his Puritan forefathers "would have held to be a deadlier crime than that stigmatized by the scarlet letter" (p. 183). Thus the narrator himself pays his own tribute to the split language game of the Puritan code. This narrator, with his unconcealed hatred of the rigidity of Puritanism but with his unresolved ambivalence toward Puritan norms, suggests that Hester's secret affinities with witches or heretics like Ann Hutchinson are a deviation not only from Puritan belief but also from the "nature of womankind." Yet it is precisely those attributes condemned by the narrator which make for the strength of Hester as a literary character. The latter by far outweighs whatever weight the narrator's morality can gain in guiding the readers' responses. Thus Hester's portrayal as a literary character reenacts a pattern of seduction for the community of readers very much similar to the one Hester herself uses to change the attitude of the Puritan community toward her. As she seduced the community into a reevaluation of her social role, so the reader is seduced to side with her against the morality of the narrator. Hester challenges not only the image of the Puritan woman both of the seventeenth and the nineteenth centuries, but also the norms of a romantic imagination of femininity. The aesthetic ambiguity that arises from the polarization of an unconventional female character portrayed and judged by a conventional narrator is clearly resolved in Hester's favor—all the more so since the narrator's very moralizations can hardly conceal his secret sympathy and fascination. Thus the text works against the norms its narrator explicitly professes. This does not mean, however, that Hester does not remain a victim of the Puritan norms and of the social environment in which she lives. But she survives her victimization as a person—and this seems to be decisive from the textual perspective. Her decision not to flee the community that has stigmatized her makes her victimization, from a reader's point of view, fall back all the more vehemently on the violence and destructiveness inherent in the Puritan norms of "femininity" and "female deviancy."

Thus Hester's tacit language game not only changes the community's attitude toward her, but also asserts itself aesthetically against the official language game of the narrator. Just as Hester could use the scarlet *A* against the grain of its codified cultural reading according to Puritan norms, so the reader can read the text against the grain of those very norms embodied by the narrator. Letter and text, as emblematic as they might originally have been conceived, thus open themselves up for historically changing readings. *The Scarlet Letter*, as sign and as text, instead of attempting to refer to a historical reality of the witch, plays its game with the flexibility of the witch stereotype and the phantasms it nourishes. Thus it becomes a "purloined letter," purloined from its cultural codification as much as from its fixation to a referent. This is why Hawthorne's novel reveals more of the witch than those texts that conventionalize the historical witches into a literary monument or a romantic myth. While conventional witchcraft romances cannot afford to portray the reality of witches and therefore depend on reviving mere phantasms of the witch, Hawthorne uses these phantasms to demonstrate how to make a witch or how to avoid becoming one.

NOTES

This chapter is dedicated to the memory of Carlos Dominguez.

1. I have used the Penguin edition (1970) of Nathaniel Hawthorne's *The Scarlet Letter*. With respect to the cultural formation of a witchcraft pattern, see Claudia Honegger, ed., *Die Hexen der Neuzeit: Studien zur Sozialgeschichte eines kulturellen Deutungsmusters* (Frankfurt: Suhrkamp, 1978), introduction.
2. I use the term "social semantics" in the sense of Niklas Luhman, *Gesellschaftsstruktur und Semantik: Studien zur Wissenssoziologie der modernen Gesellschaft* (Frankfurt: Suhrkamp, 1980).
3. Though I have developed my arguments by reading fictions which deal with the Salem events, these arguments could be generalized beyond this historical frame. The focus on seventeenth-century New England Puritanism as a narrower historical context is motivated by my choice of *The Scarlet Letter* as the central paradigm.

4. See Perry Miller, *The New England Mind: The Seventeenth Century* (Cambridge, Mass.: Harvard University Press, 1963).

5. For further references, see G. Harrison Orians, "New England Witchcraft in Fiction," *American Literature* 2 (1930–31), 54–71. Orians discusses some of the above-mentioned texts in more detail.

6. Norbert Elias, *Über den Prozess der Zivilisation: Soziogentische und psychogenetische Untersuchungen* (Bern: Francke AG, 1969).

7. With respect to a desymbolization of social patterns and their internalization as clichés, see Alfred Lorenzer, *Sprachzerstörung und Rekonstruktion: Vorarbeiten zu einer Metatheorie der Psychoanalyse* (Frankfurt: Suhrkamp, 1970).

8. This has even led to a recent dispute in a medical journal where a doctor argued that Chillingworth actually murdered Dimmesdale with these plants.

9. With respect to the psychological implications of a mirror stage, see D. W. Winnicott, *Playing and Reality* (London 1971); and Jacques Lacan, *Écrits* (Paris: Editions du Seuil, 1966), pp. 93–100.

10. The reversibility of the letter has also been analyzed under a different perspective in Peggy Kamuf, "Hawthorne's Genres: The Letter of the Law Appliquée," in *After Strange Texts: The Role of Theory in the Study of Literature*, ed. Gregory S. Jay and David L. Miller, pp. 69–84.

11. Hawthorne's notion has, in fact, certain affinities to Sartre's idea of the "derealization" of an "imaginary personality."

12. For a more detailed analysis of the affinities between Hester and Ann Hutchinson, see Michael J. Colacurcio, "Footsteps of Ann Hutchinson: The Context of *The Scarlet Letter*," ELH 39 (1972), 459–94.

13. This is one of the most controversial issues among the literary critics, and it is specifically related to the ending of the text, which many readers consider unsatisfying, if not disturbing. I will argue for a textual perspective that is critical of the narrator's moralistic point of view. For a recent discussion of this issue see David Leverenz, "Mrs. Hawthorne's Headache: Reading *The Scarlet Letter*," in *The (M)other Tongue: Essays in Feminist Psychoanalytic Interpretation*, ed. S. N. Garner, C. Kahane, and M. Sprengnether (Ithaca: Cornell University Press, 1985), pp. 194–216.

PART FOUR

Lacan, Baudrillard, Irigaray: "Masculine" and "Feminine" in the Rhetoric of French Theory

Confessing Lacan

Like a contagion, Jacques Lacan's recent influence is ubiquitous; his terminology, such as "the Other" and the "Symbolic Order," generously populates literary critical discourse.[1] For Shoshana Felman, Lacan's theoretical value constitutes a "reading lesson" which attempts nothing less than "the adjustment or translation of our modes of thinking and of operating to the still unassimilated radicality of the Freudian revolution."[2] The zeal with which purveyors of Lacanian theory peddle his discourse suggests an influence so prodigious that I am tempted to compare its effect to seduction. By "seduction" I mean to indicate the traces of power and desire, including the erotics of reading and sex/gender differences enacted in the process of reading, that punctuate the performances—or staged readings—of two critical responses which transmit Lacanian psychoanalytic theory.

Lacan's blandishments reside in style. Constructed from his own lexicon, aphorisms such as "the unconscious is the discourse of the Other" offer enticing sparks of accessibility in an otherwise obscure, even resistant discourse. The heterogeneity of Lacan's linguistic style—the aphorisms and neologisms, the impossibly dense formulations, and various associations from disparate disciplines of knowledge—fuels his theoretical appeal by dramatizing the structure of desire. Just as desire is predicated on a condition of deferral where gratification continually recedes one's grasp, so does Lacan's discourse seem to promise, while inevitably postponing, a fuller understanding of human subjectivity. While the same may be observed about Freud, what makes Lacan different is the way his style repeatedly foregrounds through its performance this breach between the desire for and the possession of knowledge.

Because of his opaque style,[3] Lacan's discourse forces a confrontation with the process of reading as the slippery construction of meaning out of words in a text—a process not dissimilar to making sense out of unconscious material. Various readers have posed an analogy between reading Lacan and doing psychoanalysis. Jane Gallop's *Reading Lacan* (1985) works from precisely this similarity: "This book presupposes . . . that the *Écrits* seem to put the reader through an experience analogous to analysis: complete with passion, pain, desire to know, transference."[4]

Another analogy, one explicitly drawn from Lacan, associates the discourse of psychoanalysis with the discourse of the hysteric. Lacan describes psychoanalysis as the hystericisation of discourse, while readers have compared Lacan's texts to the hysteric's language: full of holes and wordplay, refusing the conventions of ordering and definition which would seem to make meaning available. If reading Lacan is like doing psychoanalysis, and the discourse of psychoanalysis is like hysterical discourse, do readers of Lacan suffer from signs of hysteria?

Hysterical discourse tends to utilize the confessional mode, telling stories through the grammar of the textual body by means of the self-reflexivity of the intrusive "I." Stuart Schneiderman's *Jacques Lacan: The Death of an Intellectual Hero* (1983) and Gallop's *Reading Lacan* assimilate personal disclosures into their accounts of Lacan, although the styles and effects of confession in these two books differ significantly.

By "confessional mode" I wish to designate a discourse marked in some sense by autobiographical disclosure. It is impossible to delimit subjective boundaries exhaustively; and certainly Lacan's model of subject/object positions contextualizes this difficulty. Nevertheless, I call "confessional" those textual moments of the intrusive "I" where attention swerves from the subject of Lacan's texts to the narrating subject. The disjunctions between the subject positions of the deictic "I" and the reflexive "I" suggest holes of hysterical discourse. Confessional interpretation, moreover, conjoins the subject positions of analyst and analysand, a strategy Gallop both addresses and employs.

Along with these similarities between psychoanalytic and hysterical discourses, the enigma of seduction haunts the scenes of Schneiderman and Gallop reading and transmitting Lacan. Like Freud's primary and secondarily revised theories of hysteria, the confessional mode figures in Gallop and Schneiderman as both resistance to the seduction of Lacanian theory and a disguised strategy of appropriation of the power of textual or interpretive seduction. Freud's initial seduction theory posited an historical incident of childhood seduction, whether attempted or accomplished, whose memory the hysteria is designed to repress/reveal through conversion symptoms. Typically, the precipitating event involved a young girl, who later became hysterical, and an older man, often a relation or family friend, who made sexual advances toward the girl. Freud's revised or subsequent theory speculated instead that no real seduction scene occurred, but that the hysteria camouflaged an unbearable memory of the hysteric's desire to seduce the person to whom she attributes the act of seduction. As for the historical facts of the events in the lives of these patients, the question of accomplished or imagined seduction remains a moot point. Freud exploited this impossible recuperation as leverage to revise his seduction theory. The first theory acknowledged this actual seduction as well as the hysteric's resistance to it, while the later reading attributed to the hysteric a troublesome desire to seduce.[5]

Using confession as a strategy of response to Lacan's theoretical seduction, Jane Gallop's discursive operations "resist" through recognition the enticements of what she calls her "reading transference" to Lacan, although her "feminist reading practice" stages its own temptations. Stuart Schneiderman's confessions, on the other hand, signify exclusively an effort to appropriate the power of seduction from his psychoanalytic father, Lacan.

Echoing Freud's formulation that "hysterics suffer mainly from reminiscence,"[6] Schneiderman writes: "This book is a reminiscence . . . a first-person narrative."[7] Rather than explicate Lacan's theories, Schneiderman, in an enticingly firsthand account, sketches out scenes of Lacan's consulting room and training seminars. In a conversational manner, studded with American idioms, Schneiderman's relationship to his audience is personable, with frequent addresses of "I" and "you," suggesting intimate tones from the analyst's couch. Attracted to Schneiderman's chattiness, readers can enjoy soap-operatic gossip of Lacan's sexual exploits in the backseat of a taxi[8] and then dismiss Lacan rather than struggle without reward through his texts, which resist but also deserve attempts at understanding. Conversely, Schneiderman's "up-close portrait" might encourage readers to pursue their textual relationship with Lacan, since it seductively offers images of the man behind the abstractions of Lacanian discourse, like the lure of the imaginary order's mirror stage which mollifies the harshness of the symbolic order.

More difficult to summarize is Gallop's style, which, like hysterical fragmentation, takes up a cast of voices spanning the positions of analyst and analysand. As analyst, Gallop personifies the scholarly translator, the professional literary critic, and the psychoanalytic reader who seizes on points of textual ambiguity as symptomatic moments which she investigates for "rootstocks" of significance. As analysand, Gallop includes the confessions of a Lacanian disciple caught up in the mirror structure of her own transference. Bisecting the body of her text, which investigates six *écrits* of Lacan, Gallop's "Interstory" occupies the innermost space of *Reading Lacan*, providing the reader with the "inner" story for reading Gallop. Using a diary format, Gallop conveys her own brief experience in Freudian psychoanalysis and its relevance to the production of the present book, while she also uncovers her vexed political relation to the institution of psychoanalysis, represented here by her male analyst, and elsewhere by Lacan.

Gallop's role-playing translates the classic hysteric's questions about sexual identity ("Who am I?" "Am I a woman?" "Am I a man?") into questions about linguistic identity in different cultural and disciplinary spaces. Her various positions ask: Who am I in psychoanalytic discourse? Who am I in feminist discourse? Who am I in academic discourse? Who am I in 'personal' discourse? Aware that all discourse is reflexive at some level, Gallop expresses her uneasiness through a hysterical symptom: "As I struggle with this portion of my reading/writing, struggle with my own narcissistic investment in my own phallus (femininely latent of course), a nausea, a paralysis creeps over me."[9] It is possible to read Gallop's hysterical symptom here as an indication of her desire to seduce others with her "reading/writing," which she conveys through the parenthetically covered image of her "femininely latent" phallus. "Phallus" means the objective authority of the traditional critic, yet in a sense, Gallop's feminist reading practice might constitute a screen for a desire to seduce discursively, something she partially dislodges through her constant reflexivity in recounting the process of this "reading/writing."

Also featuring discursive blandishments, if in a less complicated fashion, Schneiderman exploits the confessional mode to frame his entire book on Lacan. He writes, "Rather than offer a critical commentary on Lacan's texts or an elaboration of his theory, I want to reenact my experience of psychoanalysis with Jacques Lacan, rhetorically."[10] Schneiderman's approach here lapses into the Lacanian imaginary order's mirror correspondence of the self-identical, an inevitable and problematic feature of the biography he attempts to produce. Capitalizing on the identification between his analyst and his subject, Schneiderman fills in necessary gaps between Lacan as theoretician and Lacan as clinician with a tricky construct he calls

"Lacan the man." Similarly, Schneiderman slips out of his account-
ability for a distinction between the narrative "I" as critical analyst and as analysand. "Rather than . . . critical commentary . . .
or an elaboration of [Lacan's] theory," Schneiderman substitutes this
textual rendition of "my experience of psychoanalysis with Jacques
Lacan." Moving along the vertical or upright axis of language, Schneiderman's "reenactment" functions as metaphoric substitution for
Lacan's theory.[11]

Schneiderman twice cites the *Confessions* of St. Augustine, the
patriarch of the confessional genre in Western literature. Remarking
that his arrival in Paris to seek out Lacan was "not what one would
call a momentous event," Schneiderman explains: "It is no sense
of false modesty that prevents me from comparing it to the arrival
of Augustine in Carthage."[12] The dramatic effect of this professed
misalliance begs the question of resemblance. The comparison to
Augustine is particularly apt. Similar to the path of a psychoanalysis, Augustine's confessions center around a crisis in signification
which is reconciled through a conversion experience. A new key to
the meaning of human subjectivity for both Augustine, as Christian
disciple, and Schneiderman, as Lacanian disciple, involves the practice of reading. Augustine's conversion, however, presents a precise
reversal or mirror image of the shift in reading strategies suggested
by Schneiderman's transformation. Augustine's *Confessions* climax
with the scene of his conversion, where he learns to privilege figurative reading, by the spirit, and disavow literal reading; Schneiderman's conversion constitutes a new reading practice: he moves from
an English professor who reads for content to a Lacanian analyst
who, focusing instead on the materiality of language and the play
of the signifier, reads for style. The confessional mode of Schneiderman's discourse on Lacan overlaps with the Augustinian notion
of conversion. Behind both accounts is a kind of seduction scene.
Each narrative functions as testimony to a discursive restructuring of
subjectivity through a revised approach to texts; and it is this transformation which registers the enticements of interpretive theory.

After quoting Augustine's description of his arrival in Carthage,
Schneiderman appends: "Whether or not this has anything to do with
me, it is as good a Lacanian definition of neurosis as I have ever read."
Even though Schneiderman omits an explicit account of his analytic
sessions—a hole in his text—the question of "whether or not this
has anything to do with me" hovers provocatively around the edges
of what the jacket copy calls "a close-up portrait of this controversial

figure." Repeated reminders of the possibility of confession, disclosures direct from Lacan's psychoanalytic couch, undercoat Schneiderman's narrative.

In a hybrid account of Lacan's theory and practice of the infamous short session, Schneiderman provides a titillatingly graphic description of the scene of his psychoanalysis, Lacan's waiting and consulting rooms. Luring the reader into the position of voyeur, the narrator enters the inner sanctum, exposing the rarefied parts of Lacan's professional space, an area now foreclosed—as Schneiderman reminds us repeatedly—because Lacan is dead. Using the second person, the narrator encourages the reader's identification with the analysand, presumably Schneiderman, as he plays on the desire of readers to attain this enviable, impossible position.

> To reach Lacan's office you walked to the end of the courtyard until you found a door on the right. . . . The waiting room was small, with just enough room for a loveseat and two easy chairs. . . . Resting on the table was a piece of wood . . . shaped precisely like an oversized phallus, the kind you would expect to find in a scene from de Sade. At other times this piece of wood resembled the trunk of an elephant raised as it would be were the elephant to talk.[13]

Suggesting the polymorphously perverse, "a scene from de Sade," Schneiderman's description incorporates both sexual and romantic imagery. While the phallic objects and the coveted journey into the mysterious inner depths of Lacan's chambers suggest male and female genitalia, the connection between the elephant's trunk and speech recalls Lacan's observation that sexual identity is a function of language and culture—what Lacan called the symbolic order. From here follows an association between language and seduction; the ability to speak, to manipulate words, even to formulate theories, parallels sexual power.[14]

Schneiderman delineates the structure of analytic sessions with Lacan, where the analyst is "a very gracious host" until the beginning of the "analysis proper"—the first experience of the short session whose duration might be only a few minutes. Schneiderman writes, "The ending of the session, unexpected and unwanted, was like a rude awakening, like being torn out of a dream by a loud alarm. (One person likened it to *coitus interruptus*.)"[15] Like memoirs of a bygone love affair, the drift of these confessional moments reflects Schneiderman's privileged status as the only American who did it with Lacan. In turn, his psychoanalytic seduction by Lacan, clinically called "transference," offers a means to entice readers to read his book.

Somewhat congruously, Gallop reproduces the scene of her failed attempt to gain access to Lacan's lodgings as she likens herself to the unrequited lover in Edith Wharton's *The Age of Innocence* who stands outside the Parisian flat of the woman he has loved unseen for many years. Since Lacan observed that where there is transference, there is love, the amorous contours of these presentations dramatize a clinical transference in Schneiderman's case, and a reading transference which Gallop's book both replicates and interrogates.

In these vignettes the gender confusions of hysteria surface.[16] Schneiderman figures ambiguously as Lacan's feminized lover, while Gallop occupies a man's position in her parable. Freud defines hysterical attacks as erotic daydreams which intrude on "ordinary life."[17] The two daydreams, which impinge in the form of confession on the two accounts of Lacanian theory, carry sexual valences. Schneiderman's scene of psychoanalytic love with Lacan recommends an analogy between the analytic session and coitus, a comparison recalling Freud's observation that "a convulsive hysterical attack is an equivalent of coition"[18] and Lacan's association between the discourses of hysteria and psychoanalysis. Who assumes the masculine and feminine identities in Schneiderman's scene? As in traditionally defined sex roles, Lacan's power as analyst puts him in a masculine position and Schneiderman in a feminine one. This alignment makes sense if we consider transference as a form of seduction in which the analyst, an older, more "psychoanalytically experienced"[19] man, masters the patient, who occupies a more vulnerable position. But framing the eroticized description of Schneiderman's psychoanalysis with Lacan is the fact, reported in the jacket copy, that Schneiderman now "practices Lacanian analysis." Once in the feminine position of submission to the transference, Schneiderman's eventual succession to the place of the analyst presides over his narrative.

Since Gallop's investment in Lacan's texts as the locus of knowledge, and concomitantly as the object of desire, constitutes a "reading transference," her daydream of unfulfilled love takes shape through her association with a fictional character, Newland Archer, who "has long loved in his mind" a woman. In Wharton's novel, Archer decides not to consummate a long-deferred encounter because, or so Gallop justifies, "he could not really see her whom he had loved for so long."[20] The bisexuality of Gallop's "femininely latent" phallus, which figures in her hysterical symptom, rises to the surface here in two ways: through her analogical identification as a male lover and through her translation of a denied encounter with Lacan into a matter of (fictionalized) choice. In both Gallop's and Schneiderman's scenes with Lacan, issues of control intersect with sex-gender positions.

For both writers the confessional strain is clearly motivated by transference. According to Lacan, "As soon as the subject who is sup-posed to know exists somewhere . . . there is transference."[21] With regard to what she repeatedly labels as a reading transference, Gal-lop notes that Lacan's language makes painfully explicit the usually domesticated process of reading, producing feelings of inadequacy and vulnerability, much like the analysand's experience of psycho-analysis. Gallop further speculates: "Lacan's writings seem to pro-duce this effect. But is this due to his style and its ability to mimic psychoanalysis? Or is it perhaps because the reader desires to 'get psychoanalysis,' to get that other scene from reading Lacan's text, that she produces the experience Lacan describes as transference?"[22] It is not only Lacan's style that drives the analogy, but also a belief that these texts possess knowledge, a knowledge whose recondite form seems to multiply its value, just as academic culture, exten-sively permeated by psychoanalytic thought, privileges unconscious knowledge. This belief in the (illusory) site of knowledge, whether a text or a person, produces a transference effect.

To the extent that transference signifies assimilation as repe-tition of the structure of earlier relationships (in Gallop's case, to texts), and is marked by belief in "the subject presumed to know," it implies a form of seduction. One is drawn without conscious choice to replicate previous affective ties. The association between hysteria and seduction, established through Freud's case studies and elabo-rated in relation to transference and countertransference by con-temporary psychoanalytic and feminist readings, surfaces in Lacan's observation that the effect of psychoanalysis is to "hystericize" the patient in the transference. This verbal "hystericize" corresponds to "seduce." The erotic element in transference, the love that accompa-nies the analysand's belief in a "subject presumed to know," bespeaks the sexual component in seduction. Since the desire to know moti-vates transferential belief, the desire for the substance or "body" of Lacanian theory is a transformation of desire for a sexual body. Gal-lop's passionate rereadings of Lacan's texts, which she confesses she has deciphered some twenty times in the past decade, attest to an interminable desire: "I cannot, however, have him [Lacan], cannot satisfy my desire to know, in any lasting or universal way."[23]

Can a reading transference qualify as a scene of seduction? Forms of the words "lure," "lead," and "entice" recur in Gallop's account of the process of reading Lacan. She describes "the lure of the text as bait"[24] where Lacan's style, promoting the hook which secures the reader's cathexis onto the text, exploits the signifier's power of suspense. By deferring meaning, Lacan's abstractions and puns facilitate the possibility of seduction in the form of a reading investment spurred by a desire to know. Suggesting this reading transference, Gallop includes her own provocative confession in response to a passage in *Écrits*: "There is more I want to say, but I cannot, now. I would like to say something about the dazzling style and force, about the extraordinary performance that is this text ["The Freudian Thing"] . . . I feel some inhibition against touching the beautiful, crazy, violent portions of the text, some taboo against understanding how they work."[25] The erotics encoded in this act of reading underscore Gallop's transference onto Lacan. This articulation of a space of silence and submission, her "inhibition against touching" Lacan's words, operates seductively to pique the reader's curiosity about a text eliciting such passionate response. Moreover, this confessional gesture, like Lacan's style, stages a deferral, translating into a different form Gallop's domination since her resistance to reading further does foreclose Lacan's text. Elsewhere, as in the final chapter of *Reading Lacan*, Gallop's reading repeatedly breaks through this "taboo" and " 'tears off a piece' of Lacan," ravishing "not . . . much more than one paragraph" of Lacan's *Écrits* with thirty pages of her interpretive "touching."[26]

In *The Daughter's Seduction* Gallop personifies Lacan's style as a ladies' man, a prick: "a narcissistic tease who persuades by means of attraction and resistance, not by orderly systematic discourse."[27] Confessional intrusions in both Gallop's and Schneiderman's accounts of Lacan also upset "orderly systematic discourse," occluding boundaries between subject/object positions, between memoir and criticism, between transference—to use Gallop's dichotomy—and interpretation.

Whether a reading or a clinical transference, what prompts the description of this experience into these two books? Does transference compel or does it justify these confessions? The confessional moments might offer a keyhole into the transference, but the concept of transference might also signify a loophole providing legitimacy for confession. As Peter Brooks notes, the desire to tell one's story motivates the narrative act, while it "seeks to seduce and to subjugate the listener."[28] Certainly it is possible to read these confessional moments as expressing a compulsion to disclose, quickened by the scenes of psychoanalysis which traverse the two accounts. But Schneiderman's use of confession seems to reinforce the power structure Michel Foucault associates with the cultural ritual of confession, whereas Gallop attempts to expose this political paradigm through her dramatic deployments of alternating subject and object positions.

A seduction theory of reading transference suggests the operations of dominance and submission; and any explication of seduction must consider schemes of gender. The original seduction[29] theory represents Freud's attempts to explain behavior prevalent in his female patients with regard to sexualized relationships (whether real or imaginary) with dominant males in their lives. Maria Ramas, among others, has pointed to the crucial connection between seduction and the politics of interpretation; and in "Enforcing Oedipus: Freud and Dora" Madelon Sprengnether similarly describes "seduction via interpretation" and "verbal seduction" with regard to Freud's attempted linguistic influence over Dora. Thus, feminists have been led to ask to what extent the privilege to speak and to confer meaning, which might also be the power to seduce through language, is culturally encoded as a male prerogative. Indeed, one may well ask whether every account of seduction, even the textual enticements Gallop construes as reading transference, is marked by gender patterns of dominance and submission.[30]

In narration, a structure of dominance and submission suggests an analogy to Freud's double theory of seduction. The narrator arouses and manipulates the reader's desire for narration; while in a different sense, the reader's desire for textual seduction signifies a reversal of power where the reader wishes to overwhelm or seduce the text with her own interpretations. Reader-response theory takes up this second position, assigning the power in the act of reading to the reader. Poststructuralist theories, specifically Lacan's notion of the split subject constituted through language, would locate dominance in the position of textuality, where the reader (and here the writer is also a reader) unwittingly submits to the power of language. Ross Chambers has described a similar bifurcated theory of textual seduction. He defines the narrator and reader as seducer and seduced where linguistic seduction is "the necessary means . . . whereby a text succeeds in acquiring a readership"; but he observes a reversal in this relationship with regard to postmodernist texts.[31] Realignment of dominance and submission in a theory of discursive seduction privileges the irreducible otherness of the seduced, or, in other words, imagines the unclosable gap between the reader and the text.

Advancing what Gallop construes as a feminist reading practice, the confessional moments in her book participate in her project to question and revise categories and patterns of authority. In this sense, her confessions of transference counter the convention of critical reading as an act of power, since Gallop argues that transference necessarily structures every interpretive act. In this position, the literary reader is the analysand who presumes that the text, even the author of the text, contains knowledge the reader desires to possess. Analysis of this transference in any reading, Gallop urges, unmasks the structuring of the authority of a particular interpretation by revealing its inadequacy or vested interests.

Gallop's reading strategy challenges a tradition of phallic criticism, where unacknowledged masculine perspectives constitute unanalyzed structures of transference. She writes: "I believe that the pretense of a masterful grasp of Lacan serves only to consolidate the oppressive mystification of the Lacanian institution. Lacan talks insightfully about the analyst as the illusion of the 'subject presumed to know.' I am trying to undo that illusion . . . the phallic illusion[s] of authority."[32] With regard to the relation between theory and the confessional "I," Gallop explains, "My point is not to reduce theory to subjectivity but to see the ways the levels intertwine and thus to understand both better."[33] Implicit in this practice is a critique of the power relations inscribed in every reading. As a gesture toward uncovering a "massive" transference onto Lacan and psychoanalysis that structures her interpretive acts, Gallop confesses frustrations in reading Lacan, fantasies about her relationship with this subject she knows only through texts, and her foray into the consulting room as trainee to confer an illusory legitimacy on her theory and practice.

Gallop's alloy of transference and interpretation problematizes the "correct distance" institutionally sanctioned and reinforced between subject/object positions, between analyst and analysand, between the disciplinary divisions of psychoanalysis and literature. In this light, she offers a confessor's manifesto: "I . . . am trying to write in a different relation to the material, from a more unsettling confrontation with its contradictory plurivocity, a sort of encounter I believe is possible only if one relinquishes the usual position of command, and thus writes from a more subjective, vulnerable position."[34] Relinquishing "the usual position of command" however, the confessional mode entices the reader to pursue a text not so much about Lacan's theory as about Gallop's reading, so that the *Reading* which precedes *Lacan* in the title arrangement also overwhelms Lacan performatively. Seduction, which seeks to disguise even while it exploits power relations, operates here by transforming the "subjective, more vulnerable position" into the locus which decodes the conventional packaging of authority. But by doing so, confession subtly usurps and restores a different, if subjective, sovereignty.

The structure of *Reading Lacan* (which also has an introduction, "Prefatory Material,"[35] and a concluding "Postory") resembles a case study, a genre whose ancestry includes the confession. Like her hysterical counterpart, Dora, Gallop terminates her own psychoanalysis with a male Freudian after a couple of months, but unlike Dora, she incorporates her version of this experience as the centerpiece of her text. Not only does this confessional "Interstory" attempt to fill in the gap constructed by Dora's silence, a blank space variously distorted and abused, but in doing so Gallop seeks to convert psychiatric female hysteria into feminist resistance.[36] Gallop's mix of confessional interpretation punctures, by means of her acknowledged reading transference, the hegemony of (Lacanian) psychoanalysis by calling attention to the seductions of theory where belief in Lacan's text as a subject of knowledge inevitably structures her reading.

The confessional reading Gallop employs is seductive because it offers strategies for the inadequate or unqualified reader (i.e., everyone, according to Lacan, who reads Lacan) to assert provisional mastery over the blindnesses or unintended (or unattended) meanings in the text such as typos and parapraxes. Continually directing attention toward herself through the intrusive "I," Gallop's theatricality emphasizes a "narcissistic investment" in her desire to display her multiple readings. But this dramatic presentation incurs risks. Gallop's imitation of Lacan's linguistic play, an attempt at appropriated seduction, as well as the psychoanalytically inscribed compulsion to tell all, lure Gallop to the perilous brink of what she calls a "pathology of interpretation."[37] Here the cost of her reading transference onto Lacanian psychoanalysis emerges: anything signifies a symptomatic moment. As a result, Gallop confesses a breakdown in her typewriter and reports her misreading of only one "1" in Ellie Ragland-Sullivan's first name—an observation that somewhat softens Gallop's caustic "[sic]" after quoting Ragland-Sullivan's misspelling of Fredric Jameson's first name. Overdetermined semiosis, a consequence of the impulse to confess every detail in the process of producing a reading, is one textual symptom of Gallop's seduction by Lacanian theory.

For Gallop, confessional interpretation aims to encourage Lacan's acceptance among American feminists. Gallop wants to reconcile through her reading practice her commitment to feminism with her evident investment in the historically male-identified psychoanalytic institution. Allowing the confessional "I" to speak, even to disrupt the trajectory of her "masterly" critical discourse on Lacan's texts, Gallop's verbal performance connects feminism and Lacanian psychoanalysis in practice. This reconciliation remains less convincing in theory since the book's attention, at least, does favor psychoanalysis over feminism. Yet even this irremediably split subject coincides with Lacan's idiom.

If Gallop utilizes confession to reveal the underpinnings of hegemony in critical discourse, Schneiderman manages personal disclosure simply to shore up his own authority. The reiteration of two facts—repetitions the reader cannot fail to miss—bolster Schneiderman's claim to be the singular heir of Lacanian thought in the United States: he did psychoanalysis with Lacan and Lacan is dead. As the "legitimate" American son by way of his analytic and pedagogic relation to Lacan, Schneiderman states: "I had the distinction of being the only American to train with Lacan."[38] By right of his transference, Schneiderman monopolizes the right of transmission, whereas in Gallop's reading practice the effects of transference necessarily complicate any effort toward transmission.

As evidence of his authority, through this textual dramatization of the law of primogeniture, Schneiderman's style is preemptive. Acting out his "birthright," he shoulders aside rival sibling readers. Divided into a prologue and eight untitled chapters, *Jacques Lacan: The Death of an Intellectual Hero* contains no table of contents, no index, no bibliography, no footnotes, and only a few quotations, without any documentation. No source other than Schneiderman or Lacan speaks in this book. Lacan is dead and this crucial fact is repeated from the title on the cover to the book's penultimate sentence.

The words "hero" in the title and "prologue" labeling the first section suggest the fictive status of Schneiderman's (re)invention of Lacan. Through this textual act of transmission, not only does the author seek to replace the "hero"—who, after all, is dead—he inevitably rewrites him. In this way, Schneiderman has reversed the seduction inscribed in his own clinical transference onto Lacan. Appropriating the power to seduce, he transposes Lacan's theory through repeated acts of ventriloquism by virtue of his former double relation to Lacan as analysand and student.

Does Lacan succeed as an "intellectual hero" in Schneiderman's "close-up" poetics? Or does this account, glittering with gossip as well as glib formulas of Lacan's theory and practice signify "the death of an intellectual hero"—the legendary killing of the father? Does this text urge, "Where Lacan was, there Schneiderman (in America) claims to be"?

In a sense, the confessional mode tries to resolve the problem of transmission. Through autobiographical disclosure, Schneiderman's authority to convey the words of the father takes up a hierarchical arrangement where the right to represent Lacan descends on a vertical axis from father to son. Gallop's confessions, on the other hand, bespeak the daughter's deferred or cheated inheritance. Unable to reach the living Lacan, her relationship is through texts—a metonymic or horizontal affiliation.

Gallop uncovers an ideology of the dead father suggestive in light of Schneiderman's refrain that Lacan is dead. She writes, "Is the image of the dead author a reader's fantasy of perfect mastery? A fantasy for the critic who would identify with such mastery as reader-writer? . . . Proclaiming the death of the author asserts that one does not care, is not at all troubled by the still unknown source."[39] If, as Gallop observes, "to read as if Lacan were simply dead would be to protect his mastery," then Schneiderman can best assert his Lacanian inheritance as indisputable inasmuch as his claim rests on a metaphysics of presence. Not only did Schneiderman indubitably work directly with Lacan, but also Lacan is unquestionably dead. Schneiderman's compulsion to repeat these facts is embellished by his inclusion of the pathological explanation of Lacan's death: "Lacan died of postoperative complications after a tumor was removed from his intestines. Specifically, his kidneys failed, he lapsed into a coma, and he died."[40] Schneiderman's efforts to confirm the actual death of Lacan are an essential strategy in his appropriation of the interpretive rights, or the seductive power, of the (dead) father.

In contrast to Schneiderman's preemptive exclusionary style, Gallop's brazen repartee with citations from other Lacanian explicators accentuates the sibling rivalry suppressed in Schneiderman's book. Gallop continually upstages competitive readers and basks in the interpretive limelight as the purveyor of the provisional last word on Lacan. In turn, this dramatization of sibling rivalry is offset through the confessional moments where Gallop acknowledges her intense desire to "get Lacan right" and to achieve his impossible approbation.

Analogous to Freud's conversion symptoms, confession stands in Gallop's textual body for the vexed condition of (discursive) seduction. In addition, it figures as resistance because it draws attention to the tension between at least two linguistic subjectivities. By displacing Lacan's theory through her confessions, Gallop textually wards off Lacanian engulfment even though the nature of these confessions accedes to her attraction to Lacan's authority in psychoanalytic thought. Like Freud's earlier seduction theory, Gallop's hysterical discourse in response to Lacan signals repudiation of a seduction which has already taken place. The insistence of the intrusive "I" constitutes a defense reaction against the overwhelming objectifications of theory.

Like Freud's revised seduction theory, Gallop's confession in response to Lacan also signifies a screen for transferential seduction whereby she utilizes confession as an appropriation of the power to seduce discursively. Freud's imaginary scene of seduction translates here into not only the desire to be seduced by the father— the phallocentric bearer of authoritative knowledge—but also the desire to be the father in terms of theoretical influence. Weakening the resistance to Lacan which Lacan's obscure discourse often provokes, Schneiderman's personal disclosures lure the reader into engagement, but this textual intercourse is with Schneiderman's words, not Lacan's. As self-appointed heir of Lacanian theory in the United States, Schneiderman's narrator attempts substitution for his now deceased psychoanalytic father. This differs from Gallop's confessions, which also act as bait, because she features an occasional interlude of analytical regard for her own linguistic fanfares.

On the reading stages of *Jacques Lacan: The Death of an Intellectual Hero* and *Reading Lacan* the seduction of confession, motivated by the seduction of theory, qualifies both discursive performances. While Schneiderman's confessions appropriate through identification the father's desire to seduce, Gallop's strategy problematizes seduction by the father. Choreographing these textual encounters with Lacan, the operations of power and gender inflect the arrangement and uses of the confessional "I." My reading implies that both interpretation and seduction function through cultural codes as predominantly paternal prerogatives where the daughter can accede to these positions of power through imitation and play, metonymic activities; while the son aims to replace the father, a metaphoric substitution.

Although Lacan's theory of subjectivity draws knots around any notion of a coherent self, Schneiderman's confessions, despite his disclaimer of selfhood in a gesture of allegiance to Lacanian doctrine, are fashioned in the spirit of the confessional fathers, Augustine and Rousseau, where the signifier of the self-adequate subject, Schneiderman's narrative "I," reigns consistently to the end. Operating otherwise, Gallop's intrusive "I," with its roots in feminist discourse, seeks to unsettle the classical opposition between subject and object. The theoretical, in at least two senses, seduction of Gallop by psychoanalysis and feminism transfers onto her textual allure. Combining both the roles of interpreting analyst and confessing patient, Gallop's feminist reading practice offers an enticing correlative to the seductive scene of psychoanalytic discourse.

NOTES

I wish to thank Helena Michie and Nora Mitchell for their encouragement on an earlier version of this paper presented at the 1986 MLA special session, "The Reception to Lacan in America."

1. Juliet Flower MacCannell makes this observation in her *Figuring Lacan* (Lincoln: University of Nebraska Press, 1986), pp. 1–2.
2. Shoshana Felman, *Jacques Lacan and the Adventure of Insight* (Cambridge, Mass.: Harvard University Press, 1987), p. 20.
3. As James Glogowski reminded Lacan's readers in his paper "The Unconscious Aspect of Lacan's Text," presented at the 1986 MLA special session, "The Reception to Lacan in America," Lacan's texts are predominantly transcripts from his lecture notes for his training seminars. This discourse was designed to be spoken and heard from the stage rather than read elsewhere.
4. Jane Gallop, *Reading Lacan* (Ithaca: Cornell University Press, 1985), p. 53.
5. See Jeffrey Masson, *The Assault on Truth: Freud's Suppression of the Seduction Theory* (New York: Farrar, Straus, and Giroux, 1984); and Marianne Krüll, *Freud and His Father*, trans. Arnold J. Pomerans (New York: W. W. Norton and Co., 1986).
6. Sigmund Freud, *Studies on Hysteria*, in *The Standard Edition of the Complete Psychological Works of Sigmund Freud*, ed. and trans. James Strachey et al., 24 vols. (London: Hogarth Press, 1953–74) (hereafter cited as *S.E.*), vol. 3, p. 7.
7. Stuart Schneiderman, *Jacques Lacan: The Death of an Intellectual Hero* (Cambridge, Mass.: Harvard University Press, 1983), p. 27.
8. The operation of gossip in critical discourse holds its own seductive appeal. Schneiderman's particular use of gossip might constitute an "antiheroics," deflating the transferential illusion of the infallible master. Juliet Flower MacCannell alludes to a slightly different form of hearsay —academic gossip—when she reports what Paul de Man relayed to her about Lacan's wife, Sylvia, although she qualifies that she knows "nothing of the historical accuracy of the gossip Prof. de Man shared with me." (See *Figuring Lacan*, p. 34, note 6.)
9. Gallop, *Reading Lacan*, p. 131.

10. Schneiderman, *Jacques Lacan*, p. vi.
11. Drawing from the linguistics theory of Ferdinand de Saussure, Roman Jakobson postulates that binarily opposed polarities structure language. The vertical and horizontal axes signify respectively the processes of selection and combination. Metaphor is based on the principle of selection where one signifier replaces another, while metonymy emphasizes combination, or a signifier in relation to another signifier.

    Because of its hierarchical structure, the vertical axis is often associated with the paternal metaphor or masculine-identified arrangements of domination and submission. The horizontal axis, with its metonymic structure of affiliation and deferral, suggests the feminine. This does not mean that the structure of language is sex-linked, but rather that Western culture has established and reinforced gender-specific patterns which can be compared to this bipolar system of language. I argue here that Schneiderman's use of confession, replacing Lacan's theory, operates as metaphor and this strategy figures in a hierarchical arrangement. Gallop's heuristics, in contrast, operate along the metonymic plane. See chapter 5, "Metaphor and Metonymy ('The Agency of the Letter')" in *Reading Lacan* for Gallop's reading application of linguistics. For a more extensive discussion of Gallop's use of metaphor and metonymy, see Phil Barrish, "Rehearsing a Reading," *Diacritics* 16, no. 4 (Winter 1986).
12. Schneiderman, *Jacques Lacan*, p. 27.
13. Ibid., pp. 129–30.
14. Jacques Derrida combines logocentrism and phallocentrism in Western culture into "phallogocentrism." He observes: "It is one and the same system: the erection of a paternal logos . . . and of the phallus as 'privileged' signifier (Lacan)." Quoted in Jonathan Culler, *On Deconstruction: Theory and Criticism after Structuralism* (Ithaca: Cornell University Press, 1982), p. 172.
15. Schneiderman, *Jacques Lacan*, p. 132.
16. Freud observes: "Hysterical symptoms are the expression on the one hand of a masculine unconscious sexual phantasy, and on the other hand of a feminine one"; *S.E.*, 9:165.
17. Ibid., 159–60.
18. Ibid., 234.
19. More 'linguistically experienced,' Lacan holds sway over Schneiderman since one supposes Lacan's French more secure than Schneiderman's. Nowhere, however, does Schneiderman state in what language his analytic sessions were conducted. Because he emphasizes that Lacan is "untranslatable"—Schneiderman's rationale for not quoting Lacan in English—I can only assume that these sessions were spoken in French.
20. Gallop, *Reading Lacan*, p. 35.
21. Jacques Lacan, *The Four Fundamental Concepts of Psycho-Analysis*, trans. Alan Sheridan (New York: W. W. Norton and Co., 1981), p. 232.
22. Gallop, *Reading Lacan*, p. 44.

23. Ibid., p. 185.

24. Ibid., p. 31.

25. Ibid., p. 110.

26. Ibid., p. 185.

27. Jane Gallop, *The Daughter's Seduction: Feminism and Psychoanalysis* (Ithaca: Cornell University Press, 1982), p. 37. The very same observation applies to Gallop's style, particularly evident in *Reading Lacan*. Somewhat different from Lacan, though, she foregrounds her style by the "self-consciousness" which accompanies and layers her readings. See discussion above on Gallop's "narcissistic investment" in her "reading/writing."

28. Peter Brooks, *Reading for the Plot: Design and Intention in Narrative* (New York: Vintage Books, 1985), p. 61.

29. "Seduction" implies some degree of mutuality, yet the notion of mutuality (to the extent that it implies choice) is complicated when lines of power offset the relation between participants. Feminist thought has guided attention to the gender lines of power. In the context of Freud's seduction theory, we must reconsider mutuality in adult/child relations as well as the ways in which the unconscious complicates the operations of seduction and mutuality.

30. Maria Ramas, "Freud's Dora, Dora's Hysteria" and Madelon Sprengnether, "Enforcing Oedipus: Freud and Dora," both reprinted in *In Dora's Case: Freud—Hysteria—Feminism*, ed. Charles Bernheimer and Claire Kahane (New York: Columbia University Press, 1985).

31. Ross Chambers, *Story and Situation: Narrative Seduction and the Power of Fiction* (Minneapolis: University of Minnesota Press, 1984), pp. 6–14.

32. Gallop, *Reading Lacan*, p. 20.

33. Ibid., p. 147.

34. Ibid., p. 19.

35. This "Prefatory Material" is subdivided into "PrefaStory" and "PrefatHEory." Taken together, the internal capitalizations spell out "SHE," the privileged combined signifier and proposed orientation of Gallop's feminist reading practice. Moreover, these accidentals code the confessional moments, the story portions, as feminine, while theory is aligned with the masculine. Although this gender encoding seeks to recognize the political context of Gallop's book on Lacanian psychoanalysis, a subject often vehemently criticized by feminists as masculine-oriented, there is something unsettling in the way her own codes reinforce the very binary opposition she interrogates.

36. Kristina Straub makes a similar observation in her review essay, "Psychoanalytic Relation and Feminist Praxis in *Reading Lacan*," *Literature and Psychology* 32, no. 4 (1986). Her article offers some suggestive insights on Gallop's "ambiguous" relation to psychoanalysis.

    Gallop also ends the "Interstory" section by announcing that she has returned, but with a critical difference, to the consulting room: "As I finish off my manuscript, I am currently in therapy, have been for three months, with a woman psychologist who is neither a physician nor a psychoanalyst" (p. 113). The confessional moments attest to the incompatibility between Gallop's feminism and psychoanalysis. During her months in traditional psychoanalysis, she confides, Gallop was unable to write her book. This codicil, her final dated entry in the "Interstory," suggests that she has reached a reconciliation, or rather a new marriage, between feminism and psychological "self"-scrutiny.

John Muller, in his review essay, "Lacan's Transmission" (forthcoming), cites Gallop's unresolved transference as the cause of the substantive weakness of the second half (the portion after "Interstory") of *Reading Lacan*: "It shows us how a 'reading transference' becomes contaminated by an analytic transference." Muller does not read the political statement staged by Gallop's confessions, and privileges without scrutiny a clinical or "real" transference over a reading transference.

37. Gallop, *Reading Lacan*, p. 131.
38. Schneiderman, *Jacques Lacan*, p. 28.
39. Gallop, *Reading Lacan*, p. 183.
40. Schneiderman, *Jacques Lacan*, p. 23.

Baudrillard's Bad Attitude

By now it's clear to everyone that Jean Baudrillard has a bad attitude. He writes with an animus that is not exactly antisocial, but
is rather the result of oversocialization. His is not then the voice of
the delinquent, the pariah, or, as has often been suggested, not least
by himself, the nihilist. With Baudrillard, it is more apt to speak of
a vendetta, a highly ritualized feud with culture itself, for there is
nothing in the realm of cultural events and objects with which he
does not have a bone to pick. This kind of social temper (practically
a distemper) unavoidably lends itself to an apocalyptic tone and sees
the end of history in any and almost every object of contemplation he
encounters: a jogger with his Walkman, seen alone on a beach, pun-
ishing his body in the solitary, suicidal sacrifice of all of his physical
energy—to what end? Or the muscle-woman whose self-developed
vaginal muscles allow her, Baudrillard claims, to reproduce exactly
masculine penetration—the embodiment of autoreferentiality?

For the true apocalyptic, the kind of question which Baudrillard
likes to cite as symptomatic—"What are you doing after the orgy?"
—is always a rhetorical one. For Baudrillard, however, it is simply
a banal question, for if it suggests the end of history, then it is a
particular *idea* of history that has ended; an idea which Baudrillard
invokes by way of the great nineteenth-century themes of "nature,"
"production," and "desire," but which is based upon an earlier and
abiding faith in the rationality of social forms. It is therefore an
apocalypse that is fatal to European philosophy alone, for it has long
since been a socialized component of everyday life in the (wild) technological West in the name of "utopia achieved."

Baudrillard is resolved to show the full extent of the sphere of
banality, with its built-in apocalypse, that characterizes modern consumer culture. He is less concerned to investigate the historical conditions from which the "obscene" social forms of postmodern hyper-

reality have arisen. In this respect, he strikes a new note in cultural criticism. Unlike the traditional conservative critique of technological culture, which ranges from the embattled aristocratism of Spengler, Gasset, Eliot, and the Agrarians, to the ardent Luddism of Leavis and MacDonald, Baudrillard has no organic past to prefer over modernity. Unlike the mandarin formalism of the Frankfurt school, he has no faith in the redemptionary power of avant-garde culture. And as for McLuhan's theses, he has inverted them one by one, transforming the post-Gutenberg implosion of a brave new humanism into the implosion of the social itself, now reduced to a flat, screenlike surface which simulates a sense of occasion without depth, affect, or history.

So too, in his work from the early seventies (in *The Mirror of Production* and *For a Critique of the Political Economy of the Sign*), Baudrillard had put to the sword the Marxist and Freudian traditions in a trenchant criticism of their attempts to rationalize and systematize the character and effects of capital and the unconscious. Thereby delivered from the kind of materialist methodologies that many of his contemporaries were still trying to reformulate in a poststructuralist way, Baudrillard had long since renounced the possibility of *transcendental* critique. On the contrary, his has been the voice of immanence, crying in the manmade wilderness of an information culture that owns and processes our very critical responses for us.

Without an attitude toward history, Baudrillard himself is perhaps yet another symptom of a culture for which history, at best, is manufactured in Disneyland and other centers of simulation. There is indeed in Baudrillard's attitude a strong element of what more morally-minded critics would call "collusion"; an active or willful complicity with the given, and, consequently, a reluctance to interpret the latent, or ideological, features of the culture at large. In effect, he is less concerned with the ways in which culture is produced than he is obsessed with the mode of disappearance or brute sense of desertion which characterizes the staged productions of an ever more disenchanted (in Weber's sense) world. Rather than account for what remains of history, he sees no further than the fact of its extinction.

For Baudrillard, however, whose own moralism seems to be appropriately confined to the descriptive mode (*O tempora! O mores!*), the choice of collusion, ironic or not, is itself a site of contestation. In a culture which tries to simulate our responses for us, contestation no longer involves choosing between several, available modes of open confrontation; now, it is strategic, covert, cryptic and illusion-ary—a Gramscian war of position rather than a war of maneuver. Set against the grand Utopian sweep of his precursors' adventures in cul-tural criticism, Baudrillard's strategies cannot help but be viewed as a lowering of the stakes; to outdo the inauthentic in inauthenticity is hardly the most heroic, or militant, course of action to advocate. In a world, nonetheless, in which the real has been reduced to a "stock-pile of dead matter, dead bodies, dead language—a sedimentary resi-due,"[1] the old, militant, even "virile" faith in producing new versions of reality is no longer a powerful source of alternative action. That is a banal strategy, and can never be anything but necroscopic (the bane of our existence) because it is aimed at a world beyond the world of appearances. Baudrillard's strategies, by contrast, are fatal and necromantic; their destiny, if you like, is not anatomical, but is bound up with the vicissitudes of the symbolic universe and its shimmering fabric of signs. In this respect, they can be added to the growing body of parasitical discourses—mimickry, disarticula-tion, plagiarism—advanced by theorists who have sought to fashion a politics out of the poststructuralist critique.

Baudrillard's own attempts to formulate such a politics have undergone a significant shift since the time of *For a Critique of the Political Economy of the Sign* and its largely abstract proposition of a "symbolic exchange" beyond the mere circulation of use-value. If Baudrillard, buoyed up by his new visibility as a cultural prophet, has tried to internalize discursively this symbolic exchange in his more recent work, then it is because he has given himself over to the deep immanence of a position that renounces the traditional rights of the universal intellectual who exercises the transcendental privilege of imagining a Utopian future for a particular, dominated social group. At the heart of this shift is his abiding faith in the reversibility of signs, and the corresponding thesis that all discourse is threatened by this black magic of signs turning themselves into their contrary meanings.

In *De la séduction* (1979), Baudrillard outlines a particular way of describing this thesis. Seduction, with its dependence on artifice and inauthenticity, is a "feminine" challenge to the "masculine" prin-ciples of the nineteenth-century bourgeois worship of nature and production. Seduction is thus the feminine reverse of sex, meaning, and power, which is to say that the feminine seduces the mascu-line, it does not oppose the masculine. It is not surface as opposed to depth—it renders indistinct such oppositions—and in this it re-sembles the qualities of the simulacrum (neither copy nor original), the theoretical mass-object with which Baudrillard has been most famously associated. Seduction, for example, disrupts the hermeneutic of depth which psychoanalysis invokes in its distinction between manifest and latent. For Baudrillard, the repression of the power of seduction stands at the origin of Freud's scientific imposture of codifying the laws of the unconscious. (So too, Saussure's science of linguistics flourishes at the cost of his repression of the linguistic play discovered in the earlier *Anagrammes*.)

This is a different claim, of course, from that of Jeffrey Masson, whose attacks on Freudianism are predicated upon the actuality of real experiences of seduction. Unlike Masson, Baudrillard would not object to Freud's discovery of the importance of fantasy in infantile sexuality. Rather, it is Freud's devotion to an objective, mechanistic code of interpretation that offends Baudrillard, because it promises to distinguish between the fantasmatic and the lived real. The Freudian hermeneutic would threaten to expose the trompe l'oeil effects of our psychic life, and thereby restore historicity, landscape, vanishing point, and natural light to a scene that for Baudrillard is essentially simulated. In his preferred structure of power relations, then, knowledge or mastery of the real is a hoax; the real source of power lies, if anywhere, in learning how to manipulate the symbolic world of appearances, and its privileged operation is that of seduction.

What is most troubling about *De la séduction*, however, are the moments in which Baudrillard levels his appraisal of the feminine/ seductive at feminists for whom anatomy is an essentialist frame of reference, and for whom femininity is opposed to, and not differentiated from, masculinity. Baudrillard's advice is to forgo this strategy, and to recognize, instead, that the feminine, like seduction, is the dominant, constitutive form of the symbolic order; masculine truth, by contrast, is only a repressive, institutionalizing secondary order of meanings. Whatever is to be gained by this advice *in abstracto* is lost through Baudrillard's inability to recognize the urgency of a wide range of feminist strategies, crucial to a feminist politics that has survived through its claims of relative autonomy. Although she herself has described at length the progressive links between seduction and feminist strategies, Jane Gallop is surely correct to record how she feels "insulted" by Baudrillard's advice.[2]

Gallop's more specific objection, however, is to Baudrillard's attitude toward writing. Because it is so heavily dependent upon categories and distinctions, his mode of polemic, she claims, is far from seductive. In fact, Gallop would have us understand that Baudrillard is, in spite of himself, too much on the side of masculine truth, and that he has not accepted "the necessity for entanglement, contradiction and loss of mastery" through which writers, advised thus by poststructuralism, have forsaken their authorial will to power. This characterization, however, will seem inappropriate to habitual readers of Baudrillard's work who have been both disarmed and exhilarated by his bad attitude toward the evidence of logical assertion. It is true that Baudrillard proceeds methodologically by category and distinction. But each successive distinction breaks up, as if by some nuclear chain reaction, into further demarcated categories, each with its own set of vertiginous discriminations: obscenity/secrecy, obscene/scene, banality/fatality, pornography/trompe l'oeil, perversion/seduction, simulated seduction/true seduction, fascination/simulation, disenchanted simulation/enchanted simulation, hyperreality/autofascination, etc. This process of fission is incessant, while it serves no finely moral end other than its own inexorable logic. Even if it delivers each fresh distinction with a ceremonious air of foreknowledge, it is a perfect example of Kant's "purposiveness without purpose." Some readers will say that Baudrillard works this method to excess, thereby exhausting the rationalist logic that underpins it. Thus, if it is indeed seductive, then it is because it relentlessly parodies the Socratic method, invoking the mode of discrimination as a moral imperative of form in itself. Others will point out that such a fugitive method is always his best chance of escaping from a tight polemical corner, and that it is a serviceable strategy well known to those who find themselves in a position to exercise power and exact domination.

Whatever the damage to logic, or to truth, we are so claustrally locked into this methodology as readers of Baudrillard that we become overacquainted with its conventional responses. Meaghan Morris has written well of the "adjectival escalation" involved in the comparativist leap that takes us beyond each successive category in the name of a generic equation: "more X than X" ("more real than the real," "more true than the true," "more commodified than the commodity."[3] The reading effect of this "ecstasy of the comparative" is like "hallucinating on platitude," to use the phrase that Baudrillard himself employs to describe an audience at a hyperrealist sculpture exhibition. Morris declares this to be the perfect description of the "pleasures of hype" that are evoked by Baudrillard's fatal charms. Hype, then, or hyperbole in an age of mass cozenage. It is no surprise to find that this is Baudrillard's trope, and that the worst of his fears is to come across readers who cannot be seduced, or hyp(e)-

notized. For these would be undersocialized readers, ill equipped to respond to, let alone activate, the reversibility of signs. Such a reader would be immune to the runaway rate of inflation which informs Baudrillard's trope.

Hype contaminates as much as it communicates. In fact, its viral spread, like the "white lymph" of Baudrillard's contaminating media images, is ubiquitous in the voracious communications universe which Baudrillard has described in a highly influential series of articles and books, running from "Requiem for the Media" to *Les stratégies fatales*. In his recent book, *Amérique*, he expects to meet his match in the land of hype. For it is into the deserts of the West that he ventures in order to lose the way of the world, and reclaim another, much older voice, that cries in the wilderness.

Baudrillard's adventures on the North American continent are, of course, backed up by a long history of rhetorical inflation. Early European travelers to the New World, charged with the promise of fantastic riches, adopted hyperbole as the sovereign trope of their rhetoric of discovery. More recently, in a justly celebrated essay, "Travels in Hyperreality," a modern Renaissance man, Umberto Eco, has written in luxuriating prose about an America that "has to be discovered." He is referring to the national culture of kitsch, sham, and fakery that Eco, like Baudrillard, finds everywhere emblematized in the obsessive exhibition of copies, in every form imaginable, of European art objects.

Eco's journey in search of the "absolute fake" takes him from the numerous wax models of *The Last Supper* to be found all over California, to the Ringling Museum of Art in Florida, owned by the circus family; he moves between the sublime scholarship of the Getty Museum to Disneyland, the "Sistine Chapel" of degenerate utopias, where imitation reaches its zenith, and where reality will always be inferior. In his trip from one sanctuary of the genuine to the next, Eco is careful to note the link between the worship of art and the vacuum of history which supports and maintains the discourse of popular respect for these transplantations of the Old World into the New. Like all *marxisant* visiting intellectuals, he is properly fascinated and repelled by a culture which so obsessively pursues the "real thing," while he generously adds his own voice, overladen with its own surfeit of showy burlesque, to the chorus of kitsch affect radiating out from the artificial paradises he visits. Of the "barbarian grandeur" of Hearst's San Simeon castle, he reflects: "It is like making love in a confessional with a prostitute dressed in a prelate's liturgical

robes reciting Baudelaire while ten electronic organs reproduce the
Well Tempered Clavier played by Scriabin."[4] We recognize in this the
voice of the intellectual gone slumming.

More ostentatious yet, at least in its attempt to outdo the ostentatious vulgarity of its object, is Eco's hallucinatory projections of
the Madonna Inn, the "poor man's" version of Hearst Castle:

> Let's say that Albert Speer, while leafing through a book on Gaudi,
> swallowed an overgenerous dose of LSD and began to build a nuptial
> catacomb for Liza Minnelli. But that doesn't give you an idea. Let's
> say Arcimboldi builds the Sagrada Familia for Dolly Parton. Or: Car-
> men Miranda designs a Tiffany locale for the Jolly Hotel chain. Or
> D'Annunzio's Vittoriale imagined by Bob Cratchit. Calvino's *Invisible
> Cities* described by Judith Krantz and executed by Leonor Fini for the
> plush-doll industry. Chopin's Sonata in B flat minor sung by Perry Como
> in an arrangement by Liberace and accompanied by the Marine Band.
> No, that still isn't right.[5]

Eco succeeds to ever more tiresome flights of camp fantasy, for he
is just as disingenuously in pursuit of the "real description" as the
middle-class tourist is supposed to be in pursuit of the "real thing."

Like a traditional anthropologist, Eco feels that he should be
able to make sense of this culture, since he is a European, deeply
engaged in art and history, who alone possesses a language that is
capable of assimilating this hybrid object-world. For the European
intellectual, then, America's culture of simulation lies in wait like
some immense and continuous found object, while he can say that
"American intellectuals are quite right to refuse to go" to places like
Disneyland, presumably because they are too close to home. Eco,
of course, recognizes home when he sees it, in Louisiana, where he
checks in to measure the real New Orleans against its recreation in
Disneyland. In New Orleans, to his relief, "history still exists and
is tangible," the city "passes out memories generously like a great
lord"; it doesn't have to pursue the "real thing."[6] In this milieu,
the lures and workings of ideology are more familiar to Eco. In the
hinterland of hyperreality, ideology itself is an effect, staged for consumption and profit, and therefore devoid of its seductive trappings
which the European intellectual is so used to exposing on his or her
own turf.

By virtue of dressing down, and working up, his pop mode, Eco
seems nonetheless to want to take his share of responsibility for a
culture that will guarantee the survival of Europe in the same way
that Rome sought to preserve Greek culture, albeit in the form of

copies. Who, after all, is right? One need only invoke Benjamin's famous thesis, which questions the morality of all cultural transactions: "There is no document of civilization which is not at the same time a document of barbarism. And just as such a document is not free of barbarism, barbarism taints also the manner in which it was transmitted from owner to owner."[7] Eco's traveler is willing to accept the burden of European guilt not only for art's "barbarism" but also for history's associated excesses. It would be kindly to think that he undertakes his ambassadorial journey in the good faith of turning Tocqueville on his head.

"Travels in Hyperreality" is everywhere resonant with the more questionable attitude of Baudrillard toward the American "state culture" of hyperreality. For in Baudrillard's *Amérique* we find a different kind of traveler, a European who is privileged to know that "Europe" completely disappears in "America" (it is not preserved in any representational form, no matter how secondary), and who, unlike Eco, in his sightseeing trips to the monuments of culture, pursues this knowledge quite literally to the ends of the earth in the desert regions of the West.

For Baudrillard, America is where there is no seduction; it is a social space that is immune to the multilayered *commedia dell'arte* of European life and culture. More alien yet, it is the only truly primitive society, an artificial paradise which thrives upon the miracle of *obscenity*, his term for connoting simulation, transparency, fascination for the empty, the hyperreal, the cryogenized body, the evacuation of history. Like a gigantic hologram, its information is totally contained in each and every one of its components—a Burger King, a parking lot, a Studebaker—and it can thus be telescopically reduced into successive microcosmic models of the national essence: the West, California, Disneyland, Las Vegas/Death Valley. America has always behaved as if it were an achieved utopia, and so Baudrillard finds that it subscribes to the same moral, utopian perspective (politics is never an issue in this country) held by those eighteenth-century gentlemen who fashioned Puritan dissent into a revolution of egalitarian originality.

By contrast, Europe is the home of the *scene*, with its Renaissance Italianate origin in illusion, depth, perspective and trompe l'oeil—the home, in short, of seduction. But Europe has lived by the universal—reason, history, Marxism, man—and will die by the universal. Finally, it will be debilitated by the sirens of the West, who preach, rather than sing, that a fierce ecological morality must thrive alongside the deathly logic of capitalism, and that each and every technology must always appear in its primitive state of development —hygienic, natural, indifferent to its production.

Baudrillard invests this scenario between European scenery and American obscenity with the studied devotion of a biblical zealot. Evidence of postapocalyptic life—what are you doing after the orgy? —when everything is available and nothing is wanting, is a hysterical simulation of social relations that have long since lost any secret promise of hidden authenticity. Paradise is hell. Sexuality is a game and not a mode of social articulation. Politics is merely a death mask. Culture is a wilderness to which intellect and aesthetics are ritually sacrificed. Although *Amérique* contains its share of urban investigations, it is hardly surprising to find Baudrillard taking to the wilderness in the best tradition (*vox clamans*) of the desert prophet. Of course, it turns out to be a desert without a garden, a journey that offers elemental proof that ascesis and denial are not sites of opposition, but rather the purest symptoms of a society fascinated with the emptiness of its forms.

Echoing Victor Hugo, Frank Lloyd Wright said: "The Desert is where God is and Man is not." But Wright's comment evokes only that desert tradition which produced the paranoid solipsism of the patristics. The other, older desert tradition is that of communal exile of the early Christians, a history that presents us with a desert that is not at all deserted, but populated with all manner of cultures, commercial, nomadic, outlawed and communitarian alike. In *Scenes in American Deserta*, a book that anticipates *Amérique* and to which Baudrillard refers in passing, the English architecture critic Reyner Banham revives the extensive English genre of desert travel literature, the finest example of which is Charles Doughty's epic *Travels in Arabia Deserta*, and behind which genre Banham detects the nordic, Protestant obsession with the populated, if not entirely inhabited, desert culture of the Old Testament.[8] Accordingly, while Banham finds personal moments of Anglican epiphany in the course of his American travels, these are moments suggested not by some irreducible communion with the otherness of nature/God, but rather by the arbitrary, quirky, and always humanized event: an illusory point of view on a desert landscape that reveals some vast disproportion or discrepancy on the perspectival scale; or else a passing encounter with one of the capricious "desert freaks" who roam the landscape and set up temporary domiciles in its nooks and crannies. In fact, Banham begins to take his place among the complex subculture of these desert freaks, who compare and exchange knowledge about the fat corpus of desert literature and desert lore as eagerly as hi-tech hackers swap information about software. His desert is full of scenes, and thus sites of seduction, because it is a place where anything is thinkable once one has been captured by the lure of its many optical illusions. It is no surprise, for example, that the rich lore of UFO subculture has its origins in desert sightings, or that the unthinkable nightmare of the atomic bomb and advanced missile systems have their material reality, past and present, there.

For Banham, finally, the desert is a "slow burn," the result of a lived experience that is at home in the desert, and not in ascetic exile. Nothing could be further from Baudrillard's desert, which has little to do with nature and even less to do with humanity. In fact, his desert is saturated with "unculture"; it may even be a profound critique of culture, radically indifferent to the aesthetics of "disappearance" that Baudrillard both exalts and vilifies as obscenity of the first order. Ultimately, it is immoral and thus exhilarating, because of its extreme deliverance from lived, social space, temporality and desire. This desert is obscene and fascinating, because it has eliminated every possible means of seduction. Everywhere else, nature (especially European nature) is full of meaning, whereas here Baudrillard is confronted only with the external catastrophe of nonmeaning. Of course, he sees no strip-mining, no Indian reservations, and few traces of the long history of human migration across the West (just as he sees no ghetto, or rustbelt, in the city). Baudrillard's desert is a "desert forever," and thus a neutral surface which, while it speaks from the margins of American culture, wants to prove that neutrality and superficiality are just as much at home here as they are at the hi-tech core.

On another level, the desert is a stunning example of what, notoriously, Baudrillard finds merely fascinating and not seductive in pornography. What is obscene about the pornographic image is the "fascination of being seduced by a dead object," and therefore the attempt to seduce through hypervisibility: everything is on show, nothing is hidden:

> [Pornography is] the disembodied passion of a look without an image. For a long time now our mediated spectacles have been crossing the border into the realm of speculation. This stupefaction is what is obscene, it is the glazed extreme of the body. The glazed extreme of sex, it is an empty scene where nothing happens and yet one that fills the viewfinder. It might just as easily be the stage for information, or for politics, as for sex! Nothing happens and yet we are saturated by it.[9]

Pornography, for Baudrillard, is self-evidently *there*. In pornography, however, we do not see the image for what it represents, we see the image for what it is—the product of a generic set of representational codes and conventions. For Baudrillard, the "hypervisibility" of the pornographic image and its corresponding loss of "scene" saturate the medium. As a result, the real can be only a continuation of representation by other means. There is no need to account for the nature of representation itself and its various constructions of subjectivity (or more important, its nonconstruction of female subjectivity).

So too, Baudrillard's "obscenario" fails to recognize that "seeing everything" is a media convention which pays its own ambiguous tribute to fantasy in pornography as constitutionally as it does in the exposé of political scandals, the consequences of which often take the form of a national ritual of televised hearings and inquiries. Indeed, the very existence of pornography is protected under a set of constitutionally extended liberties similar to those which guarantee the public right to hear everything. Naive, resistant to seduction, and painfully moralistic, such conventions/rights, to the Baudrillardian European, will speak only to the excesses and not to the achievements of the American democracy cult.

Is it Baudrillard's suspicion of the democratic guarantee of rights and access which finally explains what I have called his bad attitude? If, as I believe, this is the root of the Baudrillard problem, then it is an attitude that we can find enshrined, in many different forms, in the more commonly held perceptions of modern neoconservatism—in other words, the consensus of interests which has agreed to see capitalism, but not to see through it. Like other Europeans, Baudrillard has arrived at this position in his own way and in his own time, and his critical voice retains the radical or oppositional rhetorical edge which is foreign to the ex-liberals who characterize the American neoconservative scene. But his is nonetheless a critique of excess, of hyperinformation, of overrepresentation. It is nowhere a critique of the excesses of a centralized elite in power. In fact, his abiding faith in seduction *tout court* could easily be read as a faith in older, European, and preliberal versions of power, as power was once exercised through spectacle and other forms of public (though not necessarily popular) theatricality.

Finally, his critique of excess strikes hard at the superstructures raised upon basic democratic foundations. Whether in the desert, at a female mud-wrestling show, or confronting some smooth, hi-tech surface, I find that Baudrillard is prone to that slip of the tongue which speaks "excess" for "access," and which has been so fundamental to neoconservative thought that kicks into reverse gear at the spectacle of the egalitarian gains of the sixties. Whether or not this is merely an expression of hype—a Baudrillardian strategy of high mimickry which parasitically weakens its host discourse—remains to be seen. Of this much we can be sure, however. If he does not come to "Amérique" to praise Tocqueville, he does not go out of his way to bury Tocqueville's highhanded legacy of suspicion and disdain for the continuing experiment of democracy, ever stifled but still alive and kicking. And if he comes to make his peace with capitalism, then he is wise to head for the deserts; he knows that there is little hope of finding the "peace which passeth understanding" in the inner cities.

NOTES

1. Jean Baudrillard, *De la séduction* (Paris: Galilée, 1979), p. 70.
2. Jane Gallop, "French Theory and the Seduction of Feminism," in *Men in Feminism*, ed. Alice Jardine and Paul Smith (New York: Methuen, 1987).
3. Meaghan Morris, "Room 101 or a Few Worst Things in the World," in *Seduced and Abandoned: The Baudrillard Scene*, ed. André Frankovits (Glebe, Australia: Stonemoss, 1984), pp. 91–117.
4. Umberto Eco, *Travels in Hyperreality*, trans. William Weaver (New York: Harcourt, Brace, Jovanovich, 1986), pp. 23–24.
5. Ibid.
6. Ibid., pp. 29–30.
7. Walter Benjamin, "Theses on the Philosophy of History," in *Illuminations*, ed. Hannah Arendt, trans. Harry Zohn (New York: Harcourt Brace, 1968), p. 257.
8. Reyner Banham, *Scenes in American Deserta* (Salt Lake City: Peregrine Smith, 1982).
9. Jean Baudrillard, "What Are You Doing after the Orgy?" *Artforum* (October 1983), 43. A selected Baudrillard bibliography: *Le système des objets* (Paris: Gallimard, 1968); *The Mirror of Production* (1973), trans. Mark Poster (St. Louis: Telos Press, 1975); *For a Critique of the Political Economy of the Sign* (1972), trans. Charles Levin (St. Louis: Telos Press, 1981); *In the Shadow of the Silent Majorities* (1978), trans. Paul Foss, Paul Patton, and John Johnston (New York: Semiotext(e), 1983); *Simulations* (1981), trans. Paul Foss, Paul Patton, and Philip Beitchman (New York: Semiotext(e), 1983); *Les stratégies fatales* (Paris: Grasset, 1983); *Amérique* (Paris: Grasset, 1986); *Cool Memories: 1980–1985* (Paris: Galilée, 1987).

Romancing the Philosophers: Luce Irigaray

Luce Irigaray's English-speaking readers are sometimes surprised to learn that she considers her object of analysis not psychoanalysis per se but rather, philosophical discourse in general: "the one that lays down the law to the others . . . the discourse on discourses."[1] This discovery may be unsettling in countries where philosophy shares neither the prestige nor the tradition that Irigaray attributes to the "master discourse," and where feminist readers sometimes object to her engagement with kinds of theory that they see as either misogynistic or irrelevant, or both. Moreover, through the accidents of translation and differences in cultural context, even those who are sympathetic toward her work have tended to emphasize its critique of psychoanalysis at the expense of her philosophical project. Now that the complete texts of *Speculum of the Other Woman* and *This Sex Which Is Not One* are available in English, we are in a better position to evaluate the magnitude and daring of this project, a radical reinterpretation of Western philosophic tradition, which, in her view, includes psychoanalysis as "a possible enclave of philosophic discourse."[2]

Put schematically, *Speculum* is a massive dismantling of the "phallogocentric" mechanisms of Western metaphysical tradition, which relegates the feminine to the position of the object, matter, or material against which the masculine subject defines itself, thereby subordinating the feminine to an economy of exchange among masculine subjects. *This Sex* serves both as a kind of postface to *Speculum*, amplifying and illustrating its ideas, and as a moving call for a "speaking (as) woman" (*parler-femme*), a mode of expression capable of embodying what Irigaray takes to be feminine desire. Both in the

A different form of this essay appeared in the Minnesota Review *n.s. 29 (Fall 1987).*

original French and in the fragmentary translations available until recently, these books have already had a major impact on feminist theory of various persuasions, literary criticism, and film theory, as readers have assimilated their strangeness and massive complexity. But just as her writing began to seem readable, almost accessible, Irigaray appeared to take off in another direction. For in *Amante marine, de Friedrich Nietzsche* (1980), *Passions élémentaires* (1982), *L'Oubli de l'air* (1982), and "Fecondité de la caresse" (1983), Irigaray pursued her reinterpretation of philosophy in a style so unfamiliar even to those trained in its traditions that many readers wondered whether her original project had not gone astray. As if in anticipation of their bafflement, Irigaray commented on her unusual method in *Speculum*, "Philosophical mastery . . . cannot simply be approached head on, nor simply within the realm of the philosophical itself. Thus it was necessary to deploy other languages . . . so that something of the feminine as the limit of the philosophical might finally be heard."[3] This essay discusses the deployment of those other languages in her recent attempts to initiate a sideways dialogue with the masters of philosophy whom she tried to approach head-on in her earlier writing.

From the start, Irigaray was aware that her oblique linguistic strategies could lead to misunderstanding, given the generally accepted requirements for logical coherence and discursive clarity. In *Speculum*, however, she was already pushing against these forms of intelligibility, which, in her view, result in a conception of theory and method "that has always also led us away, led us astray, by fraud and artifice, from woman's path" to knowledge. She concluded that "in order to reopen woman's path, in particular in and through language, it was therefore necessary to note the way in which the method is never as simple as it purports to be, the way in which the teleological project [that] . . . the method takes on is always a project, conscious or not, of turning away, of deviation, and of reduction, in the artifice of sameness, of otherness. In other words, speaking at the greatest level of generality so far as philosophical methods are concerned: of the feminine."[4] Theory itself had seduced or turned its followers away from the feminine, while taking unto itself the privilege of speaking as the universal. But how was the silenced feminine to reassert itself within a system that denied its existence? By countering one form of seduction with another: "It was necessary to destroy, but, as René Char wrote, with nuptial tools. . . . To put it another way: the option left to me was to have a fling with the philosophers, which is easier said than done."[5] Having a fling with the philosophers, seducing them on their own ground, was the only recourse of the feminine, given the position to which it had been relegated.

But, Irigaray asked, "what path can one take to get inside their ever so coherent systems? . . . (how) to go back inside the philosopher's house" to attract his attention? Two interim strategies are possible for female subjects. The first, to accept the roles already assigned to the feminine in relation to the masculine, either as "reproductive material" (maternal space or matter), or as "duplicating mirror" (whose function is to send back the masculine subject's self-reflection). Moreover, if a woman plays either of these roles, she must do so seductively: "The philosopher's wife must also . . . be beautiful, and *exhibit all the attractions of femininity*, in order to distract a gaze too often carried away by theoretical contemplations."[6] Irigaray equates this traditionally feminine pose with Freudian femininity: a seductive masquerade in which the woman displays her charms because she knows this is what the man wants of her.[7] Such femininity is always alienated, since it permits the woman to experience desire not in her own right but only as the man's desire situates her. The second strategy for the philosopher's spouse is what Irigaray calls "mimicry" (*mimétisme*), the deliberate assumption of the feminine posture assigned to her within the realm of discourse in order to uncover the mechanisms by which it represses her.[8]

But if the woman does not wish to marry the philosopher, which means espousing his ideas about her, how is she to engage his attention? In her writings published between 1980 and 1983, Irigaray sets out to romance her philosophical partners in a "langage amoureux," an amorous language that begins with a seductive stance in order to move beyond it. Although it could be said that in these encounters with Nietzsche, Heidegger, the pre-Socratics, and Levinas, "Irigaray's writing takes the form of a lover's discourse,"[9] her textual politics differ from those of Roland Barthes: his *A Lover's Discourse* (1977) is written from within a masculine subject's psychology of the amorous imagination, where the loved one is so much the absent other of Lacanian theory that the speaker abandons any attempt to appropriate his alterity. In contrast to this situation, Irigaray initiates dialogue with her philosopher-lovers by weaving herself in and out of their arguments, thus insinuating the feminine into their systems. Nor does Irigaray write in the manner of Derrida's equally seductive *La Carte postale* (1980), although *Amante marine*, her first experiment in this new style, only lightly veils the presence of Derrida behind her actual interlocuter, Nietzsche (whose figure of woman as "a name for (the) untruth of truth" Derrida had explored in *Spurs*, without, however, giving a voice to any actual female speaker.)[10] She may, in fact, be responding obliquely to Baudrillard's provocative vision of "a universe where the feminine is not that which opposes itself to the masculine, but that which *seduces* the masculine."[11] The purpose of her newly amorous language is to begin "speaking (as) woman"—the project elaborated in her earlier books—and to do so not theoretically but seductively: to beguile her philosophical partners into a recognition of sexual difference.

This sly enterprise disconcerted many feminist readers for whom Irigaray's position appeared to be summed up in the lyrical concluding essay of *This Sex*, "When Our Lips Speak Together." In this first deployment of an amorous language, the speaker imagines a dialogue between female lovers whose resemblance is the basis for their fluid and changing mutuality, figured in the double subject (*tu/je*) with which Irigaray rewrites the subject/object relation as it has been constructed in Western philosophy. With the publication of her subsequent books, however, it became clear that this essay was not a definitive statement, but a hyphen or bridge between the more theoretical texts that preceded it and the more poetic ones that followed (although to make such clear distinctions is to misread Irigaray's project). As several critics have observed, the speaker of "When Our Lips" is haunted by the presence of another woman outside the *tu/je* couple—the mother whose pardon she seeks in a startling parenthesis. This maternal presence emerges like the return of the repressed in her next published work, "And the One Doesn't Stir without the Other" (1979).[12] There, the daughter's appeal to the mother mimes their knotted relationship in the almost visceral quality of the syntax, which suggests blockage and paralysis while only gesturing at their potential release. The final text of this transitional stage, *Le Corps-à-corps avec la mère* (1981), makes clear Irigaray's commitment to an erotics of writing in which feminine modes of embodiment and contact may provide the way out of such paralysis. She advocates not an intellectual tête-à-tête but a physical "corps-à-corps," a close combat between mother and daughter that may allow both to regain the primary narcissism that is the precondition for the love of another.[13] Thus, her amorous language develops from but is not limited by the female homosexuality of "When Our Lips Speak Together" and is grounded in a relation to the material that Irigaray considers the vital starting place for both sexes and all modes of sexual relationship.

Furthermore, such language would no longer be based on the

morphology of the phallus as transcendental signifier and ground of meaning, but on an interplay or "nuptials" (*noces*) between the revitalized female body and a male body newly aware of its interrelation with and recognition of the female partner. Here too, Irigaray had anticipated conceptually what remained for her to write in another language, as she made clear in a 1977 interview: "Historically, [men] have chosen sex and language against or in spite of the body. . . . It would be necessary for women to be recognized as bodies with sexual attribute(s), desiring and uttering, and for men to rediscover the materiality of their bodies. There should no longer be this separation: sex/language on the one hand, body/matter on the other. Then, perhaps, another history would be possible."[14] In such a history, Irigaray would seek to reembody the disembodied Cartesian subject— the *cogito*, a subject who thinks himself as both incorporeal and universal, or sexually neutral. Because the practice of metaphysics has seemed to take the thinker beyond the physical, she seeks to put thinking back in touch with its material sources in a kind of reverse incarnation. Like Heidegger, an important partner in these philosophical dialogues, she would reimmerse thought in the physical world that it has forgotten.

This reverse incarnation is, clearly, neither a scientific model nor an ontological statement. It is, rather, both an evocation of an archaic and fluid worldview that predates or excedes our own more narrowly materialist model of understanding, and a dream of a corporeal philosophy appropriate to the bodies and desires of women. (As such, it also resembles the strategic fables of signification suggested by the figures of the speculum or curved mirror and the lips that are never simply open or closed, in *Speculum* and *This Sex* respectively.) In her most recent texts, Irigaray evokes a conceptual space that has, in her view, been repressed by philosophy since the pre-Socratics: the "elemental" worldview preceding our own "reasoned" science in which the earth, air, fire, and water combine and interact to generate forms of life still in a state of becoming, within the human microcosm as well as in the larger macrocosm. She observed recently of her work since 1980, "I wanted to go back to this natural material which makes up our bodies, in which our lives and environment are grounded: the flesh of our passions."[15] Thus, beginning with *Amante marine*, she planned "a kind of tetralogy which would have touched on the problem of the four elements . . . applied to philosophers closer to us" in order to reopen the philosophical tradition to the specificity of the feminine.[16] This return to a prerational, elemental, and transmutational model provided the conceptual context in which sexual difference could be thought through in more appropriate circumstances. As Elizabeth Gross observes, "This elementary language has the dual advantage of providing a corporeal model of sexual difference, as well as using a terminology, repressed or latent within our history, to describe the powerful relations that constitute love, exchange and social organization."[17]

In *Amante marine*, the first book of the tetralogy, Irigaray works out her own position with, and against, the writings of Nietzsche as the first modern philosopher who himself considered metaphysics a misunderstanding of the body. It is intended not as a book *about* Nietzsche but as a "corps-à-corps" in which Irigaray weaves her own voice in and out of his discourse.[18] Like Nietzsche, Irigaray is by turns poetic, oracular, epigrammatic and deliberately unsystematic, for she wants us to reconsider the material bases that underlie the demand for coherence and system in Western metaphysics. Consequently, she examines Nietzsche from the position of the fluids that she associates with the feminine: "I chose to examine Nietzsche in terms of water because it is the place of the strongest interpellation, it is the element of which he is the most afraid. In *Zarathustra*, we hear his fear of the deluge. Water is what disturbs rigidity of both ices and mirrors (frozen forms and mirrors). It is a pole which I wouldn't call opposite but different, in relation to the sun."[19] In her interpretive rereading, the female speaker tries to cajole the philosopher into desiring her as herself by paradoxically impersonating three figures about whom Nietzsche wrote—Ariadne, Athena, and Persephone—each as "a mask made to order to seduce" him.[20] The first section speaks in the voice of Ariadne, who rescued Theseus from the labyrinth, married Dionysus, and appears to be Zarathustra's ideal woman.[21] Irigaray adopts this voice because Ariadne, like all mythological figures, is fluid, metamorphic, and, in Irigaray's reading, capable of resisting the philosopher's definition of her as *his* feminine. But the philosopher tries to enclose Ariadne within his own labyrinth because she knows the way out of closed systems, and in *Ecce Homo*, asserts "who besides me knows what Ariadne is? She's a riddle, an answer to . . . solar solitude."[22] Thus, he tries to contain the woman to make her the guardian of his being. However, when Ariadne rejects his "noces de glace," the icy marriage that would deny her autonomy, he reencloses himself in his eternal recurrence, the very labyrinth in which he sought to imprison her. Irigaray concludes that each sex could have been the other's labyrinth and the other's way out, if only the philosopher could "drop all disguises and displays and at last, go on a fling."[23]

If Ariadne speaks to Nietzsche from the watery realm of the first seas to confound his landlocked logic, *Passions élémentaires* (1982), the second work of Irigaray's tetralogy, enacts the dividing up of the earth in what is simultaneously a prebiblical evocation of desire as the substratum of existence and a new Genesis. This hymn to erotic love is played out in an archaic conceptual landscape where male and female participate in the redefinition of the world along with the rediscovery of the elements, as if they were once again taking part in that harmonic discord "in which opposites unite in an intense melee."[24] Here, love, the strongest of the passions, can be reinvented as a "corps-à-corps" of opposites who meet in a creative encounter rather than in a seductive power play: "Love is the mode of becoming which appropriates the other to itself by consuming it, introjecting it into the self until it disappears. Or else love is the movement of becoming that allows the one and the other to grow. For such love to exist, each one must keep an autonomous body. One must not be the source of the other, nor the other of the one. Two lives must embrace and fecundate each other with no preconceived goal for either."[25] But enacting such a passion depends upon the recognition of each other's difference, the precondition for "a model of exchange that acknowledges two different sexes as both givers and receivers."[26]

Passions élémentaires also dreams of a world where identities, both "elemental" and sexual, are not confining. Like the oppositions between earth and air, fire and water, sexual difference there is not irremediable as in our world, nor do corporeal boundaries create unbridgeable separations. Bodily morphology does not appear to delimit Irigaray's dream of embracing that which is both like and unlike the self. Her speaker addresses the unnamed masculine lover in terms that reinvent both the cosmos and the body as newly permeable and capable of different relations between near and far, interior and exterior, masculine and feminine, along with all the other oppositions: "Before the separation of the sky from the earth, the continents from the sea, the dark from the light. A mingling of rock, fire, water, ether. Where violence is still wed to softness. The heroic body spilling over with tenderness. Its arms still those of an original innocence. Which confounds all decisive distinctions and returns all divisions to their original nuptials."[27] Irigaray deliberately invokes the language of the pre-Socratics in order to express her vision of a psychic space that precedes our familiar logic of identity. In this more "feminine" (pre-oedipal?) place, where touch and tact have not yet been subordinated to the imperious discriminations of sight, the new mode of circular exchange may at last be possible.

In "Fecondité de la caresse," a related mediation on, and with, Emmanuel Levinas's "The Phenomenology of Eros," Irigaray returns again to "that which was in the beginning": eros prior to the formation of the subject(s) of sexual difference.[28] Levinas, who was the student of both Husserl and Heidegger, has produced an unusual crossing of philosophic traditions by opening the questions of identity and transcendence first formulated in Greek to the perspective of Hebraic ethical thought. Derrida observes of Levinas's work, "This thought summons us to a dislocation of the Greek logos, to a dislocation of our identity, and perhaps of identity in general; it summons us to move forward toward . . . an *exhalation*, toward a prophetic speech."[29] His thought would liberate Western philosophy from the totalizing concepts that dominate it through their repression of otherness, alterity, and difference. Levinas calls instead for an ethical relation to the other as the only path toward transcendence, but he does so as one for whom this "opening" must proceed from within experience itself. For, in his view, we are first of all beings responsive to the sensuous world, to its elemental qualities, its luminosity, elasticity, savor, and vibrancy, before we are beings with a sense of the other as a call to ethical responsibility. In this respect for the other as other, a form of desire that does not seek to seduce or consume, Levinas sees the only basis for metaphysical transcendence.

Derrida also observes that Levinas rejects the supposedly universal or neutral discursive stance in his writing (especially in "The Phenomenology of Eros"), where "the philosophical subject is man (vir)."[30] In response to Levinas's deliberate assumption of a masculine subject, Irigaray again speaks from the position of the feminine, about which he philosophizes but to which he cannot give voice. Thus, where Levinas writes of the lover's responsibility toward the feminine as the "loved one" (*aimée*), Irigaray distinguishes between this passive mode of femininity and that of the more active "beloved" (*amante*), a subject in her own right like the masculine "lover" (*amant*).[31] Furthermore, she extends Levinas's emphasis on the ethical relation with the other to the question of sexual difference—the respectful recognition and love of both partners in their "nuptials." This erotic encounter would allow them to return to "the innocence that never took place with the other as other," where the lover's touch invites the woman "to become what I have not yet become. To realize a birth still in the future. Plunging me back into the maternal womb and beyond that conception, awakening me to another." Thus, because the caress can allow the lonely subject(s) to recollect the original maternal space without reviving desires for mastery or possession, Irigaray describes it as "this always still-preliminary gesture which precedes any union and comes first in all nuptials." Her vision of eros extends the biblical idea of carnal knowledge as a mode of knowing the other by making love to it rather than by imposing our familiar mental categories upon it. For the caress "weds without consuming," regenerates and returns to the other its bodily contours and profound inwardness.[32]

Of his own debt to Heidegger, Levinas recently asserted that his teacher's reinterpretation of metaphysics has "completely altered the course and character of European philosophy," and that, furthermore, "one cannot seriously philosophize today without traversing the Heideggerian path."[33] If Levinas's own example confirmed Irigaray's view of philosophy as an ethical inquiry that needed to be reimmersed in the elemental, there were still related paths for her to traverse in Heidegger's writing: first, in relation to his return to the Greek language as the material basis of Western philosophy, and then, to his "ecologistic" belief that the totalizing stance of post-Cartesian metaphysics had produced the destructive technologies that might annihilate the material bases of our existence. From the start, her amorous language showed the impact of Heidegger's call for a more reverential mode of thinking (as opposed to theorizing) and a different poetics of statement, one closer to the gestural languages of poetry and creative forms that enact what they seek to know rather than speaking objectively or from a distance. But in her view, Heidegger's return to a more embodied philosophy still neglects an elemental dimension of being: the "spatiality that precedes any localization, . . . substratum that is simultaneously immobile and mobile, permanent and flowing," the element of air.[34]

Thus, her next book, *L'Oubli de l'air chez Martin Heidegger*, the third and last book of the proposed tetralogy, observes that in his attempt to get beyond metaphysics, Heidegger still bases his thought on an unexplored materialism, that of "solid ground, that 'illusion' of a path which holds firm beneath his feet." For in her view, "as long as Heidegger does not leave the 'earth,' he does not leave metaphysics behind."[35] And yet, she observes, he was drawn to those airy "openings" and "clearings" in the thought-forest where one might be astonished by "Being." Thus, she finds it surprising that Heidegger did not consider the air an aspect of this central philosophical question, whose propositions all depend upon it as their primary space and irreducibly constituent element. Moreover, for Irigaray, the element of air is also linked to the original human condition, the debt that both sexes owe to the material source of their being—the life-generating powers of the feminine. In *L'Oubli de l'air*, however, Irigaray does not speak from the position of the feminine and all but abandons the stylistic strategies of her amorous language: rather than using the intimate *tu* of the earlier works in the tetralogy, she addresses her interlocutor as *vous*, and rarely uses apostrophe to engage them in dialogue. In place of the seductive voice of Ariadne, the amorous speaker of *Passions*, or the prophetic tone of "Fecondité," Irigaray adopts a more familiar, reasoned philosophical style and lets occasional first-person declarations slip back into her insistent mode of questioning. Once a few airy spaces have been opened in the solidity of systematic thought, however, a more ecstatic tone returns when she dwells on Heidegger's readings of Holderlin, where the philosopher asserts that the poet is a kind of prophet who grounds the sacred by naming it: "To the poet is entrusted the vocation of watching over/guarding this primordial openness which covers and uncovers the sacred with language." Like the lovers of her amorous dialogues, the poet, and the poet-philosopher, inhabit "l'entre-deux," the "space between," which for Irigaray is the home of the sacred.[36]

For this reason, *L'Oubli de l'air* ends in celebration of those amorous thinkers who, like the poets, allow language to speak in, and through, their writing: "They attract each other in the mystery of a verb in search of its incarnation. Entrusting themselves, immoderately, to that which makes up the body and the flesh of all speech: air, breath, song. . . . These prophets sense that if something of the divine can still come to us, it will happen through the abandonment of self-interest/ulterior motives. Of any language and meaning already turned out. In risk. Only that kind of risk that leads where no one can predict."[37] How did Irigaray arrive at this vatic conception of philosophy? Obviously, Heidegger's call for a "thinking poetry" or a "poetizing thought" (*das dichtende Denken*), as well as Derrida's related use of a "sensible language" attentive to its sensuous surface, provide the stylistic ambiance in which Irigaray's other languages are deployed. Like them, she writes against expectations, in resistance to idealist notions of a transcendence in which corporeal reality is left behind in order to attain the realm of pure ideas or mental representations.[38] Such writers' stylistic idiosyncracies cannot be divorced from their thought because its inner processes are embedded or embodied in their linguistic textures. But unlike these partners in her rethinking of philosophy, Irigaray also writes to create the possibility of a philosophical subject as woman. For perhaps no other subject could imagine erotic union as a potential third term between masculine and feminine—an intermediate space where both can meet in mutual admiration and respect.

Thus, what began as a dismantling or deconstruction of philosophy came to overlap with a creative or reconstructive enterprise, as Irigaray implied by borrowing from René Char the image of "destroying with nuptial tools." Char's oxymoronic figure suggests the meeting place of opposites (masculine/feminine, mind/body, subject/object, philosophy/poetry) in a general "entre-deux" of thought. In a similar spirit, Irigaray's recent work emphasizes this space between as "l'intervalle," a mediate position between two polarized terms which requires us to abandon "either/or" thinking in favor of a "both/and" model.[39] For she abandons the definitions and distinctions of conventional discourse to explore those intermediary rhythms and spaces in the human passions (such as admiration of the other, the caress, and the moment of the nuptials) where a regenerating sense of mutuality can still be found.

To be sure, such writing is deliberately unstable, rejecting the necessity for a solid ground beneath its own slipperiness. Like Derrida, Irigaray refuses the demand for fixed philosophical positions in what can only be described as a highly performative kind of writing. Such writing can also be said to be seductive, if by this word one understands a certain deliberate reversibility.[40] Readers may respond with fascination, bafflement, or anger, depending upon their willingness to be led astray. In other words, their very ability to read her amorous language may depend upon their receptivity to difference and undecidability. The appeal of such writing derives, in large part, from its transgressive nature and its promise of forbidden pleasures, as Irigaray's own reading practice implies: "I had the feeling that in Nietzsche, there was a new kind of philosophical language because of the writing, the always very dense work of the writing. That was often connected to the critical language, that is to say, through language, through the deconstruction of the language, so that another one could be invented. In a way, Nietzsche made me take off and go soaring. I had the feeling that I was in the midst of poetry, which made me perfectly happy. One could consider that there is a philosophical thought in this."[41] One could also consider that there are worse things than being swept away by the charms of amorous philosophy.

NOTES

1. Luce Irigaray, *This Sex Which Is Not One*, trans. Catherine Porter with Carolyn Burke (Ithaca: Cornell University Press, 1985), p. 149. See also Irigaray, *Speculum of the Other Woman*, trans. Gillian C. Gill (Ithaca: Cornell University Press, 1985). I am indebted to Gill's unpublished introduction to *Speculum*.

2. Irigaray, *This Sex*, p. 160. For an introduction to her earlier work, see Carolyn Burke, "Irigaray through the Looking Glass," *Feminist Studies* 7, no. 2 (1981), 288–306.

3. Irigaray, *This Sex*, pp. 149–50.

4. Ibid., p. 150.

5. Ibid.

6. Ibid., p. 151.

7. Irigaray builds on the ideas of Joan Riviere, "Womanliness as a Masquerade," *International Journal of Psychoanalysis* 10 (1929), 303–13. Riviere's article is reprinted in *Formations of Fantasy*, ed. Victor Burgin et al. (London: Methuen, 1986), which also contains a very useful essay by Stephen Heath, "Joan Riviere and the Masquerade."

8. See the account of "mimicry" in Irigaray, *This Sex*, pp. 76–77, and compare the discussions of this concept in Nancy K. Miller, "Emphasis Added: Plots and Plausibilities in Women's Fiction," *PMLA* 96 (1981), 38; and Mary Jacobus, "The Question of Language: Men of Maxims and *The Mill on the Floss*," in *Writing and Sexual Difference*, ed. Elizabeth Abel (Chicago: University of Chicago Press, 1982), pp. 40–41 and *passim*. It is unclear just how mimicry differs from masquerade, except that the former seems to be a more passive, self-subordinating acceptance of femininity, while the latter is a more active, self-assertive strategy or practice. Stephen Heath sees mimicry as "a kind of strategic reduplication of masquerade" and notes that for this reason, Irigaray has difficulty in defining mimicry as a concept: "She can only make the difference in her writing" (personal communication, June 27, 1987).

9. Elizabeth Berg, "The Third Woman," *Diacritics* 12 (1982), p. 16. Berg adds, "All of Irigaray's work is in some sense to be understood as a dialogue with Lacan, although his name is spectacularly missing from her books."

10. Jacques Derrida, *Spurs/Eperons*, trans. Barbara Harlow (Chicago: University of Chicago Press, 1979), p. 51; the citation is taken from a passage in which Derrida discusses the woman's seduction "from a distance," as "the feminine operation," to which Irigaray replies in her writing starting with *Amante marine*. On this question, see Elizabeth Gross, "Derrida, Irigaray, and Deconstruction," in *Leftwing* (Intervention 20) (Sydney: Intervention Publications, 1986), n.p.

11. Jean Baudrillard, *De la séduction* (Paris: Galilée, 1979), p. 18. (All translations are my own unless otherwise noted.) See pp. 19–22 (especially Baudrillard's reductive reading of *This Sex Which Is Not One*), which

makes clear his hostility to feminism in general and Irigaray in particular. Unlike Baudrillard, who claims that "woman is only appearance," a seductive surface which "defeats the profundity of the masculine" (p. 22), Irigaray neither advocates seductiveness for its own sake nor identifies it in any definitive manner with the feminine.

12. See Hélène V. Wenzel, "Introduction to Luce Irigaray's 'And the One Doesn't Stir without the Other,' " and Wenzel's translation of Irigaray, *Et l'une ne bouge pas sans l'autre*, both in *Signs* 7, no. 1 (1981), 56–59, 60–67; also Jane Gallop, *The Daughter's Seduction: Feminism and Psychoanalysis* (Ithaca: Cornell University Press, 1982), pp. 113–18, where Gallop sets up a deliberately theatrical opposition between Irigaray and Kristeva.

13. Irigaray, *Le Corps-à-corps avec la mère* (Montreal: Les éditions de la pleine lune, 1981). Cf. Julia Kristeva's use of the "corps-à-corps" in "Stabat Mater," *Poetics Today* 6, nos. 1–2 (1985), 147: "Women no doubt reproduce between them the peculiar, forgotten forms of close combat in which they engaged with their mothers."

14. Irigaray, "Women's Exile," *Ideology and Consciousness* 1 (1977), 76.

15. Irigaray, "Femmes Divines," *Critique* 454 (1985), 294–308; trans. Stephen Muecke as "Divine Women," *Local Consumption Occasional Paper 8* (Sydney: Local Consumption, 1986), p. 1.

16. Irigaray, *Le Corps-à-corps avec la mère*, p. 43. Although Irigaray never mentions Bachelard, his work on the elements provides another intellectual context for her own project, in which, as Margaret Whitford puts it, "what we take to be universal and objective is in fact male, so that the four elements, in their turn, are subtended by a more basic scheme than Bachelard's, namely the male/female distinction." See Whitford, "Luce Irigaray and the Female Imaginary: Speaking as a Woman," *Radical Philosophy* 43 (1986), 4.

17. Elizabeth Gross, "Irigaray and the Divine," *Local Consumption Occasional Paper 9* (Sydney: Local Consumption, 1986), p. 10. On the question of the elements in particular and on Irigaray's recent work in general, I am indebted to Gross's excellent analysis.

18. Irigaray, *Amante marine de Friedrich Nietzsche* (Paris: Minuit, 1980), a section of which is translated by Sara Speidel as "Veiled Lips," in *Mississippi Review* 11, no. 3 (1983), 98–119. Cf. Irigaray's account of this text as "not a book *on* Nietzsche but *with* Nietzsche" as "an amorous partner" (*Le Corps-à-corps avec la mère*, p. 44). In order to talk with the philosopher rather than about him, Irigaray adopts several disorienting textual strategies: her own words and those of her interlocutor are intermingled, and she deliberately dispenses with the usual scholarly conventions governing citations and other textual references.

19. Irigaray, *Corps-à-corps avec la mère*, p. 43; and cf. *This Sex*, pp. 106–18.

20. Irigaray, *Amante marine*, p. 65.

21. See Speidel's informative note on Nietzsche's references to Ariadne, in

"Veiled Lips," p. 127, n. 16. Walter Kaufman identifies both the "anima" and Cosima Wagner as Nietzsche's Ariadne in *Nietzsche: Philosopher, Psychologist, Antichrist* (Princeton: Princeton University Press, 1974), pp. 33–34, and cites the following remark by Nietzsche: "A labyrinthian man never seeks the truth but always only his Ariadne—whatever he may tell us."

22. Friedrich Nietzsche, *Ecce Homo*, vol. 8, trans. Walter Kaufman (New York: Vintage, 1969), p. 308.

23. Irigaray, *Amante marine*, p. 80.

24. Irigaray, *Passions élémentaires* (Paris: Minuit, 1982), p. 125.

25. Ibid., pp. 32–33.

26. Gross, "Irigaray and the Divine," p. 127.

27. Irigaray, *Passions élémentaires*, p. 125.

28. Luce Irigaray, "The Fecundity of the Caress," trans. Carolyn Burke, in *Face to Face with Levinas*, ed. Richard A. Cohen (Albany: SUNY Press, 1986), pp. 231–56. The original appeared in *Exercises de la patience* 5 (1983), 119–37, and was reprinted as the final chapter of Irigaray's *Ethique de la différence sexuelle* (Paris: Minuit, 1984), pp. 173–99.

29. Jacques Derrida, *Writing and Difference*, trans. Alan Bass (Chicago: University of Chicago Press, 1978), p. 82.

30. Ibid., pp. 320–21, n. 92.

31. Because of the lack of gender inflections in English, the parallel between *amant* and *amante* (as contrasted to *aimée*) cannot be rendered here.

32. Irigaray, "The Fecundity," pp. 231–33.

33. Emmanuel Levinas, in *Face to Face with Levinas*, ed. Richard A. Cohen (Albany: State University of New York Press, 1986), p. 15.

34. Luce Irigaray, *L'Oubli de l'air chez Martin Heidegger* (Paris: Minuit, 1983), p. 15.

35. Ibid., p. 10. The proposed fourth volume, a dialogue with Marx in terms of fire, was never completed. Cf. Irigaray, *Corps-à-corps avec la mère*, p. 44. Two other texts published during this period and related to Irigaray's projected tetralogy are "Ou et comment habiter?" in *Les Cahiers du GRIF* 26 (1983), 139–43; and *La Croyance même* (Paris: Galilée, 1983).

36. Irigaray, *L'Oubli de l'air*, p. 104.

37. Ibid., p. 156.

38. On Heidegger's notion of "thinking poetry," see George Steiner, *Martin Heidegger* (New York: Penguin, 1980), pp. 32, 39, 51; and on Derrida's "sensible language," see Mark Krupnick, in *Displacement: Derrida and After*, ed. M. Krupnick (Bloomington: Indiana University Press, 1983), pp. 21–28. Irigaray's own vision of a "transcendental sensible," as a possibility to follow on a transformed notion of sexual difference, appears in her *Ethique de la différence sexuelle*, p. 124.

39. On the "intervalle," see Irigaray, *Ethique de la différence sexuelle*, pp. 15–21, 41–59.

40. Cf. Baudrillard, *De la Séduction*, p. 10: "All discourse is threatened by this sudden reversibility or absorption into its own signifiers, without a trace of meaning. This is why all the disciplines, which hold as axiomatic the coherence and finality of their own discourse must exorcise it [reversibility]. This is where seduction and femininity converge, have always converged." By reversibility, Baudrillard intends the undecidable, "feminine" dimension of signification or that which refuses to take a stand in relation to referentiality. Cf. Andrew Ross, "Baudrillard's Bad Attitude," and Sharon Willis, "Seductive Spaces: Private Fascinations and Public Fantasies in Popular Cinema," this volume.

41. Irigaray, *Corps-à-corps avec la mère*, p. 45.

Notes on Contributors

CHARLES BERNHEIMER teaches Romance Languages and Comparative Literature at the University of Pennsylvania. He is author of the forthcoming *Figures of Ill Repute: Representing Prostitution in Nineteenth Century France* and *Flaubert and Kafka: Studies in Psychopoetic Structure*, as well as numerous articles on nineteenth- and twentieth-century European literature. He coedited *In Dora's Case: Freud—Hysteria—Feminism*.

SUSAN DAVID BERNSTEIN teaches English at the University of Wisconsin, Madison. She is currently writing about confession, gender, and the body in nineteenth-century British novels and has published articles on Charlotte Brontë and Emily Dickinson.

CAROLYN BURKE is a Research Associate in Humanities at the University of California at Santa Cruz. The author of numerous articles on French feminist writers and on female modernists, she is now translating Luce Irigaray's *L'Ethique de la difference sexuelle* and completing a biography of Mina Loy.

MARTHA NOEL EVANS, author of *Masks of Tradition: Women and the Politics of Writing in Twentieth-Century France*, teaches French and Women's Studies at Mary Baldwin College in Virginia. She has translated Jacques Lacan and Shoshana Felman, and published articles on psychoanalysis and on nineteenth- and twentieth-century French literature. She is currently writing a book on hysteria.

LAWRENCE FRANK, author of *Charles Dickens and the Romantic Self*, teaches English at the University of Oklahoma. He has published numerous articles on psychoanalysis and literature. His current project is a book titled *The Eternal City: A Metaphor for the Mind*.

SHIRLEY NELSON GARNER teaches English at the University of Minnesota. She is coeditor of *The (M)other Tongue: Essays in Feminist Psychoanalytic Interpretation* and of *Interpreting Women's Lives: Theories of Personal Narratives*. Author of articles on Shakespeare and on various women writers, she is currently writing a series of autobiographical essays and coediting *Shakespearean Tragedy and Gender.*

DIANNE HUNTER teaches English at Trinity College, Connecticut. She is the author of psychoanalytic and feminist studies of myth, literature, and drama. Her current writing projects focus on hysteria and dramatic literature.

CLAIRE KAHANE teaches English at the State University of New York at Buffalo, where she directs the Center for the Psychological Study of the Arts. She is coeditor of *In Dora's Case: Freud—Hysteria—Feminism* and *The (M)other Tongue: Essays in Feminist Psychoanalytic Interpretation,* and editor of *Psychoanalyse und das Unheimliche.* She has authored articles on Gothic fiction, hysteria and literature, the comic-grotesque, Virginia Woolf, and Flannery O'Connor. Her current project studies hysteria, feminism, and the emergence of modernist form.

JUDITH MAYNE teaches French and Women's Studies at Ohio State University. She is the author of *Private Novels, Public Films* and *Kino and the Woman Question.* She has published numerous articles on Soviet, French, German, and American cinema; and on women, feminist film theory, and literature. Her current project is a book on feminism and women filmmakers.

ALICIA OSTRIKER, a critic and poet, teaches English at Rutgers University. Her critical works include *Vision and Verse in William Blake, Writing Like a Woman,* and *Stealing the Language: The Emergence of Women's Poetry in America.* She has published six books of poetry, most recently *The Mother/Child Papers, A Woman under the Surface,* and *The Imaginary Lover.*

ANDREW ROSS teaches English at Princeton. He is the author of *The Failure of Modernism* and of *No Respect: Intellectuals and Popular Culture* and editor of *Universal Abandon? The Politics of Postmodernism.*

GABRIELE SCHWAB, author of *Samuel Beckett's Endgame with Subjectivity: Towards a Psychoaesthetic Theory of Modern Drama* and *Subjects without Selves: Subjectivity and Aesthetics of Response in Modern Fiction,* teaches English and Comparative Literature at the University of California, Irvine. She has published numerous essays and articles on literature and literary theory.

SHARON WILLIS teaches French at the University of Rochester. She is the author of *Marguerite Duras: Writing on the Body* as well as numerous essays on feminist theory, film theory, and the psychology of the visual. She is currently preparing a book on sexual difference and cultural difference in contemporary American film.

Index